12.80

Chocolate

Chocolate

p

This is a Parragon Book
First published in 2001

Parragon
Queen Street House
4 Queen Street
Bath BA1 1HE, UK

Copyright © Parragon 2001

ISBN: 0-75254-886-7

Printed in Indonesia

NOTE

This book uses metric and imperial measurements. Follow the same units of measurement throughout; do not mix metric and imperial.
All spoon measurements are level: teaspoons are assumed to be 5 ml, and tablespoons are assumed to be 15 ml. Unless otherwise stated,
milk is assumed to be full fat, eggs and individual vegetables such as potatoes are medium,
and pepper is freshly ground black pepper.

Recipes using raw or very lightly cooked eggs should be
avoided by infants, the elderly, pregnant women, convalescents, and anyone suffering from an illness.

Contents

Introduction 8 Regional Cooking 10–13
Using Chocolate 14 How to Use This Book 17

Cakes, Gateaux & Loaves

Hot Desserts

Savouries

Cold Desserts

Small Cakes & Cookies

Sweets & Drinks

Introduction

Chocolate! – even the word is an enticing mixture of indulgence tinged with a touch of sinfulness, and the product itself more than lives up to its promise. The mere mention of anything associated with this mouthwatering confection can cause a dreamy look to come into the eyes of the chocoholic.

The cocoa tree, *Theobroma cacao*, originated in South America, and from the early 7th century it was cultivated by the Maya, who established a flourishing trade and even used the cocoa bean as currency. In 1502, Christopher Columbus took the cocoa bean to Spain, but it wasn't until later that Cortés introduced *xocotlatl*, a recipe brought from the Mexican court of Montezuma for a drink made of crushed roasted cocoa beans and cold water, thickened with cornflour and frothed with a swizzle stick. Vanilla, spices, honey and sugar were added to improve the flavour of this thick and bitter brew, and over time it came to be served hot. Cocoa was believed to cure a variety of physical illnesses, and to promote stamina.

In the 17th century, the popularity of cocoa spread to the rest of Europe. France was the first country to fall to its charms, then Holland, where Amsterdam became the most important cocoa port beyond Spain. From there cocoa went to Germany, then north to Scandinavia, and also south to Italy – by which time it had become a major source of revenue.

Cocoa arrived in England in the mid 17th century, and chocolate houses quickly began to rival the newly established coffee houses.

In the early 19th century, Dutch chemist Coenraad Van Houten invented a press to extract the fat from the beans, and developed a method of neutralizing the acids. In this way, he was able to produce almost pure cocoa butter, and a hard 'cake', which could be milled to a powder for use as a flavouring. As a result, it became possible to eat chocolate as well as to drink it.

It was soon discovered that the rich cocoa butter made a delicious confection, and chocolate production began in earnest. In Britain, Fry's chocolate appeared in 1847, and in

Switzerland the famous chocolate companies were established. In 1875 chocolate was combined with condensed milk to produce the first milk chocolate. At around this time, Lindt found a way of making the smooth, melting chocolate still associated with his company today. About 20 years later, Hershey introduced his famous chocolate bar in the United States, where chocolate is perhaps better loved than anywhere else.

Today, cocoa trees are grown in Africa, the West Indies, the tropical areas of America, and the Far East. Harvested cocoa beans are left in the heat of the sun to develop their chocolate flavour, then afterwards the beans are shelled, and the kernels are processed to produce cocoa solids. Finally, the cocoa butter is extracted and further processed to become chocolate, in all its many guises.

Regional Cooking

The Europeans, following their long association with cocoa as a drink, soon discovered the delights of chocolate, and set about using it to create some of the most delicious classic dessert recipes – rich, creamy, and incredibly good to eat.

In Austria, tortes are very popular, particularly Anna Sacher's delectable Sachertorte, which dates from 1883. The French offer a melting roulade, a light-as-air mixture that is cooked in a long rectangle, then rolled around a filling – there is plenty of scope for variations on this basic recipe. Also from France comes mousse, a melt-in-the-mouth dessert based on chocolate and eggs, to which can be added double cream, brandy, rum – or even champagne.

The Italians really know how to impress with their chocolate desserts. The frothy zabaglione, laced with marsala, is whisked over hot water until thick, and served immediately – so it needs patient guests and a confident cook! Tiramisu is based on a smooth and versatile cream cheese, mascarpone, which is layered with coffee-drenched sponge and chunks of chocolate. And the Italians are of course wonderful at making ice-cream – the combination of chocolate and mint is a classic favourite. For special occasions, two Tuscan specialities are Panforte di

Siena – a rich, chocolate-flavoured mixture of dried fruit, nuts and honey – and Florentines, thin, crispy biscuits topped with chocolate.

From Germany comes the Black Forest gateau, a chocolate cake soaked in liqueur and filled with whipped cream and cherries. Adapted into a trifle, this makes a very special dessert.

Regional Cooking

It may seem a strange and newly fashionable idea to combine the creamy sweetness of chocolate with the hot and fiery chilli, but in fact chilli was one of the flavourings used in the original cocoa drink, *xocotlatl*, and the combination is still used in Mexican cookery today. That chocolate and chilli have an affinity is evident in one of the most popular Mexican dishes, Mole Poblano (see

page 106), a blend of toasted fresh chillies, onions, garlic, tomatoes, spices, nuts, raisins – and chocolate, which is even used to garnish the dish. Chocolate also adds flavour and richness to Mexican beef stews.

More conventionally, chocolate is used in desserts such as Empanadas (see page 92), little parcels of banana and chocolate in filo pastry, and chocolate meringues, served with strawberries and chocolate-flavoured cream. The Mexicans also make a modern version of the original cocoa drink, which is spiced with cinnamon and thickened with tortilla flour.

In North America, where home-baked cookies and traybakes are such a feature of everyday life and social occasions, chocolate is a very popular ingredient. From here come such tempting treats as the moist,

chewy, chocolate brownie, crisp chocolate chip cookies, and rocky road bites, which often find their way into ice-cream. Some recipes reflect the area in which a recipe originated – one that particularly catches the attention is Mississippi Mud Pie, definitely not a dish for the faint-hearted! And Devil's Food Cake, with its sumptuous chocolate frosting, is just as the name suggests – positively wicked!

Using Chocolate

Chocolate is delicious whether cooked or uncooked. It comes in many forms, of course, and here is a selection of some of the most popular ones, which can all be used in a wide variety of mouthwatering recipes.

Dark Chocolate

Dark chocolate that contains around 50% cocoa solids is ideal for most everyday cooking purposes. For special recipes, choose a luxury or continental chocolate with a cocoa solid content of 70–75% for a richer, more intense flavour.

White Chocolate

For colour contrast, especially for cake decoration, white chocolate is unbeatable. However, white chocolate has a lower content of cocoa butter and cocoa solids, so choose a luxury cooking variety and take care not to overheat it when melting it.

Chocolate Chips

Available in dark, milk or white chocolate, these chips are useful for baking and decoration. They are especially good in biscuits and cookies, as well as sweets and a whole range of delicious confections.

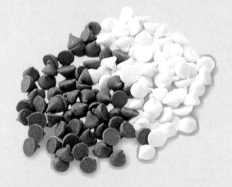

Milk Chocolate

This variety has a milder, creamier flavour. It is also useful for decorations. Care must be taken when melting it, however, because milk chocolate is more sensitive to heat than dark chocolate is.

Chocolate-flavoured Cake Covering

This product has an inferior flavour, but it is useful for making decorations because of its high fat content. As a compromise, add a few squares to a good-quality chocolate.

Cocoa Powder

Cocoa powder should be bought unsweetened. It tastes bitter, and gives a good, strong chocolate flavour in cooking. It is mostly used in cakes.

Most chocolate, including cocoa powder, can be stored for up to a year if it is kept in a cool, dry place away from direct heat or sunlight.

Preparing Chocolate

To melt chocolate on a stove:

1 Break the chocolate into small, equal-sized pieces and put it into a heatproof bowl.

2 Place the bowl over a pan of hot, simmering water, making sure the base of the bowl does not come into contact with the water.

3 Once the chocolate starts to melt, stir gently until smooth, then remove from the heat.

Note: Do not melt chocolate over direct heat (unless melting with other ingredients – in this case, keep the heat very low).

To melt chocolate in a microwave oven:

1 Break chocolate into small pieces and place in a microwave-proof bowl.

2 Put the bowl in the microwave oven and melt. As a guide, melt 125g/4½ oz dark chocolate on High for 2 minutes, and white or milk chocolate on Medium for 2–3 minutes.

Note: As microwave oven temperatures and settings vary, you should consult the manufacturer's instructions first.

3 Stir the chocolate, leave to stand for a few minutes, then stir again. If necessary, return it to the microwave for a further 30 seconds.

Chocolate Decorations

Decorations add a special touch to a cake or dessert. They can be interleaved with non-stick baking parchment and stored in airtight containers. Dark chocolate will keep for 4 weeks, and milk or white chocolate for 2 weeks.

Caraque

1 Spread the melted chocolate over a clean acrylic chopping board and leave it to set.

2 When the chocolate has set, hold the board firmly, position a large, smooth-bladed knife on the chocolate and pull the blade towards you at an angle of 45°, scraping along the chocolate to form the caraque. You should end up with irregularly shaped long curls (see below).

3 Using the knife blade, lift the caraque off the board.

Quick Curls

1 For quick curls, choose a thick bar of chocolate, and keep it at room temperature.

2 Using a sharp, swivel-bladed vegetable peeler, scrape lightly along the chocolate to form fine curls, or more firmly to form thicker curls.

Leaves

1 Use freshly-picked leaves with well-defined veins that are clean, dry and pliable. Holding a leaf by its stem, paint a smooth layer of melted chocolate onto the underside with a small paint brush or pastry brush.

2 Repeat with the remaining leaves, then place them, chocolate side up, on a baking sheet lined with silicone paper.

3 Refrigerate for at least an hour until set. When set, peel each leaf away from its chocolate coating.

How to Use This Book

Each recipe contains a wealth of useful information, including a breakdown of nutritional quantities, preparation and cooking times, and level of difficulty. All of this information is explained in detail below.

The number of chef's hats represents the difficulty of each recipe, ranging from easy (1 chef's hat) to difficult (5 chef's hats).

This amount of time represents the preparation of ingredients, including cooling, chilling and soaking times.

This represents the cooking time.

The ingredients for each recipe are listed in the order that they are used.

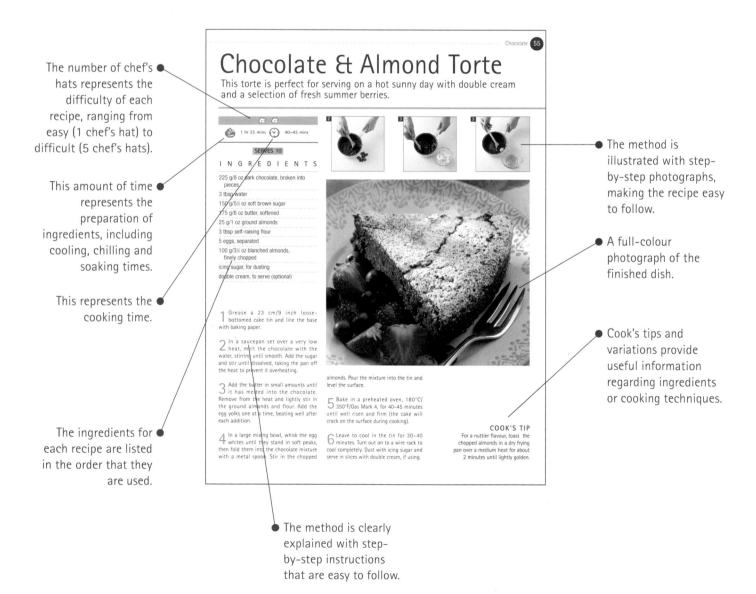

The method is illustrated with step-by-step photographs, making the recipe easy to follow.

A full-colour photograph of the finished dish.

Cook's tips and variations provide useful information regarding ingredients or cooking techniques.

The method is clearly explained with step-by-step instructions that are easy to follow.

The inset recipe page reads:

Chocolate 55

Chocolate & Almond Torte

This torte is perfect for serving on a hot sunny day with double cream and a selection of fresh summer berries.

1 hr 25 mins   40–45 mins

SERVES 10

INGREDIENTS

225 g/8 oz dark chocolate, broken into pieces

3 tbsp water

150 g/5½ oz soft brown sugar

175 g/6 oz butter, softened

25 g/1 oz ground almonds

3 tbsp self-raising flour

5 eggs, separated

100 g/3½ oz blanched almonds, finely chopped

icing sugar, for dusting

double cream, to serve (optional)

1 Grease a 23 cm/9 inch loose-bottomed cake tin and line the base with baking paper.

2 In a saucepan set over a very low heat, melt the chocolate with the water, stirring until smooth. Add the sugar and stir until dissolved, taking the pan off the heat to prevent it overheating.

3 Add the butter in small amounts until it has melted into the chocolate. Remove from the heat and lightly stir in the ground almonds and flour. Add the egg yolks one at a time, beating well after each addition.

4 In a large mixing bowl, whisk the egg whites until they stand in soft peaks, then fold them into the chocolate mixture with a metal spoon. Stir in the chopped almonds. Pour the mixture into the tin and level the surface.

5 Bake in a preheated oven, 180°C/350°F/Gas Mark 4, for 40–45 minutes until well risen and firm (the cake will crack on the surface during cooking).

6 Leave to cool in the tin for 30–40 minutes. Turn out on to a wire rack to cool completely. Dust with icing sugar and serve in slices with double cream, if using.

COOK'S TIP
For a nuttier flavour, toast the chopped almonds in a dry frying pan over a medium heat for about 2 minutes until lightly golden.

Cakes, Gateaux & Loaves

It is hard to resist the pleasure of a sumptuous piece of chocolate cake and no chocolate book would be complete without a selection of cakes, gateaux and loaves – there are plenty to choose from in this chapter. The more experimental amongst you can vary the fillings or decorations according to what takes your fancy. Alternatively, follow our easy step-by-step instructions and look at our glossy pictures to guide you to perfect results.

The gateaux in this book are a feast for the eyes, and so are the delicious cakes, many of which can be made with surprising ease. The loaves are the perfect indulgence for teatime and can be made with very little effort. So next time you feel like a mouthwatering slice of something, these recipes are sure to be a success.

Chocolate Almond Cake

Chocolate and almonds complement each other perfectly in this delicious cake. Be warned though, one slice will never be enough!

3 hrs   40 mins

SERVES 8

INGREDIENTS

175 g/6 oz dark chocolate

175 g/6 oz butter

125 g/4½ oz caster sugar

4 eggs, separated

¼ tsp cream of tartar

6 tbsp self-raising flour

125 g/4½ oz ground almonds

1 tsp almond essence

TOPPING

125 g/4½ oz milk chocolate

2 tbsp butter

4 tbsp double cream

TO DECORATE

25 g/1 oz toasted flaked almonds

25 g/1 oz dark chocolate, melted

1 Lightly grease and line the base of a 23 cm/9 inch round springform tin. Break the chocolate into small pieces and place in a small pan with the butter. Heat gently, stirring until melted and well combined.

2 Place 100 g/3½ oz of the caster sugar in a bowl with the egg yolks and whisk until pale and creamy. Add the melted chocolate mixture, beating until well combined.

3 Sieve the cream of tartar and flour together and fold into the chocolate mixture with the ground almonds and almond essence.

4 Whisk the egg whites in a bowl until standing in soft peaks. Add the remaining caster sugar and whisk for about 2 minutes by hand, or 45–60 seconds, if using an electric whisk, until thick and glossy. Fold the egg whites into the chocolate mixture and spoon into the

tin. Bake in a preheated oven, 190°C/375°F/Gas Mark 5, for 40 minutes, until just springy to the touch. Leave to cool.

5 Heat the topping ingredients in a bowl over a pan of hot water. Remove from the heat and beat for 2 minutes. Leave to cool for 30 minutes. Transfer the cake to a plate and spread with the topping. Scatter with the almonds and drizzle with melted chocolate. Leave to set for 2 hours before serving.

Chocolate Tray Bake

This is a good family cake that keeps well. Baked in a shallow rectangular cake tin, it is ideal for selling at a cake stall or charity coffee morning.

10 Mins   30–40 mins

SERVES 15

INGREDIENTS

350 g/12 oz self-raising flour, sifted

3 tbsp cocoa powder, sifted

225 g/8 oz caster sugar

225 g/8 oz soft margarine

4 eggs, beaten

4 tbsp milk

50 g/1¾ oz milk chocolate chips

50 g/1¾ oz dark chocolate chips

50 g/1¾ oz white chocolate chips

icing sugar, to dust

1 Grease a 33 x 24 x 5 cm/13 x 9 x 2 inch cake tin with a little butter or margarine.

2 Place all of the ingredients except for the chocolate chips and icing sugar in a large mixing bowl and beat together until smooth.

VARIATION

For an attractive finish, cut thin strips of paper and lay them in a criss-cross pattern across the top of the cake. Dust with icing sugar, then remove the paper strips.

3 Beat in the milk, dark and white chocolate chips.

4 Spoon the mixture into the prepared cake tin and level the top. Bake in a preheated oven, 180°C/350°F/Gas Mark 4,

for 30–40 minutes, until risen and springy to the touch. Leave to cool in the tin.

5 Once cool, dust with icing sugar. Cut into squares to serve.

Chocolate & Pineapple Cake

Decorated with thick yogurt and canned pineapple, this is a low-fat cake, but it is by no means lacking in flavour.

40 mins | 20–25 mins

SERVES 9

INGREDIENTS

150 g/5½ oz low-fat spread

125 g/4½ oz caster sugar

100 g/3½ oz self-raising flour, sifted

3 tbsp cocoa powder, sifted

1½ tsp baking powder

2 eggs

225g/8 oz canned pineapple pieces in natural juice

125 ml /4 fl oz low-fat thick natural yogurt

about 1 tbsp icing sugar

grated chocolate, to decorate

1 Lightly grease a 20 cm/8 inch square cake tin.

2 Place the low-fat spread, caster sugar, flour, cocoa powder, baking powder and eggs in a large mixing bowl. Beat with a wooden spoon or electric hand whisk until smooth.

3 Pour the cake mixture into the prepared tin and level the surface. Bake in a preheated oven, 190°C/325°F/Gas Mark 5, for 20–25 minutes or until springy to the touch. Leave the cake to cool slightly in the tin before transferring to a wire rack to cool completely.

4 Drain the pineapple, chop the pineapple pieces and drain again. Reserve a little pineapple for decoration,

then stir the rest into the yogurt and sweeten to taste with icing sugar.

5 Spread the pineapple and yogurt mixture over the cake and decorate with the reserved pineapple pieces. Sprinkle with the grated chocolate.

COOK'S TIP

Store the cake, undecorated, in an airtight container for up to 3 days. Once decorated, refrigerate and use within 2 days.

Chocolate & Orange Cake

An all-time favourite combination of flavours makes this cake ideal for a tea-time treat. Omit the icing, if preferred, and sprinkle with icing sugar.

1 hr   25 mins

SERVES 8

INGREDIENTS

175 g/6 oz caster sugar

175 g/6 oz butter or block margarine

3 eggs, beaten

175 g/6 oz self-raising flour, sifted

2 tbsp cocoa powder, sifted

2 tbsp milk

3 tbsp orange juice

grated rind of ½ orange

ICING

175 g/6 oz icing sugar

2 tbsp orange juice

1 Lightly grease a 20 cm/8 inch deep round cake tin.

2 Beat together the sugar and butter or margarine in a bowl until light and fluffy. Gradually add the eggs, beating well after each addition. Carefully fold in the flour.

3 Divide the cake mixture in half. Add the cocoa powder and milk to one half, stirring until well combined. Flavour the other half of the mixture with the orange juice and rind.

4 Place spoonfuls of each mixture into the prepared tin and swirl together with a skewer, to create a marbled effect. Bake in a preheated oven, 190°C/375°F/Gas Mark 5, for 25 minutes or until springy to the touch.

5 Leave the cake to cool in the tin for a few minutes before transferring to a wire rack to cool completely.

6 To make the icing, sift the icing sugar into a mixing bowl and mix in enough of the orange juice to form a smooth icing. Spread the icing over the top of the cake and leave to set before serving.

VARIATION

Add 2 tablespoons of rum or brandy to the chocolate mixture instead of the milk. The cake also works well when flavoured with grated lemon rind and juice instead of the orange.

Family Chocolate Cake

A simple-to-make family cake ideal for a treat. Keep the decoration as simple as you like – you could use a shop-bought icing or filling, if liked.

1 hr   20 mins

SERVES 8

INGREDIENTS

125 g/4½ oz soft margarine

125 g/4½ oz caster sugar

2 eggs

1 tbsp golden syrup

125 g/4½ oz self-raising flour, sifted

2 tbsp cocoa powder, sifted

FILLING AND TOPPING

50 g/1¾ oz icing sugar, sifted

2 tbsp butter

100 g/3½ oz white or milk cooking chocolate

a little milk or white chocolate, melted (optional)

1 Lightly grease two 18 cm/7 inch shallow cake tins.

2 Place all of the ingredients for the cake in a large mixing bowl and beat with a wooden spoon or electric hand whisk to form a smooth mixture.

3 Divide the mixture between the prepared tins and level the tops. Bake in a preheated oven, 190°C/325°F/Gas Mark 5, for 20 minutes or until springy to the touch. Cool for a few minutes in the tins before transferring to a wire rack to cool completely.

4 To make the filling, beat the icing sugar and butter together in a bowl until light and fluffy. Melt the cooking chocolate and beat half into the icing mixture. Use the filling to sandwich the 2 cakes together.

5 Spread the remaining melted cooking chocolate over the top of the cake. Pipe circles of contrasting melted milk or white chocolate and feather into the cooking chocolate with a cocktail stick, if liked. Leave to set before serving.

COOK'S TIP

Ensure that you eat this cake on the day of baking, because it does not keep well.

Chocolate & Vanilla Loaf

An old-fashioned favourite, this cake will keep well if stored in an airtight container or wrapped in foil in a cool place.

50 mins   30 mins

SERVES 10

INGREDIENTS

175 g/6 oz caster sugar

175 g/6 oz soft margarine

½ tsp vanilla essence

3 eggs

225 g/8 oz self-raising flour, sifted

50 g/1¾ oz dark chocolate

icing sugar, to dust

1 Lightly grease a 450-g/1-lb loaf tin.

2 Beat together the sugar and soft margarine in a bowl until light and fluffy.

3 Beat in the vanilla essence, then gradually add the eggs, beating well after each addition. Carefully fold in the self-raising flour.

4 Divide the mixture in half. Melt the dark chocolate and stir into one half of the mixture until well combined.

COOK'S TIP
Freeze the cake undecorated for up to 2 months. Defrost at room temperature.

5 Place the vanilla mixture in the tin and level the top. Spread the chocolate layer over the vanilla layer.

6 Bake in a preheated oven, 190°C/375°F/Gas Mark 5, for 30 minutes or until springy to the touch.

7 Leave to cool in the tin for a few minutes before transferring to a wire rack to cool completely.

8 Serve the loaf dusted with icing sugar.

Chocolate Tea Bread

What can be better in the afternoon than sitting down with a cup of tea and a slice of tea bread made with chocolate?

45 mins   1 hr

SERVES 4

INGREDIENTS

175 g/6 oz butter, softened

100 g/3½ oz light muscovado sugar

4 eggs, lightly beaten

225 g/8 oz dark chocolate chips

100 g/3½ oz raisins

50 g/1¾ oz chopped walnuts

finely grated rind of 1 orange

225 g/8 oz self-raising flour

1 Lightly grease a 900-g/2-lb loaf tin and line the base with baking paper.

2 Cream together the butter and sugar in a bowl until light and fluffy.

3 Gradually add the eggs, beating well after each addition. If the mixture begins to curdle, beat in 1–2 tablespoons of the flour.

4 Stir in the chocolate chips, raisins, walnuts and orange rind. Sieve the flour and carefully fold it into the mixture.

5 Spoon the mixture into the prepared loaf tin and make a slight dip in the centre of the top with the back of a spoon.

6 Bake in a preheated oven, 170°C/325°F/Gas Mark 3, for 1 hour or until a fine skewer inserted into the centre of the loaf comes out clean.

7 Leave to cool in the tin for 5 minutes, before carefully turning out and leaving on a wire rack to cool completely.

8 Serve the tea bread cut into thin slices.

VARIATION

Use white or milk chocolate chips instead of dark chocolate chips, or a mixture of all three, if desired. Dried cranberries instead of the raisins also work well in this recipe.

Apricot & Chocolate Ring

A tasty tea bread in the shape of a ring. You could use sultanas instead of the apricots, if preferred.

🥮 1 hr   🕐 30 mins

SERVES 12

INGREDIENTS

6 tbsp butter, diced

450 g/1 lb self-raising flour, sifted

4 tbsp caster sugar

2 eggs, beaten

150 ml/5 fl oz milk

FILLING AND DECORATION

2 tbsp butter, melted

150 g/5½ oz no-soak dried apricots, chopped

100 g/3½ oz dark chocolate chips

1–2 tbsp milk, to glaze

25 g/1 oz dark chocolate, melted

1 Grease a 25 cm/10 inch round cake tin and then line the base with baking paper.

2 Rub the butter into the flour until the mixture resembles fine breadcrumbs. Stir in the caster sugar, eggs and milk to form a soft dough.

COOK'S TIP

This cake is best served very fresh, ideally on the day it is made. It is fabulous served slightly warm.

3 Roll out the dough on a lightly floured surface to form a 35 cm/14 inch square.

4 Brush the melted butter over the surface of the dough. Mix together the apricots and chocolate chips and spread them over the dough to within 2.5 cm/1 inch of the top and bottom.

5 Roll up the dough tightly, like a Swiss roll, and cut it into 2.5 cm/1 inch slices. Stand the slices in a ring around the edge of the prepared tin at a slight tilt. Brush with a little milk.

6 Bake in a preheated oven, 180°C/350°F/Gas Mark 4, for 30 minutes or until cooked and golden. Leave to cool in the tin for about 15 minutes, then transfer to a wire rack to cool.

7 Drizzle the melted chocolate over the ring, to decorate.

Chocolate Fruit Loaf

A very moreish loaf that smells divine whilst cooking.
It is best eaten warm.

1 hr 40 mins   30 mins

SERVES 10

INGREDIENTS

350 g/12 oz strong white flour

25 g/1 oz cocoa powder

2 tbsp caster sugar

6 g sachet easy-blend dried yeast

¼ tsp salt

225 ml/8 fl oz tepid water

2 tbsp butter, melted

75 g/2¾ oz glacé cherries, roughly chopped

75 g/2¾ oz dark chocolate chips

50 g/1¾ oz sultanas

75 g/2¾ oz no-soak dried apricots, roughly chopped

GLAZE

1 tbsp caster sugar

1 tbsp water

1 Lightly grease a 900-g/2-lb loaf tin. Sieve the flour and cocoa into a large mixing bowl. Stir in the sugar, dried yeast and salt.

2 Mix together the tepid water and butter. Make a well in the centre of the dry ingredients and add the liquid. Mix well with a wooden spoon, then use your hands to bring the dough together. Turn out on to a lightly floured surface and knead for 5 minutes, until a smooth elastic dough forms. Return to a clean bowl, cover with a damp tea towel and leave to rise in a warm place for about 1 hour or until doubled in size.

3 Turn the dough out on to a floured surface and knead for 5 minutes. Roll out to a rectangle about 1 cm/½ inch thick and the same width as the length of the tin. Scatter the cherries, chocolate chips, sultanas and chopped apricots over the dough. Carefully roll up the dough, like a Swiss roll, enclosing the filling. Transfer to the loaf tin, cover with a damp tea towel and leave to rise for 20 minutes or until the top of the dough is level with the top of the tin.

4 To make the glaze, mix together the sugar and water, then brush it over the top of the loaf. Bake in a preheated oven, 200°C/400°F/Gas Mark 6, for 30 minutes or until well risen. Serve.

Mocha Layer Cake

Chocolate cake and a creamy coffee-flavoured filling are combined in this delicious mocha cake.

🍰 50 mins   🕐 35–45 mins

SERVES 8

I N G R E D I E N T S

200 g/7¾ oz self-raising flour

¼ tsp baking powder

4 tbsp cocoa powder

100 g/3½ oz caster sugar

2 eggs

2 tbsp golden syrup

150 ml/5 fl oz sunflower oil

150 ml/5 fl oz milk

FILLING

1 tsp instant coffee

1 tbsp boiling water

300 ml/10 fl oz double cream

2 tbsp icing sugar

TO DECORATE

50 g/1¾ oz flock chocolate

chocolate caraque (see page 15)

icing sugar, to dust

1 Lightly grease three 18 cm/7 inch cake tins.

2 Sieve the flour, baking powder and cocoa powder into a large mixing bowl. Stir in the sugar. Make a well in the centre and stir in the eggs, syrup, oil and milk. Beat with a wooden spoon, gradually mixing in the dry ingredients to make a smooth batter. Divide the mixture between the prepared tins.

3 Bake in a preheated oven, 180°C/ 350°F/Gas Mark 4, for 35–45 minutes or until springy to the touch. Leave in the tins for 5 minutes, then turn out on to a wire rack to cool completely.

4 Dissolve the instant coffee in the boiling water and place in a bowl with the cream and icing sugar. Whip until the cream is just holding its shape. Use half of the cream to sandwich the 3 cakes together. Spread the remaining cream over the top and sides of the cake. Lightly press the flock chocolate into the cream around the edge of the cake.

5 Transfer to a serving plate. Lay the caraque over the top of the cake. Cut a few thin strips of baking paper and place on top of the caraque. Dust lightly with icing sugar, then carefully remove the paper. Serve.

Chocolate Lamington Cake

This recipe is based on a famous Australian cake named after Lord Lamington, a former Governor of Queensland.

50 mins   40 mins

SERVES 8

INGREDIENTS

175 g/6 oz butter or block margarine

175 g/6 oz caster sugar

3 eggs, lightly beaten

150 g/5½ oz self-raising flour

2 tbsp cocoa powder

125 g/4½ oz icing sugar

50 g/1¾ oz dark chocolate, broken into pieces

5 tbsp milk

1 tsp butter

about 8 tbsp shredded coconut

150 ml/5 fl oz double cream, whipped

1 Lightly grease a 450 g/1 lb loaf tin – preferably a long, thin tin measuring about 7.5 x 25 cm/3 x 10 inches.

2 Cream together the butter and sugar in a bowl until light and fluffy. Gradually add the eggs, beating well after each addition. Sieve together the flour and cocoa. Fold into the mixture.

3 Pour the mixture into the prepared tin and level the top. Bake in a preheated oven, 180°C/350°F/Gas Mark 4, for 40 minutes or until springy to the touch. Leave to cool for 5 minutes in the tin, then turn out on to a wire rack to cool completely.

4 Place the chocolate, milk and butter in a heatproof bowl set over a pan of hot water. Stir until the chocolate has melted. Add the icing sugar and beat until smooth. Leave to cool until the icing is thick enough to spread, then spread it all over the cake. Sprinkle with the desiccated coconut and allow the icing to set.

5 Cut a V-shaped wedge from the top of the cake. Put the cream in a piping bag fitted with a plain or star nozzle. Pipe the cream down the centre of the gap left by the wedge, and replace the wedge of cake on top of the cream. Pipe another line of cream down either side of the wedge of cake. Serve.

Rich Chocolate Layer Cake

Thin layers of delicious light chocolate cake sandwiched together with a rich chocolate icing.

🍰 1 hr 5 mins 🕐 30–35 mins

SERVES 10

I N G R E D I E N T S

7 eggs

200 g/7 oz caster sugar

150 g/5½ oz plain flour

50 g/1¾ oz cocoa powder

4 tbsp butter, melted

F I L L I N G

200 g/7 oz dark chocolate

125 g/4½ oz butter

4 tbsp icing sugar

T O D E C O R A T E

75 g/2¾ oz toasted flaked almonds, crushed lightly

quick chocolate curls (see page 15) or grated chocolate

1 Grease a deep 23 cm/9 inch square cake tin and then line the base with baking paper.

2 Whisk the eggs and caster sugar together in a mixing bowl with an electric whisk for about 10 minutes, or until the mixture is very light and foamy and the whisk leaves a trail that lasts a few seconds when lifted.

3 Sieve the flour and cocoa together and fold half into the mixture. Drizzle over the melted butter and fold in the rest of the flour and cocoa. Pour into the prepared tin and bake in a preheated oven, 180°C/350°F/Gas Mark 4, for 30–35 minutes or until springy to the touch. Leave to cool slightly, then remove from the tin and cool completely on a wire rack.

Wash and dry the tin and return the cake to it.

4 While the cake is cooling, make the filling. Melt the chocolate and butter together, then remove from the heat. Stir in the icing sugar, leave to cool, then beat until thick enough to spread.

5 Halve the cooled cake lengthways and cut each half into 3 layers. Sandwich the layers together with three-quarters of the chocolate filling. Spread the remainder over the cake and mark a wavy pattern on the top. Press the almonds on to the sides. Decorate with chocolate curls (see page 15) or grated chocolate.

Chocolate & Mango Layer

Canned peaches can be used instead of mangoes for this deliciously moist cake, if you prefer.

1¼ hrs   1 hr

SERVES 12

INGREDIENTS

50 g/1¾ oz cocoa powder

150 ml/5 fl oz boiling water

6 large eggs

350 g/12 oz caster sugar

300 g/10½ oz self-raising flour

800 g/1 lb 12 oz canned mangoes

1 tsp cornflour

425 ml/15 fl oz double cream

75 g/2¾ oz dark flock chocolate or grated chocolate

1 Grease a deep 23 cm/9 inch round cake tin and line the base of the tin with baking paper.

2 Place the cocoa powder in a small bowl and gradually add the boiling water; blend to form a smooth paste.

3 Place the eggs and caster sugar in a mixing bowl and whisk until the mixture is very light and foamy and the whisk leaves a trail that lasts a few seconds when lifted. Fold in the cocoa mixture. Sieve the flour and fold gently into the mixture.

4 Pour the mixture into the tin and level the top. Bake in a preheated oven, 170°C/325°F/Gas Mark 3, for about 1 hour or until springy to the touch.

5 Leave to cool in the tin for a few minutes then turn out and cool completely on a wire rack. Peel off the lining paper and cut the cake into 3 layers.

6 Drain the mangoes and place a quarter of them in a food processor and purée until smooth. Mix the cornflour with about 3 tablespoons of the mango juice to form a smooth paste. Add to the mango purée. Transfer to a small pan and heat gently, stirring until the purée thickens. Leave to cool.

7 Chop the remaining mango. Whip the cream and reserve about one quarter. Fold the mango into the remaining cream and use the mixture to sandwich the layers of cake together. Place on a serving plate. Spread some of the remaining cream around the side of the cake. Press the flock or grated chocolate lightly into the cream. Pipe cream rosettes around the top and spread the mango purée over the centre.

Devil's Food Cake

This is an American classic, consisting of a rich melt-in-the-mouth chocolate cake that has a citrus-flavoured frosting.

🍰 1 hr   🕐 30 mins

SERVES 6

I N G R E D I E N T S

100 g/3½ oz dark chocolate

250 g/9 oz self-raising flour

1 tsp bicarbonate of soda

225 g/8 oz butter

400 g/14 oz dark muscovado sugar

1 tsp vanilla essence

3 eggs

125 ml/4 fl oz buttermilk

225 ml/8 fl oz boiling water

F R O S T I N G

300 g/10½ oz caster sugar

2 egg whites

1 tbsp lemon juice

3 tbsp orange juice

candied orange peel, to decorate

4 Divide the mixture between the tins and level the tops. Bake in a preheated oven, 190°C/375°F/Gas Mark 5, for 30 minutes, until springy to the touch. Leave to cool in the tin for 5 minutes, then transfer to a wire rack and leave to cool completely.

5 Place the frosting ingredients in a large bowl set over a pan of gently simmering water. Whisk, preferably with an electric beater, until thickened and forming soft peaks. Remove from the heat and whisk until the mixture is cool.

6 Sandwich the 2 cakes together with a little of the frosting, then spread the remainder over the sides and top of the cake, swirling it as you do so. Decorate with the candied orange peel.

1 Lightly grease two 20 cm/8 inch shallow round cake tins and line the bases with baking paper. Melt the chocolate in a pan. Sieve the flour and bicarbonate of soda together.

2 Beat the butter and sugar together in a bowl until pale and fluffy. Beat in the vanilla essence and the eggs, one at a time and beating well after each addition. Add a little flour to the mixture if it begins to curdle.

3 Fold the melted chocolate into the mixture until well blended. Gradually fold in the remaining flour, then stir in the buttermilk and boiling water.

Chocolate Passion Cake

What could be nicer than passion cake with added chocolate?
Rich and moist, this cake is fabulous with afternoon tea.

45 mins   45 mins

SERVES 6

INGREDIENTS

5 eggs

150 g/5½ oz caster sugar

150 g/5½ oz plain flour

40 g/1½ oz cocoa powder

175 g/6 oz carrots, peeled, finely grated
and squeezed until dry

50 g/1¾ oz chopped walnuts

2 tbsp sunflower oil

350 g/12 oz medium fat soft cheese

175 g/6 oz icing sugar

175 g/6 oz milk or dark chocolate, melted

1 Lightly grease the base of a 20 cm/ 8 inch deep round cake tin and line it with baking paper.

2 Place the eggs and sugar in a large mixing bowl set over a pan of gently simmering water and whisk until very thick. Lift the whisk up and let the mixture drizzle back – it will leave a trail for a few seconds when thick enough.

3 Remove the bowl from the heat. Sieve the flour and cocoa powder into the bowl and carefully fold in. Fold in the carrots, walnuts and sunflower oil until just combined.

4 Pour into the prepared tin and bake in a preheated oven, 190°C/375°F/Gas Mark 5, for 45 minutes. Leave to cool slightly then turn out on to a wire rack to cool completely.

5 Beat together the soft cheese and icing sugar until combined. Beat in the melted chocolate. Split the cake in half and sandwich together again with half of the chocolate mixture. Cover the top of the cake with the remainder of the chocolate mixture, swirling it with a knife. Leave to chill or serve at once.

COOK'S TIP

The undecorated cake can be frozen for up to 2 months. Defrost at room temperature for 3 hours or overnight in the refrigerator.

Chocolate Yogurt Cake

Adding yogurt to the cake mixture gives the baked cake a deliciously moist texture.

🕐 55 mins 🕐 45–50 mins

SERVES 8

INGREDIENTS

150 ml/5 fl oz vegetable oil

150 ml/5 fl oz whole milk natural yogurt

175 g/6 oz light muscovado sugar

3 eggs, beaten

100 g/3½ oz wholemeal self-raising flour

125 g/4½ oz self-raising flour, sifted

2 tbsp cocoa powder

1 tsp bicarbonate of soda

50 g/1¾ oz dark chocolate, melted

FILLING AND TOPPING

150 ml/5 fl oz whole milk natural yogurt

150 ml/5 fl oz double cream

225 g/8 oz fresh soft fruit, such as strawberries or raspberries

1 Grease a deep 23 cm/9 inch round cake tin and line the base with baking paper.

2 Place the oil, yogurt, sugar and beaten eggs in a large mixing bowl and beat together until well combined. Sieve the flours, cocoa powder and bicarbonate of soda together and beat into the yogurt, sugar and egg mixture until well combined. Beat in the melted chocolate.

3 Pour into the prepared tin and bake in a preheated oven, 180°C/350°F/Gas Mark 4, for 45–50 minutes or until a fine skewer inserted into the centre comes out clean. Leave to cool in the tin for 5 minutes, then turn out on to a wire rack to cool completely. When cold, split the cake into 3 layers.

4 To make the filling, place the yogurt and cream in a large mixing bowl and whisk well until the mixture stands in soft peaks.

5 Place one layer of cake on to a serving plate and spread with some of the cream. Top with a little of the fruit (slicing larger fruit such as strawberries). Repeat with the next layer. Top with the final layer of cake and spread with the rest of the cream. Arrange more fruit on top and cut the cake into wedges to serve.

Chocolate Layer Log

This unusual cake is very popular with children who love the appearance of the layers when it is sliced.

55 mins

40 mins

SERVES 8

INGREDIENTS

125 g/4½ oz soft margarine

125 g/4½ oz caster sugar

2 eggs

100 g/3½ oz self-raising flour

25 g/1 oz cocoa powder

2 tbsp milk

WHITE CHOCOLATE BUTTER CREAM

75 g/2¾ oz white chocolate

2 tbsp milk

150 g/5½ oz butter

125 g/4½ oz icing sugar

2 tbsp orange-flavoured liqueur

quick chocolate curls (see page 15), to decorate

1 Grease and line the sides of two 400 g/14 oz food cans.

2 Beat together the margarine and sugar in a bowl until light and fluffy. Gradually add the eggs, beating well after each addition. Sieve together the flour and cocoa powder and fold into the cake mixture. Fold in the milk.

3 Divide the mixture between the two prepared cans. Stand the cans on a baking tray and bake in a preheated oven, 180°C/350°F/Gas Mark 4, for 40 minutes or until springy to the touch. Leave to cool for about 5 minutes in the cans, then turn out and leave to cool completely on a wire rack.

4 To make the butter cream, heat the chocolate and milk gently in a pan until the chocolate has melted, stirring until combined. Leave to cool slightly. Beat together the butter and icing sugar until light and fluffy. Beat in the orange liqueur. Gradually beat in the chocolate mixture.

5 To assemble, cut both cakes into 1 cm/½ inch thick slices, then reassemble them by sandwiching the slices together with some of the butter cream.

6 Place the cake on a serving plate and spread the remaining butter cream over the top and sides. Decorate with the chocolate curls, then serve the cake cut diagonally into slices.

Mousse Cake

With a dark chocolate sponge sandwiched together with a light creamy orange mousse, this spectacular cake is irresistible.

1¼ hrs   40 mins

SERVES 12

INGREDIENTS

175 g/6 oz butter

175 g/6 oz caster sugar

4 eggs, lightly beaten

200 g/7 oz self-raising flour

1 tbsp cocoa powder

50 g/1¾ oz dark, orange-flavoured chocolate, melted

ORANGE MOUSSE

2 eggs, separated

4 tbsp caster sugar

200 ml/7fl oz freshly squeezed orange juice

2 tsp gelatine

3 tbsp water

300 ml/10 fl oz double cream

peeled orange slices, to decorate

1 Grease a 20 cm/8 inch springform cake tin and and line the base. Beat the butter and sugar in a bowl until light and fluffy. Gradually add the eggs, beating well after each addition. Sieve together the cocoa and flour and fold into the cake mixture. Fold in the chocolate.

2 Pour into the prepared tin and level the top. Bake in a preheated oven, 180°C/350°F/Gas Mark 4, for 40 minutes or until springy to the touch. Leave to cool for 5 minutes in the tin, then turn out and leave to cool completely on a wire rack. Cut the cold cake into 2 layers.

3 To make the orange mousse, beat the egg yolks and sugar until light, then whisk in the orange juice. Sprinkle the gelatine over the water in a small bowl and allow to go spongy, then place over a pan of hot water and stir until dissolved. Stir into the mousse.

4 Whip the cream until holding its shape, reserve a little for decoration and fold the rest into the mousse. Whisk the egg whites until standing in soft peaks, then fold in. Leave in a cool place until starting to set, stirring occasionally.

5 Place half of the cake in the tin. Pour in the mousse and press the second cake layer on top. Chill until set. Transfer to a dish, pipe cream rosettes on the top and arrange orange slices in the centre.

Chocolate Roulade

Don't worry if the cake cracks when rolled – this is quite normal. If it doesn't crack, consider yourself a real chocolate wizard in the kitchen!

1 hr · 12 mins

SERVES 6

INGREDIENTS

150 g/5½ oz dark chocolate

2 tbsp water

6 eggs

175 g/6 oz caster sugar

3 tbsp plain flour

1 tbsp cocoa powder

FILLING

300 ml/10 fl oz double cream

75 g/2¾ oz sliced strawberries

TO DECORATE

icing sugar

chocolate leaves (see page 15)

1 Line a 37.5 x 25 cm/15 x 10 inch Swiss roll tin. Melt the chocolate in the water, stirring. Leave to cool slightly.

2 Place the eggs and sugar in a bowl and whisk for 10 minutes, or until the mixture is pale and foamy and the whisk leaves a trail when lifted. Whisk in the chocolate in a thin stream. Sieve the flour and cocoa together and fold into the mixture. Pour into the tin; level the top.

3 Bake in a preheated oven, 200°C/ 400°F/Gas Mark 6, for 12 minutes. Dust a sheet of baking paper with a little icing sugar. Turn out the roulade and remove the lining paper. Roll up the roulade with the fresh paper inside. Place on a wire rack, cover with a damp tea towel and leave to cool.

4 Whisk the cream. Unroll the roulade and scatter over the fruit. Spread three-quarters of the cream over the roulade and re-roll. Dust with icing sugar.

5 Place the roulade on a plate. Pipe the rest of the cream down the centre. Make the chocolate leaves (see page 15) and use them to decorate the roulade.

Chocolate & Coconut Roulade

A coconut-flavoured roulade is encased in a rich chocolate coating. A fresh raspberry coulis gives a lovely fresh contrast.

55 mins   10–12 mins

SERVES 8

INGREDIENTS

3 eggs

75 g/2¾ oz caster sugar

5½ tbsp self-raising flour

1 tbsp block creamed coconut, softened with 1 tbsp boiling water

25 g/1 oz desiccated coconut

6 tbsp good raspberry conserve

CHOCOLATE COATING

200 g/7 oz dark chocolate

5 tbsp butter

2 tbsp golden syrup

RASPBERRY COULIS

225 g/8 oz fresh or frozen raspberries, defrosted if frozen

2 tbsp water

4 tbsp icing sugar

1 Grease and line a 23 x 30 cm/9 x 12 inch Swiss roll tin. Whisk the eggs and caster sugar in a large mixing bowl with electric beaters for about 10 minutes or until the mixture is very light and foamy and the whisk leaves a trail that lasts a few seconds when lifted.

2 Sieve the flour and fold in with a metal spoon or a spatula. Fold in the creamed coconut and desiccated coconut. Pour the mixture into the prepared tin and bake in a preheated oven, 200°C/400°F/ Gas Mark 6, for 10–12 minutes or until springy to the touch.

3 Sprinkle a sheet of baking paper with a little caster sugar and place on top of a damp tea towel. Turn the cake out on to the paper and carefully peel away the lining paper. Spread the jam over the sponge and roll up from the short end, using the tea towel to help you. Place seam-side down on a wire rack and leave to cool completely.

4 Meanwhile, make the coating. Melt the chocolate and butter, stirring. Stir in the golden syrup; leave to cool for 5 minutes. Spread it over the cooled roulade and leave to set. To make the coulis, purée the fruit in a food processor with the water and sugar; sieve to remove the seeds. Cut the roulade into slices and serve with the raspberry coulis.

Almond & Hazelnut Gateau

This is a light nutty gateau sandwiched together with chocolate cream. Simple to create, it is a cake you are sure to make again and again.

2 hrs   15–20 mins

SERVES 8

INGREDIENTS

4 eggs

100 g/3½ oz caster sugar

50 g/1¾ oz ground almonds

50 g/1¾ oz ground hazelnuts

5½ tbsp plain flour

50 g/1¾ oz flaked almonds

FILLING

100 g/3½ oz dark chocolate

1 tbsp butter

300 ml/10 fl oz double cream

icing sugar, to dust

1 Grease two 18 cm/7 inch round sandwich tins and line the bases with baking paper.

2 Whisk the eggs and caster sugar in a large mixing bowl with an electric whisk for about 10 minutes or until the mixture is very light and foamy and the whisk leaves a trail that lasts a few seconds when lifted.

3 Fold in the ground almonds and hazelnuts, sieve the flour and fold in with a metal spoon or spatula. Pour into the prepared tins.

4 Scatter the flaked almonds over the top of one of the cakes. Bake both of the cakes in a preheated oven, 190°C/375°F/Gas Mark 5, for 15–20 minutes or until springy to the touch.

5 Leave the cakes to cool slightly in the tins. Carefully remove the cakes from the tins and transfer them to a wire rack to cool completely.

6 Meanwhile, make the filling. Melt the chocolate, remove from the heat and stir in the butter. Leave to cool slightly. Whip the cream until just holding its

shape, then fold in the melted chocolate until mixed.

7 Place the cake without the extra almonds on a serving plate and spread the filling over it. Leave to set slightly, then place the almond-topped cake on top of the filling and leave to chill for about 1 hour. Dust with icing sugar and serve.

Chocolate & Walnut Cake

This walnut-studded chocolate cake has a tasty butter icing. It is perfect for serving at coffee mornings because it can be made the day before.

1 hr

30–35 mins

SERVES 8

I N G R E D I E N T S

4 eggs

125 g/4½ oz caster sugar

125 g/4½ oz plain flour

1 tbsp cocoa powder

2 tbsp butter, melted

75 g/2¾ oz dark chocolate, melted

150 g/5½ oz finely chopped walnuts

I C I N G

75 g/2¾ oz dark chocolate

125 g/4½ oz butter

200 g/7 oz icing sugar

2 tbsp milk

walnut halves, to decorate

3 Leave to cool in the tin for 5 minutes, then transfer to a wire rack and leave to cool completely.

4 To make the icing, melt the dark chocolate and leave to cool slightly. Beat together the butter, icing sugar and milk in a bowl until the mixture is pale and fluffy. Whisk in the melted chocolate.

5 Cut the cold cake into 2 layers. Sandwich the 2 layers with some of the icing and place on a serving plate. Spread the remaining icing over the top of the cake with a spatula, swirling it slightly as you do so. Decorate the cake with the walnut halves and serve.

1 Grease a 18 cm/7 inch deep round cake tin and line the base. Place the eggs and caster sugar in a mixing bowl and whisk with electric beaters for 10 minutes, or until the mixture is light and foamy and the whisk leaves a trail that lasts a few seconds when lifted.

2 Sieve together the flour and cocoa powder and fold in with a metal spoon or spatula. Fold in the melted butter and chocolate, and the chopped walnuts. Pour into the prepared tin and bake in a preheated oven, 160°C/325°F/Gas Mark 3, and bake for 30–35 minutes or until springy to the touch.

Dobos Torte

This cake originates from Hungary and consists of thin layers of sponge sandwiched together with butter cream, topped with crunchy caramel.

40 mins   10–16 mins

SERVES 8

INGREDIENTS

3 eggs

100 g/3½ oz caster sugar

1 tsp vanilla essence

100 g/3½ oz plain flour

FILLING

175 g/6 oz dark chocolate

175 g/6 oz butter

2 tbsp milk

350 g/12 oz icing sugar

CARAMEL

100 g/3½ oz granulated sugar

4 tbsp water

1 Draw four 18 cm/7 inch circles on sheets of baking paper. Place 2 of them upside down on 2 baking trays.

2 Whisk the eggs and caster sugar in a large mixing bowl with an electric whisk for 10 minutes, or until the mixture is light and foamy and the whisk leaves a trail. Fold in the vanilla essence. Sieve the flour and fold in with a metal spoon.

3 Spoon a quarter of the mixture on to one of the trays and spread out to the size of the circle. Repeat with the other circle. Bake in a preheated oven, 200°C/400°F/Gas Mark 6, for 5–8 minutes or until golden brown. Cool on wire racks. Repeat with the remaining mixture.

4 To make the filling, melt the chocolate and cool slightly. Beat the butter, milk and icing sugar until pale and fluffy. Whisk in the chocolate.

5 Place the sugar and water for the caramel in a heavy-based pan. Heat gently, stirring, to dissolve the sugar. Boil gently until pale golden in colour. Remove from the heat. Pour over one cake layer as a topping. Leave to harden slightly. Mark out 8 portions with an oiled knife.

6 Remove the cakes from the paper and trim the edges. Sandwich the layers together with some of the filling, finishing with the caramel-topped cake. Place on a serving plate, spread the sides with the filling mixture and pipe rosettes around the top.

Bistvitny Torte

This is a Russian marbled chocolate cake that is soaked in a delicious flavoured syrup and decorated with chocolate and cream.

🕐 1 hr 10 mins ⏱ 30 mins

SERVES 10

INGREDIENTS

CHOCOLATE TRIANGLES

25 g/1 oz dark chocolate, melted

25 g/1 oz white chocolate, melted

CAKE

175 g/6 oz soft margarine

175 g/6 oz caster sugar

½ tsp vanilla essence

3 eggs, lightly beaten

225 g/8 oz self-raising flour

50 g/1¾ oz dark chocolate

SYRUP

125 g/4½ oz sugar

6 tbsp water

3 tbsp brandy or sherry

150 ml/5 fl oz double cream

1 Grease a 23 cm/9 inch ring tin. To make the triangles, place a sheet of baking paper on to a baking tray and place alternate spoonfuls of the dark and white chocolate on to the paper. Spread together to form a thick marbled layer; leave to set. Cut into squares, then into triangles.

2 To make the cake, beat the margarine and sugar until light and fluffy. Beat in the vanilla essence. Gradually add the eggs, beating well after each addition. Fold in the flour. Divide the mixture in half. Melt the dark chocolate and stir into one half.

3 Place spoonfuls of each mixture into the prepared tin and swirl together with a skewer to create a marbled effect.

4 Bake in a preheated oven, 190°C/375°F/Gas Mark 5, for 30 minutes or until the cake is springy to the touch. Leave to cool in the tin for a few minutes, then transfer to a wire rack and leave to cool completely.

5 To make the syrup, place the sugar in a small pan with the water and heat gently, stirring, until the sugar has dissolved. Boil gently for 1–2 minutes, then remove from the heat and stir in the brandy or sherry. Leave the syrup to cool slightly then spoon it slowly over the cake, allowing it to soak into the sponge. Whip the double cream and pipe swirls of it on top of the cake. Decorate with the chocolate triangles.

Sachertorte

This rich melt-in-the mouth cake originates in Austria. Writing the name on top requires a steady hand – drizzle a random scribble if you prefer.

3½ hrs   1–1¼ hrs

SERVES 10

INGREDIENTS

175 g/6 oz dark chocolate

150 g/5½ oz unsalted butter

150 g/5½ oz caster sugar

6 eggs, separated

150 g/5½ oz plain flour

ICING AND FILLING

175 g/6 oz dark chocolate

5 tbsp strong black coffee

175 g/6 oz icing sugar

6 tbsp good apricot preserve

50 g/1¾ oz dark chocolate, melted

1 Grease a 23 cm/9 inch springform cake tin and line the base with baking paper. Melt the chocolate. Beat the butter and 75 g/2¾ oz of the sugar until pale and fluffy. Add the egg yolks and beat together well. Add the chocolate in a thin stream, beating well. Sieve the flour and fold it into the cake mixture. Whisk the egg whites until they stand in soft peaks. Add the remaining sugar and whisk for 2 minutes by hand, or 45–60 seconds if using an electric whisk, until glossy. Fold half into the chocolate mixture, then fold in the remainder.

2 Spoon into the prepared tin and level the top. Bake in a preheated oven, 150°C/300°F/Gas Mark 2, for 1–1¼ hours until a skewer inserted into the centre comes out clean. Cool in the tin for 5 minutes, then transfer to a wire rack to cool completely.

3 To make the icing, melt the chocolate and beat in the coffee until smooth. Sieve the icing sugar into a bowl. Whisk in the melted chocolate mixture to give a thick icing. Halve the cake. Warm the jam, spread over one half of the cake and sandwich together. Invert the cake on a wire rack. Spoon the icing over the cake and spread to coat the top and sides. Leave to set for 5 minutes, allowing any

excess icing to drop through the rack. Transfer to a serving plate and leave to set for at least 2 hours.

4 To decorate, spoon the melted chocolate into a small piping bag and pipe the word 'Sacher' or 'Sachertorte' across the top of the cake. Leave the chocolate topping to harden before serving the cake.

Dark & White Chocolate Torte

If you can't decide if you prefer bitter dark chocolate or rich creamy white chocolate then this gateau is for you.

1 hr 5 mins   35–40 mins

SERVES 6

INGREDIENTS

4 eggs

100 g/3½ oz cup caster sugar

100 g/3½ oz plain flour

DARK CHOCOLATE CREAM

300 ml/10 fl oz double cream

150 g/5½ oz dark chocolate, broken into small pieces

WHITE CHOCOLATE ICING

75 g/2¾ oz white chocolate

1 tbsp butter

1 tbsp milk

4 tbsp icing sugar

chocolate caraque (see page 15)

1 Grease a 20 cm/8 inch round springform tin and line the base with baking paper. Whisk the eggs and caster sugar in a large mixing bowl with an electric whisk for about 10 minutes, or until the mixture is very light and foamy and the whisk leaves a trail that lasts a few seconds when lifted.

2 Sieve the flour and fold in with a metal spoon or spatula. Pour into the prepared tin and bake in a preheated oven, 180°C/350°F/Gas Mark 4, for 35–40 minutes, or until springy to the touch. Leave to cool slightly, then transfer to a wire rack to cool completely.

3 To make the chocolate cream, place the cream in a saucepan and bring to the boil, stirring. Add the chocolate and stir until melted. Remove from the heat, transfer to a bowl, and leave to cool. Beat with a wooden spoon until thick.

4 Cut the cold cake into 2 layers horizontally. Sandwich the layers back together with the chocolate cream and place on a wire rack.

5 To make the icing, melt the chocolate and butter together and stir until blended. Whisk in the milk and icing sugar. Continue whisking for a few minutes until the icing is cool. Pour it over the cake and spread with a spatula to coat the top and sides. Decorate the top with chocolate caraque and leave to set.

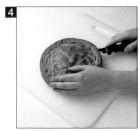

Chocolate Ganache Cake

Ganache – a divine mixture of chocolate and cream – is used to fill and decorate this rich chocolate cake, making it a chocolate-lover's dream.

2 hrs 5 mins   40 mins

SERVES 10

INGREDIENTS

175 g/6 oz butter

175 g/6 oz caster sugar

4 eggs, lightly beaten

200 g/7 oz self-raising flour

1 tbsp cocoa powder

50 g/1¾ oz dark chocolate, melted

GANACHE

450ml/16 fl oz double cream

375 g/13 oz dark chocolate, broken into pieces

TO FINISH

200 g/7 oz chocolate-flavoured cake covering

1 Lightly grease a 20 cm/8 inch springform cake tin and line the base. Beat the butter and sugar until light and fluffy. Gradually add the eggs, beating well after each addition. Sieve together the flour and cocoa. Fold into the cake mixture. Fold in the melted chocolate.

2 Pour into the prepared tin and level the top. Bake in a preheated oven, 180°C/350°F/Gas Mark 4, for 40 minutes or until springy to the touch. Leave to cool for 5 minutes in the tin, then turn out on to a wire rack and leave to cool completely. Cut the cold cake into 2 layers.

3 To make the ganache, place the double cream in a pan and bring to the boil, stirring. Add the chocolate and stir until melted and combined. Pour into

a bowl and whisk for about 5 minutes or until the ganache is fluffy and cool.

4 Reserve one-third of the ganache. Use the remaining ganache to sandwich the cake together and to spread over the top and sides of the cake.

5 Melt the chocolate-flavoured cake covering and spread it over a large

sheet of baking paper. Cool until just set. Cut into strips a little wider than the height of the cake. Place the strips around the sides of the cake, overlapping them slightly.

6 Pipe the reserved ganache in tear drops or shells to cover the top of the cake. Chill for 1 hour.

Bûche de Noël

This is the traditional French Christmas cake. It consists of a chocolate Swiss roll filled with and encased in a delicious rich chocolate icing.

🍰 1 hr   🕐 12 mins

SERVES 10

I N G R E D I E N T S

C A K E

4 eggs

100 g/3½ oz caster sugar

75 g/2¾ oz self-raising flour

2 tbsp cocoa powder

I C I N G

150 g/5½ oz dark chocolate

2 egg yolks

150 ml/5 fl oz milk

125 g/4½ oz butter

4 tbsp icing sugar

2 tbsp rum, optional

T O   D E C O R A T E

a little white glacé or royal icing

icing sugar, to dust

holly or Christmas cake decorations

1 Grease and line a 30 x 23 cm/ 12 x 9 inch Swiss roll tin.

2 Whisk the eggs and caster sugar in a bowl with an electric whisk for 10 minutes or until the mixture is light and foamy and the whisk leaves a trail. Sieve the flour and cocoa powder and fold in. Pour into the tin and bake in a preheated oven, 200°C/400°F/Gas Mark 6, for 12 minutes or until springy to the touch. Turn out on to baking paper sprinkled with a caster sugar. Peel off the lining paper and trim the edges. Cut a small slit halfway into the cake, about 1 cm/½ inch from one short end. Starting at that end, roll up, enclosing the paper. Cool on a wire rack.

3 To make the icing, break the chocolate into pieces and melt over a pan of hot water. Beat in the egg yolks, whisk in the milk and cook, stirring, until the mixture thickens enough to coat the back of a wooden spoon. Cover with dampened greaseproof paper and cool. Beat the butter and sugar until pale and fluffy. Beat in the custard and rum, if using.

4 Unroll the sponge, spread with one-third of the icing and roll up again. Place on a serving plate. Spread the remaining icing over the cake and mark with a fork to give the effect of tree bark. Leave to set. Pipe white icing at the ends to form the rings of the log. Sprinkle with sugar and decorate.

Chocolate Truffle Cake

Soft chocolate sponge topped with a rich chocolate truffle mixture makes a cake that chocoholics will die for.

4¾ hrs   20–25 mins

SERVES 12

INGREDIENTS

75 g/2¾ oz butter

75 g/2¾ oz caster sugar

2 eggs, lightly beaten

75 g/2¾ oz self-raising flour

½ tsp baking powder

25 g/1 oz cocoa powder

50 g/1¾ oz ground almonds

TRUFFLE TOPPING

350 g/12 oz dark chocolate

100 g/3½ oz butter

300 ml/10 fl oz double cream

75 g/2¾ oz plain cake crumbs

3 tbsp dark rum

TO DECORATE

Cape gooseberries

50 g/1¾ oz dark chocolate, melted

1 Lightly grease a 20 cm/8 inch round springform tin and line the base. Beat together the butter and sugar until light and fluffy. Gradually add the eggs, beating well after each addition.

2 Sieve the flour, baking powder and cocoa powder together and fold into the mixture along with the ground almonds. Pour into the prepared tin and bake in a preheated oven, 180°C/350°F/Gas Mark 4, for 20–25 minutes or until springy to the touch. Leave to cool slightly in the tin, then transfer to a wire rack to cool completely. Wash and dry the tin and return the cooled cake to the tin.

3 To make the topping, heat the chocolate, butter and cream in a heavy-based pan over a low heat and stir until smooth. Cool, then chill for 30 minutes. Beat well with a wooden spoon and chill for a further 30 minutes. Beat the mixture again, then add the cake crumbs and rum, beating until well combined. Spoon over the sponge base and chill for 3 hours.

4 Meanwhile, dip the Cape gooseberries in the melted chocolate until partially covered. Leave to set on baking paper. Transfer the cake to a serving plate; decorate with Cape gooseberries.

White Truffle Cake

A light white sponge, topped with a rich creamy-white chocolate truffle mixture, makes an out-of-this-world gateau.

🍰 3¼ hrs   🕐 25 mins

SERVES 12

INGREDIENTS

2 eggs

4 tbsp caster sugar

5½ tbsp plain flour

50 g/1¾ oz white chocolate, melted

TRUFFLE TOPPING

300 ml/10 fl oz double cream

350 g/12 oz white chocolate, broken into pieces

250 g/9 oz Quark or fromage frais

TO DECORATE

dark, milk or white chocolate caraque (see page 15)

cocoa powder, to dust

3 To make the topping, place the cream in a pan and bring to the boil, stirring to prevent it sticking to the bottom of the pan. Cool slightly, then add the white chocolate pieces and stir until melted and combined. Remove from the heat and leave until almost cool, stirring, then stir in the Quark or fromage frais. Pour the mixture on top of the cake and chill for 2 hours.

4 Remove the cake from the tin and transfer to a serving plate. Make the caraque (see page 15) and then use it to decorate the top of the cake.

1 Grease a 20 cm/8 inch round springform tin and line the base.

2 Whisk the eggs and caster sugar in a mixing bowl for 10 minutes or until very light and foamy and the whisk leaves a trail that lasts a few seconds when lifted. Sieve the flour and fold in with a metal spoon. Fold in the melted white chocolate. Pour into the tin and bake in a preheated oven, 180°C/350°F/Gas Mark 4, for 25 minutes or until springy to the touch. Leave to cool slightly, then transfer to a wire rack until completely cold. Return the cold cake to the tin.

Raspberry Vacherin

A vacherin is made of layers of crisp meringue sandwiched together with fruit and cream. It makes a fabulous gateau for special occasions.

1¾ hrs   1½ hrs

SERVES 10

INGREDIENTS

3 egg whites

175 g/6 oz caster sugar

1 tsp cornflour

25 g/1 oz dark chocolate, grated

FILLING

175 g/6 oz dark chocolate

475 ml/16 fl oz double cream, whipped

350 g/12 oz fresh raspberries

a little melted chocolate, to decorate

1 Draw 3 rectangles, 10 x 25 cm/4 x 10 inches, on sheets of baking paper, and place on 2 baking trays.

2 Whisk the egg whites in a mixing bowl until standing in soft peaks, then gradually whisk in half of the sugar and continue whisking until the mixture is very stiff and glossy.

3 Carefully fold in the rest of the sugar, the cornflour and grated chocolate with a metal spoon or a spatula.

4 Spoon the meringue mixture into a piping bag fitted with a 1 cm/½ inch plain nozzle and pipe lines across the baking paper rectangles.

5 Bake in a preheated oven, 140°C/275°F/Gas Mark 1, for 1½ hours, changing the positions of the baking trays halfway through cooking. Without opening the oven door, turn off the oven and leave the meringues inside it to cool, then peel away the paper.

6 To make the vacherin filling, melt the chocolate and spread it over 2 of the meringue layers. Leave to stand until the filling has hardened.

7 Place 1 chocolate-coated meringue on a plate and top with about one-third of the cream and raspberries. Gently place the second chocolate-coated meringue on top and spread with half of the remaining cream and raspberries.

8 Place the last meringue on the top and decorate it with the remaining cream and raspberries. Drizzle a little melted chocolate over the top of the vacherin and serve.

Tropical Fruit Vacherin

Meringue layers are sandwiched with a rich chocolate cream and topped with tropical fruit. Prepare in advance and make up just before required.

1½ hrs 1½ hrs

SERVES 10

INGREDIENTS

6 egg whites

275 g/9½ oz caster sugar

75 g/2¾ oz desiccated coconut

FILLING AND TOPPING

90 g/3 oz dark chocolate, broken into pieces

3 egg yolks

3 tbsp water

1 tbsp rum, optional

4 tbsp caster sugar

475 ml/16 fl oz double cream

selection of tropical fruits, sliced or cut into bite size pieces

1 Draw 3 circles, 20 cm/8 inch each, on sheets of baking paper, and place on baking trays.

2 Whisk the egg whites until standing in soft peaks, then gradually whisk in half of the sugar and continue whisking until the mixture is very stiff and glossy. Carefully fold in the remaining sugar and the coconut.

3 Spoon the mixture into a piping bag fitted with a star nozzle and cover the circles with piped swirls. Bake in a preheated oven, 140°C/275°F/Gas Mark 1, for 1½ hours, changing the position of the trays halfway through. Without opening the oven door, turn off the oven, leaving the meringues inside to cool, then peel away the paper.

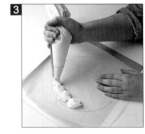

4 While the meringues are cooling, make the filling. Place the chocolate pieces, egg yolks, water, rum, if using, and sugar in a small bowl and place it over a pan of gently simmering water. Cook over a low heat, stirring, until the chocolate has melted and the mixture has thickened. Cover with a disc of baking paper and leave until cold.

5 Whip the double cream and fold two-thirds of it into the chocolate mixture. Sandwich the meringue layers together with the chocolate and cream mixture. Place the remaining cream in a piping bag fitted with a star nozzle and pipe around the edge of the meringue. Arrange the tropical fruits in the centre.

Chocolate Brownie Roulade

The addition of nuts and raisins has given this dessert extra texture, making it similar to that of chocolate brownies.

1 hr   25 mins

SERVES 8

INGREDIENTS

150 g/5 ½ oz dark chocolate, broken into pieces

3 tbsp water

175 g/6 oz caster sugar

5 eggs, separated

25 g/1 oz raisins, chopped

25 g/1 oz pecan nuts, chopped

pinch of salt

300 ml/10 fl oz double cream, whipped lightly

icing sugar, for dusting

1 Grease a 30 x 20 cm/12 x 8 inch Swiss roll tin, line with baking paper and grease the paper.

2 Place the chocolate with the water in a small saucepan over a low heat, stirring until the chocolate has just melted. Leave to cool.

3 In a bowl, whisk the sugar and egg yolks for 2–3 minutes with an electric whisk until thick and pale.

4 Fold in the cooled chocolate, raisins and pecan nuts.

5 In a separate bowl, whisk the egg whites with the salt. Fold one quarter of the egg whites into the chocolate mixture, then fold in the rest of the whites, working lightly and quickly.

6 Transfer the mixture to the prepared tin and bake in a preheated oven,

180°C/350°F/Gas Mark 4, for 25 minutes, until risen and just firm to the touch. Leave to cool before covering with a sheet of non-stick baking paper and a damp clean tea towel. Leave to stand until completely cold.

7 Turn the roulade out on to another piece of baking paper dusted with icing sugar and remove the lining paper.

8 Spread the lightly whipped cream over the roulade. Starting from a short end, roll the sponge away from you using the paper to guide you. Trim the ends of the roulade to make a neat finish and transfer to a serving plate. Leave the roulade to chill in the refrigerator until ready to serve. Dust with a little icing sugar before serving, if wished.

Chocolate & Apricot Squares

The white chocolate makes this a very rich cake, so serve it cut into small squares or bars, or sliced thinly.

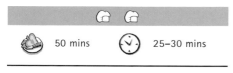

50 mins   25–30 mins

SERVES 12

INGREDIENTS

125 g/4½ oz butter

175 g/6 oz white chocolate, chopped

4 eggs

125 g/4½ oz caster sugar

200 g/7 oz plain flour, sifted

1 tsp baking powder

pinch of salt

100 g/3½ oz ready-to-eat dried apricots, chopped

1 Lightly grease a 20 cm/9 inch square cake tin and line the base with a sheet of baking paper.

2 Melt the butter and chocolate in a heatproof bowl set over a saucepan of simmering water. Stir frequently with a wooden spoon until the mixture is smooth and glossy. Leave the mixture to cool slightly.

3 Beat the eggs and caster sugar into the butter and chocolate mixture until well combined.

4 Fold in the flour, baking powder, salt and chopped dried apricots and mix together well.

5 Pour the mixture into the tin and bake in a preheated oven, 180°C/350°F/Gas Mark 4, for 25–30 minutes.

6 The centre of the cake may not be completely firm, but it will set as it cools. Leave in the tin to cool.

7 When the cake is completely cold turn it out and slice into squares or bars.

VARIATION

Replace the white chocolate with milk or dark chocolate, if you prefer.

Chocolate Slab Cake

This chocolate slab cake gets its moist texture from the soured cream which is stirred into the beaten mixture.

55 mins   40–45 mins

SERVES 10

INGREDIENTS

225 g/8 oz butter

100 g/3½ oz dark chocolate, chopped

150 ml/5 fl oz water

300 g/10½ oz plain flour

2 tsp baking powder

275 g/9½ oz soft brown sugar

150 ml/5 fl oz soured cream

2 eggs, beaten

FROSTING

200 g/7 oz dark chocolate

6 tbsp water

3 tbsp single cream

1 tbsp butter, chilled

1 Grease a 33 x 20 cm/13 x 8 inch square cake tin and line the base with baking paper. In a saucepan, melt the butter and chocolate with the water over a low heat, stirring frequently.

2 Sieve the flour and baking powder into a mixing bowl and stir in the sugar.

3 Pour the hot chocolate liquid into the bowl and then beat well until all of the ingredients are evenly mixed. Stir in the soured cream, followed by the eggs.

4 Pour the cake mixture into the prepared tin and bake in a preheated oven, 190°C/375°F/Gas Mark 5, for 40–45 minutes.

5 Leave the cake to cool in the tin before turning it out on to a wire rack. Leave to cool completely.

6 To make the frosting, melt the chocolate with the water in a saucepan over a very low heat, stir in the cream and remove from the heat. Stir in the chilled butter, then pour the frosting over the cooled cake, using a spatula to spread it evenly over the top of the cake.

COOK'S TIP

Leave the cake on the wire rack to frost it and place a large baking tray underneath to catch any drips.

Chocolate & Almond Torte

This torte is perfect for serving on a hot sunny day with double cream and a selection of fresh summer berries.

🍲 1 hr 25 mins 🕐 40–45 mins

SERVES 10

INGREDIENTS

225 g/8 oz dark chocolate, broken into pieces

3 tbsp water

150 g/5½ oz soft brown sugar

175 g/6 oz butter, softened

25 g/1 oz ground almonds

3 tbsp self-raising flour

5 eggs, separated

100 g/3½ oz blanched almonds, finely chopped

icing sugar, for dusting

double cream, to serve (optional)

1 Grease a 23 cm/9 inch loose-bottomed cake tin and line the base with baking paper.

2 In a saucepan set over a very low heat, melt the chocolate with the water, stirring until smooth. Add the sugar and stir until dissolved, taking the pan off the heat to prevent it overheating.

3 Add the butter in small amounts until it has melted into the chocolate. Remove from the heat and lightly stir in the ground almonds and flour. Add the egg yolks one at a time, beating well after each addition.

4 In a large mixing bowl, whisk the egg whites until they stand in soft peaks, then fold them into the chocolate mixture with a metal spoon. Stir in the chopped almonds. Pour the mixture into the tin and level the surface.

5 Bake in a preheated oven, 180°C/350°F/Gas Mark 4, for 40–45 minutes until well risen and firm (the cake will crack on the surface during cooking).

6 Leave to cool in the tin for 30–40 minutes. Turn out on to a wire rack to cool completely. Dust with icing sugar and serve in slices with double cream, if using.

COOK'S TIP

For a nuttier flavour, toast the chopped almonds in a dry frying pan over a medium heat for about 2 minutes until lightly golden.

Marbled Chocolate Cake

Separate chocolate and orange cake mixtures are combined in a ring mould to achieve the marbled effect in this light sponge.

🥧 1¼ hrs   🕐 30–35 mins

SERVES 8

INGREDIENTS

175 g/6 oz butter, softened

175 g/6 oz caster sugar

3 eggs, beaten

150 g/5½ oz self-raising flour, sifted

25 g/1 oz cocoa powder, sifted

5–6 tbsp orange juice

grated rind of 1 orange

1 Lightly grease a 25 cm/10 inch ovenproof ring mould.

2 In a mixing bowl, cream together the butter and sugar with an electric whisk for about 5 minutes.

3 Add the beaten egg a little at a time, whisking well after each addition.

4 Using a metal spoon, fold the flour into the creamed mixture carefully, then spoon half of the mixture into a separate mixing bowl.

5 Fold the cocoa powder and half of the orange juice into one bowl and mix gently.

6 Fold the orange rind and remaining orange juice into the other bowl and mix gently.

7 Place spoonfuls of each of the mixtures alternately into the mould, then drag a skewer through the mixture to create a marbled effect.

8 Bake in a preheated oven, 180°C/350°F/Gas Mark 4, for 30–35 minutes until well risen and a skewer inserted into the centre comes out clean.

9 Leave the cake to cool in the mould before turning out on to a wire rack.

VARIATION

For a richer chocolate flavour, add 40 g/1¾ oz chocolate drops to the cocoa mixture.

Chocolate Bread

For the chocoholics amongst us, this bread is great fun to make and even better to eat.

2 hrs   25–30 mins

MAKES 1 LOAF

I N G R E D I E N T S

450 g/1 lb strong white bread flour

25 g/1 oz cocoa powder

1 tsp salt

1 sachet easy-blend dried yeast

25 g/1 oz soft brown sugar

1 tbsp oil

300 ml/10 fl oz tepid water

1 Lightly grease a 900 g/2 lb loaf tin.

2 Sieve the flour and cocoa powder into a large mixing bowl.

3 Stir in the salt, dried yeast and soft brown sugar.

4 Pour in the oil along with the tepid water and mix the ingredients together to make a dough.

5 Place the dough on a lightly floured surface and knead for 5 minutes.

6 Place the dough in a greased bowl, cover and leave to rise in a warm

place for about 1 hour or until the dough has doubled in size.

7 Knock back the dough and shape it into a loaf. Place the dough in the prepared tin, cover and leave to rise in a warm place for a further 30 minutes.

8 Bake in a preheated oven, 200°C/400°F/Gas Mark 6, for 25–30 minutes, or until a hollow sound is heard when the base of the bread is tapped.

9 Transfer the bread to a wire rack and leave to cool. Cut into slices to serve.

COOK'S TIP

This bread can be sliced and spread with butter or it can be lightly toasted.

Raspberry Croissants

Simple to prepare, these tasty croissants are popped on the barbecue to warm through until the chocolate melts.

10 mins 10–15 mins

SERVES 4

INGREDIENTS

4 butter croissants

4 tsp raspberry preserve

75 g/2 ¾ oz dark chocolate

125 g/4 ½ oz raspberries

oil, for greasing

1 Slice the croissants in half. Spread the bottom half of each croissant with 1 teaspoon of the raspberry preserve.

2 Grate or finely chop the chocolate and sprinkle over the raspberry preserve.

3 Lightly grease 4 sheets of kitchen foil, brushing with a little oil.

4 Divide the raspberries equally among the croissants and replace the top half of each croissant. Place each croissant on to a sheet of foil, wrapping the foil to enclose the croissant completely.

VARIATION

For a delicious chocolate and strawberry filling for the croissants, use sliced strawberries and strawberry preserve instead of the raspberries.

5 Place the rack 15 cm/6 inches above hot coals. Transfer the croissants to the rack and leave them to heat through for 10–15 minutes or until the chocolate just begins to melt.

6 Remove the foil and transfer the croissants to individual serving plates. Serve hot.

Italian Chocolate Chip Bread

Serve this tasty snack plain with butter or jam or, Italian-style, with mascarpone cheese.

30 mins, plus 1½–2 hrs standing time

25 mins

MAKES 1 LOAF

INGREDIENTS

1 tsp vegetable oil, for brushing

225 g/8 oz plain flour, plus extra for dusting

1 tbsp cocoa powder

pinch of salt

1 tbsp unsalted butter, plus ½ tsp extra, melted, for brushing

1 tbsp caster sugar

1 tsp easy-blend dried yeast

150 ml/5 fl oz hand-hot water

55 g/2 oz dark chocolate chips

1 Brush a baking tray with ½ teaspoon of the oil. Sieve the flour, cocoa powder and salt into a bowl. Add the butter, cut it into the flour mixture, then stir in the sugar and yeast.

2 Gradually add the water to the mixture, stirring well to combine. When the dough becomes too firm to stir with a spoon, gather it together with your hands. Turn it out on to a lightly floured surface and knead thoroughly until smooth and elastic.

3 Knead the chocolate chips into the dough, distributing them evenly throughout. Form the dough into a round loaf, place the loaf on the baking tray, cover with oiled clingfilm and set aside in a warm place for 1½–2 hours, until doubled in bulk.

4 Remove and discard the clingfilm and bake the loaf in a preheated oven, 220°C/425°F/Gas Mark 7, for 10 minutes. Lower the temperature to 190°C/375°F/Gas Mark 5 and bake for a further 15 minutes.

5 Transfer the loaf to a wire rack and brush with melted butter. Cover with a clean tea towel until cooled.

Chocolate Marshmallow Cake

The sweetness of whipped marshmallow frosting complements the mouthwatering flavour of this moist, dark chocolate sponge.

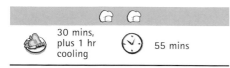

30 mins, plus 1 hr cooling

55 mins

MAKES 1 x 15 CM/6 INCH CAKE

INGREDIENTS

6 tbsp unsalted butter, plus 1 tbsp extra for greasing

225 g/8 oz caster sugar

½ tsp vanilla essence

2 eggs, lightly beaten

85 g/3 oz dark chocolate, broken into pieces

150 ml/5 fl oz buttermilk

175 g/6 oz self-raising flour

½ tsp bicarbonate of soda

pinch of salt

55 g/2 oz milk chocolate, grated, to decorate

FROSTING

175 g/6 oz white marshmallows

1 tbsp milk

2 egg whites

2 tbsp caster sugar

1 Grease an 850 ml/1½ pint ovenproof pudding basin with butter. Cream the butter, sugar and vanilla together until very pale and fluffy, then gradually beat in the eggs.

2 Melt the dark chocolate in a heatproof bowl over a pan of simmering water. When the chocolate has melted, stir in the buttermilk gradually, until well combined. Remove the pan from the heat and cool slightly.

3 Sieve the flour, bicarbonate of soda and salt into a separate bowl.

4 Alternately add the chocolate mixture and the flour mixture to the creamed mixture, a little at a time. Spoon the creamed mixture into the basin and smooth the surface.

5 Bake in a preheated oven, 160°C/ 325°F/Gas Mark 3, for about 50 minutes, until a skewer inserted into the centre of the cake comes out clean. Turn out on to a wire rack to cool.

6 Meanwhile, make the frosting. Put the marshmallows and milk in a small saucepan and heat very gently until the marshmallows have melted. Remove the pan from the heat and leave to cool.

7 Whisk the egg whites until soft peaks form, then add the sugar and continue whisking, until stiff peaks form. Fold the egg white into the cooled marshmallow mixture and set aside for 10 minutes.

8 When the cake is cool, cover the top and sides with the marshmallow frosting. Sprinkle grated milk chocolate over the frosting.

Layered Meringue Gateau

Surprisingly easy, but somewhat time-consuming to make, this magnificent gateau makes a wonderfully impressive dinner party dessert.

40 mins, plus 1 hr cooling

6 hrs, or overnight

MAKES 1 x 18 CM/7 INCH CAKE

INGREDIENTS

6 egg whites

140 g/5 oz caster sugar

175 g/6 oz icing sugar

2 tbsp cornflour

FILLING

225 ml/8 fl oz double cream

140 g/5 oz dark chocolate, broken into small pieces

4 tsp dark rum

DECORATION

150 ml/5 fl oz double cream

4 tsp caster sugar

1–2 tsp cocoa powder, for dusting

1 Prepare 5 sheets of baking paper by drawing an 18 cm/7 inch circle on each, then use them to line baking trays.

2 Whisk the egg whites until they form soft peaks. Mix together the sugar and cornflour and sieve it into the egg whites, a little at a time, whisking constantly until firm peaks form.

3 Spoon the meringue mixture into a piping bag fitted with a round nozzle. Starting from the centre, pipe five spirals, measuring 18 cm/7 inches, on each of the prepared pieces of baking paper.

4 Bake in a preheated oven, at the lowest possible temperature with the door slightly ajar, for 6 hours or overnight.

5 After baking, carefully peel the meringue spirals from the baking paper and place on wire racks to cool.

6 To make the filling, pour the double cream into a small saucepan and place over a low heat. Add the chocolate and stir until melted. Remove the pan from the heat and beat the mixture with a hand-held whisk. Beat in the dark rum, then cover with clingfilm and refrigerate overnight or for as long as the meringues are in the oven.

7 To assemble the gateau, beat the filling with an electric mixer until thick and smooth. Place three of the meringue layers on a work surface and spread the filling over them. Stack the three layers, one on top of the other, and place an uncovered meringue layer on top. Crush the fifth meringue into crumbs.

8 To make the decoration, whisk the cream with the sugar until thick. Carefully spread the mixture over the top of the gateau. Sprinkle the meringue crumbs on top of the cream and dust the centre of the gateau with cocoa powder. Serve within 1–2 hours.

No-bake Refrigerator Cake

Ideal for children to make, this cake does not require an oven and it is prepared very rapidly – but it does need to chill overnight.

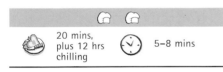

20 mins, plus 12 hrs chilling

5–8 mins

MAKES A 22 X 11 CM/ 8½ X 4¼ INCH CAKE

I N G R E D I E N T S

225 g/8 oz unsalted butter, diced

225 g/8 oz dark chocolate, broken into pieces

55 g/2 oz glacé cherries, chopped

55 g/2 oz walnuts, chopped

12 rectangular plain chocolate biscuits

1 Line a 450 g/1 lb loaf tin with greaseproof paper or baking paper.

2 Put the butter and chocolate into the top of a double boiler, or in a heatproof bowl set over a pan of barely simmering water. Stir constantly over a low heat until they have melted and the mixture is smooth. Remove from the heat and leave to cool slightly.

3 In a separate bowl, mix together the cherries and walnuts. Spoon one-third of the chocolate mixture into the prepared tin, cover with a layer of biscuits and top with half the cherries and walnuts. Make further layers, ending with the chocolate mixture. Cover with clingfilm and chill in the refrigerator for at least 12 hours. When chilled, turn the cake out onto a serving dish.

Swedish Chocolate Cake

This is the ideal snack to eat with a mid-morning cup of coffee. Serve with whipped cream for a special treat.

30 mins   1 hr

MAKES 1 x 23 CM/9 INCH CAKE

INGREDIENTS

5 tbsp unsalted butter, plus 2 tsp extra for greasing

25 g/1 oz dry white breadcrumbs

85 g/3 oz dark chocolate, broken into pieces

175 g/6 oz caster sugar

2 eggs, separated

1 tsp vanilla essence

175 g/6 oz plain flour

1 tsp baking powder

125 ml/4 fl oz single cream

1 Grease a deep 23 cm/9 inch round cake tin with butter. Sprinkle the breadcrumbs into the tin and press them on to the base and sides.

2 Place the chocolate in the top of a double boiler or in a heatproof bowl set over a pan of barely simmering water. Stir over a low heat until melted, then remove from the heat.

3 Cream the butter with the sugar until pale and fluffy. Beat in the egg yolks, one at a time, and add the vanilla.

4 Sieve one-third of the flour with the baking powder, then beat into the egg mixture. Mix together the cream and melted chocolate, then beat one-third of this mixture into the egg mixture. Continue adding the flour and the chocolate mixture alternately, beating well after each addition.

5 Whisk the egg whites in a separate bowl until they form stiff peaks. Fold the egg whites into the chocolate mixture.

6 Pour into the prepared tin and bake in a preheated oven, 150°C/300°F/Gas Mark 2, for about 50 minutes, until a skewer inserted into the centre of the cake comes out clean. Turn the cake out on to a wire rack to cool before serving.

Date & Chocolate Cake

Moist and moreish, this fruity chocolate cake will prove to be a popular after-school snack.

25 mins, plus 20 mins cooling

40 mins

MAKES 1 X 18 CM/7 INCH CAKE

I N G R E D I E N T S

115 g/4 oz unsalted butter, plus 2 tsp extra for greasing

85 g/3 oz self-raising flour, plus 1 tbsp extra for dusting

115 g/4 oz dark chocolate, broken into pieces

1 tbsp grenadine

1 tbsp golden syrup

55 g/2 oz caster sugar

2 large eggs

2 tbsp ground rice

1 tbsp icing sugar, to decorate

FILLING

115 g/4 oz dried dates, chopped

1 tbsp lemon juice

1 tbsp orange juice

1 tbsp demerara sugar

25 g/1 oz blanched almonds, chopped

2 tbsp apricot jam

1　Grease and flour two 18 cm/7 inch sandwich tins. Put the chocolate, grenadine and syrup in the top of a double boiler or in a heatproof bowl set over a pan of barely simmering water. Stir over a low heat until the chocolate has melted and the mixture is smooth. Remove from the heat and leave to cool.

2　Cream together the butter and caster sugar together until pale and fluffy, then gradually beat in the eggs and then the cooled chocolate mixture.

3　Sieve the flour into another bowl and stir in the ground rice. Fold the flour mixture into the creamed mixture.

4　Divide the mixture between the prepared tins and smooth the surface. Bake in a preheated oven, 180°C/350°F/Gas Mark 4, for 20–25 minutes, until golden and firm to the touch. Turn out on to a wire rack to cool.

5　To make the filling, put all the ingredients into a saucepan and stir over a low heat for 4–5 minutes, until fully incorporated. Remove from the heat, leave to cool and then use the filling to sandwich the cakes together. Dust the top of the cake with icing sugar to decorate.

Chocolate Bread Pudding

This chocolate pudding is served with hot fudge sauce, making it the most delicious way to use up bread that is slightly stale.

🐦🐦🐦

🍳 2¼ hours ⏲ 45 mins

SERVES 4

INGREDIENTS

6 thick slices white bread, crusts removed

450 ml/16 fl oz milk

175 g/6 oz canned evaporated milk

2 tbsp cocoa powder

2 eggs

2 tbsp dark muscovado sugar

1 tsp vanilla essence

icing sugar, for dusting

HOT FUDGE SAUCE

60 g/2 oz dark chocolate, broken into pieces

1 tbsp cocoa powder

2 tbsp golden syrup

60 g/2 oz butter or margarine

2 tbsp dark muscovado sugar

150 ml/5 fl oz milk

1 tbsp cornflour

1 Grease a shallow ovenproof dish. Cut the bread into squares and layer them in the dish.

2 Put the milk, evaporated milk and cocoa powder in a saucepan and heat gently, stirring occasionally, until lukewarm.

3 Whisk together the eggs, sugar and vanilla essence. Add the warm milk mixture and beat well.

4 Pour into the prepared dish, making sure that all the bread is completely covered. Cover the dish with clingfilm and chill in the refrigerator for 1–2 hours.

5 Bake the pudding in a preheated oven, 180°C/350°F/Gas Mark 4, for approximately 35–40 minutes, until set. Remove the pudding from the oven and allow to stand for 5 minutes.

6 To make the sauce, put the chocolate, cocoa powder, syrup, butter or margarine, sugar, milk and cornflour into a saucepan. Heat gently, stirring constantly, until smooth.

7 Dust the pudding with icing sugar and serve with the hot fudge sauce.

Hot Desserts

Chocolate is comforting at any time but no more so than when served in a steaming hot pudding. It is hard to think of anything more warming, comforting and homely than tucking into a steamed hot Chocolate Fudge Pudding or a Hot Chocolate Soufflé, and children will love the chocolate addition to nursery favourites such as Chocolate Bread & Butter Pudding. In fact, there are several old favourites that have been given the chocolate treatment, bringing

them bang up to date and putting them on the chocolate lover's map.

When you are feeling in need of something a little more sophisticated, try the new-style Chocolate Apple Pancake Stack, or Chocolate Pear & Almond Flan, or Chocolate Zabaglione for a sophisticated creamy, warm dessert set to get your tastebuds in a whirl!

This chapter is packed full of chocolate delights, with different tastes and textures to add warmth to any day.

Chocolate Queen of Puddings

An old time favourite with an up-to-date twist, this pudding makes the perfect end to a special family meal.

25 mins   40–45 mins

SERVES 4

INGREDIENTS

50 g/1¾ oz dark chocolate

475 ml/16 fl oz chocolate-flavoured milk

100 g/3½ oz fresh white or wholemeal breadcrumbs

125 g/4½ oz caster sugar

2 eggs, separated

4 tbsp black cherry jam

1 Break the chocolate into small pieces and place in a saucepan with the chocolate-flavoured milk. Heat gently, stirring until the chocolate melts. Bring almost to the boil, then remove the pan from the heat.

2 Place the breadcrumbs in a large mixing bowl with 25 g/1 oz of the sugar. Pour over the chocolate milk and mix well. Beat in the egg yolks.

3 Spoon into a 1.25 litre/2 pint pie dish and bake in a preheated oven, 180°C/350°F/Gas Mark 4, for 25–30 minutes or until set and firm to the touch.

4 Whisk the egg whites in a large grease-free bowl until standing in soft peaks. Gradually whisk in the remaining caster sugar and whisk until you have a glossy, thick meringue.

5 Spread the black cherry jam over the surface of the chocolate mixture and pile or pipe the meringue on top. Return the pudding to the oven for about 15 minutes or until the meringue is crisp and golden.

VARIATION
If you prefer, add 40 g/1½ oz desiccated coconut to the breadcrumbs and omit the jam.

Chocolate Eve's Pudding

Eve's Pudding is traditionally made with apples, but here it is made with raspberries and white chocolate sponge, with a bitter chocolate sauce.

15 mins   40–45 mins

SERVES 4

INGREDIENTS

225 g/8 oz fresh or frozen raspberries

2 eating apples, peeled, cored and sliced thickly

4 tbsp seedless raspberry jam

2 tbsp port, optional

SPONGE TOPPING

4 tbsp soft margarine

4 tbsp caster sugar

75 g/2¾ oz self-raising flour, sifted

50 g/1¾ oz white chocolate, grated

1 egg

2 tbsp milk

BITTER CHOCOLATE SAUCE

90 g/3 oz dark chocolate

150 ml/5 fl oz single cream

1 Place the apple slices and raspberries in a shallow 1.25 litre/2 pint ovenproof dish.

2 Place the raspberry jam and port (if using) in a small pan and heat gently until the jam melts and combines with the port. Pour the mixture over the fruit.

3 Place all of the ingredients for the sponge topping in a large mixing bowl and beat until the mixture is smooth.

4 Spoon the sponge mixture over the fruit and level the top. Bake in a preheated oven, 180°C/350°F/Gas Mark 4, for 40–45 minutes or until the sponge is springy to the touch.

5 To make the sauce, break the chocolate into small pieces and place in a heavy-based saucepan with the cream. Heat gently, beating until a smooth sauce is formed. Serve warm with the pudding.

VARIATION
Try using dark chocolate in the sponge, and top with apricot halves, covered with peach schnapps and apricot conserve.

Chocolate Ginger Puddings

Individual puddings always look more professional and are quicker to cook. If you do not have mini pudding basins, use small teacups instead.

10 mins

45 mins

SERVES 4

INGREDIENTS

100 g/3½ oz soft margarine

100 g/3½ oz self-raising flour, sifted

100 g/3½ oz caster sugar

2 eggs

25 g/1 oz cocoa powder, sifted

25 g/1 oz dark chocolate

50 g/1¾ oz stem ginger

CHOCOLATE CUSTARD

2 egg yolks

1 tbsp caster sugar

1 tbsp cornflour

300 ml/10 fl oz milk

100 g/3½ oz dark chocolate, broken into pieces

icing sugar, to dust

1 Lightly grease 4 individual pudding basins. Place the margarine, flour, sugar, eggs and cocoa powder in a mixing bowl and beat until well combined and smooth. Chop the chocolate and ginger and stir into the mixture.

2 Spoon the cake mixture into the prepared basins and level the top. The mixture should three-quarters fill the basins. Cover the basins with discs of baking paper and cover with a pleated sheet of foil. Steam for 45 minutes until the puddings are cooked and springy to the touch.

3 Meanwhile, make the custard. Beat together the egg yolks, sugar and cornflour to form a smooth paste. Heat the milk until boiling and pour over the egg mixture. Return to the pan and cook over a very low heat, stirring until thick. Remove from the heat and beat in the chocolate. Stir until the chocolate melts.

4 Lift the puddings from the steamer, run a knife around the edge of the basins and turn out on to serving plates. Dust with sugar and drizzle some chocolate custard over the top. Serve the remaining custard separately.

Bread & Butter Pudding

Brioche gives this pudding a lovely rich flavour, but this recipe also works well with soft-baked batch bread.

🕐 2¼ hours   🕐 35–40 mins

SERVES 4

INGREDIENTS

225 g/8 oz brioche

1 tbsp butter

50 g/1¾ oz dark chocolate chips

1 egg

2 egg yolks

4 tbsp caster sugar

425 ml/15 fl oz canned light evaporated milk

1 Cut the brioche into thin slices. Lightly butter one side of each slice.

2 Place a layer of brioche, buttered-side down, in the bottom of a shallow ovenproof dish. Sprinkle a few chocolate chips over the top.

3 Continue layering the brioche and chocolate chips, finishing with a layer of bread on top.

4 Whisk together the egg, egg yolks and sugar until well combined. Heat the milk in a small saucepan until it just begins to simmer. Gradually add to the egg mixture, whisking well.

VARIATION

For a double-chocolate pudding, heat the milk with 1 tbsp of cocoa powder, stirring until well dissolved then continue from step 4.

5 Pour the custard over the pudding and leave to stand for 5 minutes. Press the brioche down into the milk.

6 Place the pudding in a roasting tin and fill with boiling water to come halfway up the side of the dish (this is known as a bain-marie). Bake in a preheated oven, 180°C/350°F/Gas Mark 4, for 30 minutes or until the custard has set. Leave the pudding to cool for 5 minutes before serving.

Chocolate French Toasties

There is something very moreish about these delicious chocolate toasties, served with a little whipped cream and raspberry jam sauce.

10–15 mins   10–20 mins

SERVES 4

INGREDIENTS

50 g/1¾ oz dark chocolate

150 ml/5 fl oz milk

1 egg

4 tbsp seedless raspberry jam

2 tbsp rum, optional

8 thick slices white bread

butter or oil, for shallow-frying

½ tsp ground cinnamon

3 tbsp caster sugar

a little whipped cream, to serve

1 Break the chocolate into small pieces and place in a small pan with the milk. Heat gently, stirring until the chocolate melts. Leave to cool slightly.

COOK'S TIP
Young children adore this dessert. Cut the bread into fingers to make it easier for them to handle.

2 Beat the egg in a large mixing bowl and whisk in the warm chocolate milk.

3 Heat the raspberry jam gently and stir in the rum, if using. Set aside and keep warm.

4 Remove the crusts from the bread, cut into triangles and dip each one into the chocolate mixture. Heat the butter or oil in a frying pan and shallow-fry the bread triangles in batches for 2–3 minutes until just crispy, turning once.

5 Mix together the cinnamon and caster sugar and sprinkle it over the toasties. Serve with the hot jam sauce and a little whipped cream.

Chocolate Fudge Pudding

This fabulous steamed pudding, served with a rich chocolate fudge sauce, is perfect for cold winter days.

10 mins   35–40 mins

SERVES 6

INGREDIENTS

150 g/5½ oz soft margarine

150 g/5½ oz self-raising flour

150 g/5½ oz golden syrup

3 eggs

25 g/1 oz cocoa powder

CHOCOLATE FUDGE SAUCE:

100 g/3½ oz dark chocolate

125 ml/4 fl oz condensed milk

4 tbsp double cream

1 Lightly grease a 1.2 litre/2 pint pudding basin.

2 Place the ingredients for the sponge in a mixing bowl and beat until well combined and smooth.

3 Spoon into the prepared basin and level the top. Cover with a disc of baking parchment and tie a pleated sheet of foil over the basin. Steam for 1½–2 hours until the pudding is cooked and springy to the touch.

4 To make the sauce, break the chocolate into small pieces and place in a small pan with the condensed milk. Heat gently, stirring until the chocolate melts.

5 Remove the pan from the heat and stir in the double cream.

6 To serve the pudding, turn it out on to a serving plate and pour over a little of the chocolate fudge sauce. Serve the remaining sauce separately.

Chocolate Fruit Crumble

The addition of chocolate in a crumble topping makes it even more of a treat, and is a good way of enticing children to eat a fruit dessert.

  5–10 mins · 40–45 mins

SERVES 4

INGREDIENTS

400 g/14 oz canned apricots, in natural juice

450 g/1 lb cooking apples, peeled and sliced thickly

100 g/3½ oz plain flour

6 tbsp butter

50 g/1¾ oz porridge oats

4 tbsp caster sugar

100 g/3½ oz chocolate chips

1 Lightly grease an ovenproof dish with a little butter or margarine.

2 Drain the apricots, reserving 4 tablespoons of the juice. Place the apples and apricots in the prepared ovenproof dish with the reserved apricot juice and toss to mix.

3 Sieve the flour into a mixing bowl. Cut the butter into small cubes and rub in with your fingertips until the mixture resembles fine breadcrumbs. Stir in the porridge oats, caster sugar and chocolate chips.

VARIATION

Other fruits can be used to make this crumble – fresh pears mixed with fresh or frozen raspberries work well. If you do not use canned fruit, add 4 tablespoons of orange juice to the fresh fruit.

4 Sprinkle the crumble mixture over the apples and apricots and level the top roughly. Do not press the crumble down on to the fruit.

5 Bake in a preheated oven, 350°F/ 180°C/Gas Mark 4, for 40–45 minutes or until the topping is golden. Serve the crumble hot or cold.

Poached Pears in Chocolate

This elegant dessert can be served hot or cold. The pears can be poached 2 days in advance and stored in their poaching juices in the refrigerator.

10 mins   25 mins

SERVES 6

INGREDIENTS

6 firm ripe pears

100 g/3½ oz caster sugar

2 cinnamon sticks

rind of 1 orange

2 cloves

1 bottle rosé wine

CHOCOLATE SAUCE

175 g/6 oz dark chocolate

250 g/9 oz mascarpone cheese

2 tbsp orange-flavoured liqueur

1 Carefully peel the pears, leaving the stalks intact.

2 Place the sugar, cinnamon sticks, orange rind, cloves and wine in a saucepan that will hold the 6 pears snugly.

3 Heat gently until the sugar has dissolved, then add the pears to the liquid and bring to a simmer. Cover the pan and poach the pears gently for 20 minutes. If serving them cold, leave the pears to cool in the liquid, then chill until required. If serving hot, leave the pears in the hot liquid whilst preparing the chocolate sauce.

4 To make the sauce, melt the chocolate. Beat together the cheese and the orange-flavoured liqueur. Beat the cheese mixture into the chocolate.

5 Remove the pears from the poaching liquid and place on a serving plate. Add a generous spoonful of sauce on the side and serve the remainder separately.

COOK'S TIP
There is no need to waste the poaching liquid. Boil it rapidly in a clean pan for 10 minutes to reduce to a syrup. Use the syrup to sweeten fresh fruit salad or spoon it over ice cream.

Saucy Chocolate Pudding

In this recipe, the mixture separates out during cooking to produce a cream sponge topping and a delicious chocolate sauce on the bottom.

15 mins   40 mins

SERVES 4

INGREDIENTS

300 ml/10 fl oz milk

75 g/2¾ oz dark chocolate

½ tsp vanilla essence

100 g/3½ oz caster sugar

100 g/3½ oz butter

150 g/5½ oz self-raising flour

2 tbsp cocoa powder

icing sugar, to dust

FOR THE SAUCE

3 tbsp cocoa powder

4 tbsp light muscovado sugar

300 ml/10 fl oz boiling water

1 Lightly grease a 900 ml\1½ pint ovenproof dish.

2 Place the milk in a small pan. Break the chocolate into pieces and add to the milk. Heat gently, stirring until the chocolate melts. Leave to cool slightly. Stir in the vanilla essence.

3 Beat together the caster sugar and butter in a bowl until light and fluffy. Sieve the flour and cocoa powder together. Add to the bowl with the chocolate milk and beat until smooth, using an electric whisk if you have one. Pour the mixture into the prepared dish.

4 To make the sauce, mix together the cocoa powder and sugar. Add a little boiling water and mix to a smooth paste, then stir in the remaining water. Pour the sauce over the pudding but do not mix in.

5 Place the dish on to a baking tray and bake in a preheated oven, 180°C/350°F/Gas Mark 4, for 40 minutes or until the pudding is dry on top and springy to the touch. Leave to stand for about 5 minutes, then dust with a little icing sugar just before serving.

VARIATION

For a mocha sauce, add 1 tablespoon of instant coffee to the cocoa powder and sugar in step 4, before mixing to a paste with the boiling water.

Pecan & Fudge Ring

Although this can be served cold as a cake, it is absolutely delicious served hot as a pudding.

35 mins   35 mins

SERVES 6

INGREDIENTS

FUDGE SAUCE

3 tbsp butter

3 tbsp light muscovado sugar

4 tbsp golden syrup

2 tbsp milk

1 tbsp cocoa powder

40 g/1½ oz dark chocolate

50 g/1¾ oz pecan nuts, finely chopped

CAKE

100 g/3½ oz soft margarine

100 g/3½ oz light muscovado sugar

125 g/4½ oz self-raising flour

2 eggs

2 tbsp milk

1 tbsp golden syrup

1 Lightly grease a 20 cm/8 inch ring tin.

2 To make the fudge sauce, place the butter, sugar, syrup, milk and cocoa powder in a small pan and heat gently, stirring until combined.

3 Break the chocolate into pieces, add to the mixture and stir until melted. Stir in the chopped nuts. Pour into the base of the tin and leave to cool.

4 To make the cake, place all of the ingredients in a mixing bowl and beat until smooth. Carefully spoon the cake mixture over the chocolate fudge sauce.

5 Bake in a preheated oven, 180°C/350°F/Gas Mark 4, for 35 minutes or until the cake is springy to the touch.

6 Leave to cool in the tin for 5 minutes, then turn out on to a serving dish.

Chocolate Meringue Pie

Crumbly biscuit base, rich creamy chocolate filling topped with fluffy meringue – what could be more indulgent than this fabulous dessert?

25 mins   35 mins

SERVES 6

INGREDIENTS

225 g/8 oz dark chocolate digestive biscuits

4 tbsp butter

FILLING

3 egg yolks

4 tbsp caster sugar

4 tbsp cornflour

600 ml/1 pint milk

100 g/3½ oz dark chocolate, melted

MERINGUE

2 egg whites

100 g/3½ oz caster sugar

¼ tsp vanilla essence

1 Place the digestive biscuits in a plastic bag and crush with a rolling pin. Pour into a mixing bowl. Melt the butter and stir it into the biscuit crumbs until well mixed. Press the biscuit mixture firmly into the base and up the sides of a 23 cm/9 inch flan tin or dish.

2 To make the filling, beat the egg yolks, caster sugar and cornflour in a large bowl until they form a smooth paste, adding a little of the milk if necessary. Heat the milk until almost boiling, then slowly pour it on to the egg mixture, whisking well.

3 Return the mixture to the saucepan and cook gently, whisking constantly until it thickens. Remove from the heat. Whisk in the melted chocolate, then pour it on to the digestive biscuit base.

4 To make the meringue, whisk the egg whites in a large mixing bowl until standing in soft peaks. Gradually whisk in about two-thirds of the sugar until the mixture is stiff and glossy. Fold in the remaining sugar and vanilla essence.

5 Spread the meringue over the filling, swirling the surface with the back of a spoon to give it an attractive finish. Bake in the centre of a preheated oven, 170°C/375°F/Gas Mark 3, for 30 minutes or until golden. Serve hot or just warm.

Chocolate Apple Pie

Easy-to-make crumbly chocolate pastry encases a delicious apple filling studded with chocolate chips – a guaranteed family favourite.

45 mins ⏱ 40 mins

SERVES 6

INGREDIENTS

CHOCOLATE PASTRY

4 tbsp cocoa powder

200 g/7 oz plain flour

100 g/3½ oz softened butter

4 tbsp caster sugar

2 egg yolks

a few drops of vanilla essence

cold water, to mix

FILLING

750 g/1 lb10 oz cooking apples

2 tbsp butter

½ tsp ground cinnamon

50 g/1¾ oz dark chocolate chips

a little egg white, beaten

½ tsp caster sugar

whipped cream or vanilla ice cream,
  to serve

1 To make the pastry, sieve the cocoa powder and flour into a mixing bowl and rub in the butter until the mixture resembles fine breadcrumbs. Stir in the caster sugar. Add the egg yolks, vanilla essence and enough water to mix to a dough.

2 Roll out the dough on a lightly floured surface and use to line a deep 20 cm/8 inch flan or cake tin. Chill for 30 minutes. Roll out any trimmings and cut out some pastry leaves to decorate the top of the pie.

3 Peel, core and thickly slice the apples. Place half of the apple slices in a saucepan with the butter and cinnamon and cook over a gentle heat, stirring occasionally until the apples soften.

4 Stir in the uncooked apple slices, leave to cool slightly, then stir in the chocolate chips. Prick the base of the pastry case and pile the apple mixture into it. Arrange the pastry leaves on top. Brush the leaves with a little egg white and sprinkle with caster sugar.

5 Bake in a preheated oven, 180°C/350°F/Gas Mark 4, for 35 minutes until the pastry is crisp. Serve warm or cold, with whipped cream or vanilla ice cream.

Chocolate Pear & Almond Flan

This attractive dessert consists of a flan filled with pears cooked in a chocolate, almond-flavoured sponge. It is delicious served hot or cold.

30 mins   35 mins

SERVES 6

INGREDIENTS

100 g/3½ oz plain flour

25 g/1 oz ground almonds

5 tbsp block margarine

about 3 tbsp water

FILLING

400 g/14 oz canned pear halves, in natural juice

4 tbsp butter

4 tbsp caster sugar

2 eggs, beaten

100 g/3½ oz ground almonds

2 tbsp cocoa powder

few drops of almond essence

icing sugar, to dust

CHOCOLATE SAUCE

4 tbsp caster sugar

3 tbsp golden syrup

90 ml/3 fl oz water

175 g/6 oz dark chocolate, broken into pieces

2 tbsp butter

1 Lightly grease a 20 cm/8 inch flan tin. Sieve the flour into a mixing bowl and stir in the almonds. Rub in the margarine with your fingertips until the mixture resembles breadcrumbs. Add enough water to mix to a soft dough. Cover, chill in the freezer for 10 minutes, then roll out and use to line the tin. Prick the base and chill again.

2 Meanwhile, make the filling. Drain the pears well. Beat the butter and sugar until light and fluffy. Beat in the eggs. Fold in the almonds, cocoa powder and almond essence. Spread the chocolate mixture in the pastry case and arrange the pears on top, pressing down lightly. Bake in the centre of a preheated oven, 200°C/400°F/Gas Mark 6, for 30 minutes or until the filling has risen. Cool slightly and transfer to a serving dish, if wished. Dust with sugar.

3 To make the chocolate sauce, place the sugar, syrup and water in a pan and heat gently, stirring until the sugar dissolves. Boil gently for 1 minute. Remove from the heat, add the chocolate and butter and stir until melted and well combined. Serve with the flan.

Chocolate & Banana Pancakes

Pancakes are given the chocolate treatment here to make a fabulous dinner party dessert. Prepare them ahead of time for trouble-free entertaining.

🕙 10 mins   ⏲ 15 mins

SERVES 4

INGREDIENTS

3 large bananas

6 tbsp orange juice

grated rind of 1 orange

2 tbsp orange- or banana-flavoured liqueur

HOT CHOCOLATE SAUCE

1 tbsp cocoa powder

2 tsp cornflour

3 tbsp milk

40 g/1½ oz dark chocolate

1 tbsp butter

175 g/6 oz golden syrup

¼ tsp vanilla essence

PANCAKES

100 g/3½ oz plain flour

1 tbsp cocoa powder

1 egg

1 tsp sunflower oil

300 ml/10 fl oz milk

oil, for frying

1 Peel and slice the bananas and place them in a dish with the orange juice and rind and the liqueur. Set aside.

2 Mix the cocoa powder and cornflour in a bowl, then stir in the milk. Break the dark chocolate into pieces and place in a pan with the butter and golden syrup. Heat gently, stirring until well blended. Add the cocoa mixture and bring to the boil over a gentle heat, stirring. Simmer for 1 minute, then remove from the heat and stir in the vanilla essence.

3 To make the pancakes, sieve the flour and cocoa into a mixing bowl and make a well in the centre. Add the egg and oil. Gradually whisk in the milk to form a smooth batter. Heat a little oil in a heavy-based frying pan and pour off any excess. Pour in a little batter and tilt the pan to coat the base. Cook over a medium heat until the underside is browned. Flip over and cook the other side. Slide the pancake out of the pan and keep warm. Repeat until all the batter has been used.

4 To serve, reheat the chocolate sauce for 1–2 minutes. Fill the pancakes with the bananas and fold in half or into triangles. Pour over a little chocolate sauce and serve.

Apple Pancake Stacks

If you cannot wait to get your first chocolate 'fix' of the day, serve these pancakes for breakfast. They also make a perfect family dessert.

20 mins   45 mins

SERVES 4

INGREDIENTS

225 g/8 oz plain flour

1½ tsp baking powder

4 tbsp caster sugar

1 egg

1 tbsp butter, melted

300 ml10 fl oz milk

1 eating apple

50 g/1¾ oz dark chocolate chips

Chocolate Sauce (see page 80) or maple syrup, to serve

1 Sieve the flour and baking powder into a mixing bowl. Stir in the caster sugar. Make a well in the centre and add the egg and melted butter. Gradually whisk in the milk to form a smooth batter.

2 Peel, core and grate the apple and stir it into the batter with the chocolate chips.

3 Heat a griddle or heavy-based frying pan over a medium heat and grease it lightly. For each pancake, place about 2 tablespoons of the batter on to the griddle or pan and spread to make a 7.5 cm/3 inch round.

4 Cook for a few minutes until you see bubbles appear on the surface of the pancake. Turn over and cook for a further 1 minute. Remove from the pan and keep warm. Repeat with the remaining batter to make about 12 pancakes.

5 To serve, stack 2 or 3 pancakes on an individual serving plate and serve them with the hot chocolate sauce or maple syrup.

COOK'S TIP

To keep the cooked pancakes warm, pile them on top of each other with baking paper in between to prevent them sticking to one another.

Chocolate Fondue

This is a fun dessert to serve at the end of the meal. Prepare in advance, then just warm through before serving.

🍴 15 mins 🕐 5 mins

SERVES 4

INGREDIENTS

CHOCOLATE FONDUE

225 g/8 oz dark chocolate

200 ml/7 fl oz double cream

2 tbsp brandy

TO SERVE

selection of fruit

white and pink marshmallows

sweet biscuits

1 Break the chocolate into small pieces and place in a small saucepan with the double cream.

2 Heat the mixture gently, stirring constantly until the chocolate has melted and blended with the cream.

3 Remove the pan from the heat and stir in the brandy.

4 Pour into a fondue pot or a small flameproof dish and keep warm, preferably over a small burner.

5 Serve with a selection of fruit, marshmallows and biscuits for dipping. The fruit and marshmallows can be spiked on fondue forks, wooden skewers or ordinary forks for dipping into the chocolate fondue.

COOK'S TIP

To prepare the fruit for dipping, cut larger fruit into bite-sized pieces. Fruit that discolours, such as bananas, apples and pears, should be dipped in a little lemon juice as soon as it is cut.

Hot Chocolate Soufflé

Served with chocolate custard, this is a chocoholic's dream. Do not be put off by the mystique of soufflés – this one is not difficult to make.

15 mins   50–55 mins

SERVES 4

INGREDIENTS

100 g/3½ oz dark chocolate

300 ml/10 fl oz milk

2 tbsp butter

4 large eggs, separated

1 tbsp cornflour

4 tbsp caster sugar

½ tsp vanilla essence

100 g/3½ oz dark chocolate chips

caster and icing sugar, to dust

CHOCOLATE CUSTARD

2 tbsp cornflour

1 tbsp caster sugar

475 ml/16 fl oz milk

50 g/1¾ oz dark chocolate

1 Grease a 900 ml/1½ pint soufflé dish and sprinkle with caster sugar. Break the chocolate into pieces.

2 Heat the milk with the butter in a pan until almost boiling. Mix the egg yolks, cornflour and caster sugar in a bowl and pour on some of the hot milk, whisking. Return it to the pan and cook gently, stirring constantly until thickened. Add the chocolate and stir until melted. Remove from the heat and stir in the flavouring.

3 Whisk the egg whites until standing in soft peaks. Fold half of the egg whites into the chocolate mixture. Fold in the rest with the chocolate chips. Pour into the dish and bake in a preheated oven, 180°C/350°F/Gas Mark 4, for 40–45 minutes, until well risen.

4 Meanwhile, make the custard. Put the cornflour and sugar in a small bowl and mix to a smooth paste with a little of the milk. Heat the remaining milk until almost boiling. Pour a little of the hot milk on to the cornflour, mix well, then pour back into the pan. Cook gently, stirring until thickened. Break the chocolate into pieces and add to the custard, stirring until melted.

5 Dust the soufflé with sugar and serve immediately with the chocolate custard.

Chocolate Zabaglione

As this recipe only uses a little chocolate, choose one with a minimum of 70 per cent cocoa solids for a good flavour.

10 mins   5 mins

SERVES 4

INGREDIENTS

4 egg yolks

4 tbsp caster sugar

50 g/1¾ oz dark chocolate

125 ml/4 fl oz Marsala wine

cocoa powder, to dust

1 In a large glass mixing bowl, whisk together the egg yolks and caster sugar with an electric whisk until the mixture is very pale.

2 Grate the chocolate finely and fold into the egg mixture.

3 Fold the Marsala wine into the chocolate mixture.

4 Place the mixing bowl over a saucepan of gently simmering water

and set the electric whisk on the lowest speed or swap to a balloon whisk. Cook gently, whisking continuously until the mixture thickens; take care not to overcook or the mixture will curdle.

5 Spoon the hot mixture into warmed individual glass dishes or coffee cups (as here) and dust with cocoa powder. Serve the zabaglione as soon as possible, while it is warm, light and fluffy.

COOK'S TIP

Make the dessert just before serving as it will separate if left to stand. If it begins to curdle, remove it from the heat immediately and place it in a bowl of cold water to stop the cooking. Whisk furiously until the mixture comes together.

Steamed Coffee Sponge

This sponge pudding is very light and is delicious with a coffee or chocolate sauce.

🥄 10 mins   🕐 1–1¼ hrs

SERVES 4

INGREDIENTS

2 tbsp margarine

2 tbsp soft brown sugar

2 eggs

5½ tbsp flour

¾ tsp baking powder

6 tbsp milk

1 tsp coffee essence

SAUCE

300 ml/10 fl oz milk

1 tbsp soft brown sugar

1 tsp cocoa powder

2 tbsp cornflour

1 Lightly grease a 600 ml/1 pint heatproof pudding basin. Cream the margarine and sugar until light and fluffy and beat in the eggs.

2 Gradually stir in the flour and baking powder and then the milk and coffee essence to make a smooth batter.

COOK'S TIP

The pudding is covered with pleated paper and foil to allow it to rise. The foil will react with the steam and must therefore not be placed directly against the pudding.

3 Spoon the mixture into the pudding basin and cover with a pleated piece of baking paper and then a pleated piece of foil, securing around the bowl with string. Place in a steamer or large pan half full of boiling water. Cover and steam for 1–1¼ hours or until cooked through.

4 To make the sauce, put the milk, soft brown sugar and cocoa powder in a pan and heat until the sugar dissolves. Blend the cornflour with 4 tablespoons of cold water to make a paste and stir into the pan. Bring the sauce to the boil, stirring until thickened. Cook over a gentle heat for 1 minute.

5 Turn the pudding out on to a serving plate and spoon the sauce over the top. Serve.

Fudge Pudding

This pudding has a hidden surprise when cooked because it separates to give a rich chocolate sauce at the bottom of the dish.

🕐 10 mins   🕐 35–40 mins

SERVES 4

INGREDIENTS

4 tbsp margarine, plus extra for greasing

6 tbsp soft light brown sugar

2 eggs, beaten

350 ml/12 fl oz milk

50 g/1¾ oz chopped walnuts

5 tbsp plain flour

2 tbsp cocoa powder

icing sugar and cocoa, to dust

1 Lightly grease a 1 litre/1¾ pint ovenproof dish.

2 Cream together the margarine and sugar in a large mixing bowl until fluffy. Beat in the eggs.

3 Gradually stir in the milk and add the walnuts.

4 Sieve the flour and cocoa powder into the mixture and fold in gently, with a metal spoon, until well mixed.

VARIATION

Add 1–2 tablespoons of brandy or rum to the mixture for a slightly alcoholic pudding, or 1–2 tablespoons of orange juice for a child-friendly version.

5 Spoon the mixture into the dish and cook in a preheated oven at 180°C/ 350°F/Gas Mark 4, for 35–40 minutes or until the sponge is cooked.

6 Dust with icing sugar and cocoa powder and serve.

Tropical Fruit Kebabs

Spear some chunks of exotic tropical fruits on to kebab sticks,
sear them over the barbecue and serve with this amazing chocolate dip.

45 mins   5 mins

SERVES 4

I N G R E D I E N T S

DIP

125 g/4½ oz dark chocolate, broken into pieces

2 tbsp golden syrup

1 tbsp cocoa powder

1 tbsp cornflour

200 ml/7 fl oz milk

KEBABS

1 mango

1 paw-paw

2 kiwi fruit

½ small pineapple

1 large banana

2 tbsp lemon juice

150 ml/5 fl oz white rum

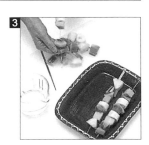

1 Put all the ingredients for the chocolate dip into a heavy-based saucepan. Heat over the barbecue or a low heat, stirring constantly, until thickened and smooth. Keep warm at the edge of the barbecue.

2 Slice the mango on each side of its large, flat stone. Cut the flesh into chunks, removing the peel. Halve, deseed and peel the paw-paw and cut it into chunks. Peel the kiwi fruit and slice into chunks. Peel the pineapple and cut it into chunks. Peel and slice the banana and dip the pieces in the lemon juice to prevent it from discolouring.

3 Thread the pieces of fruit alternately on to 4 wooden skewers. Place them in a shallow dish and pour over the rum. Leave to soak up the flavour of the rum for at least 30 minutes, until ready to barbecue.

4 Cook the kebabs over the hot coals, turning frequently, for about 2 minutes, until seared. Serve, accompanied by the hot chocolate dip.

Sticky Chocolate Puddings

These rich individual puddings with cream sauce always look and taste impressive at the end of a meal.

20 mins   1 hr

SERVES 6

INGREDIENTS

125 g/4½ oz butter, softened

150 g/5½ oz soft brown sugar

3 eggs, beaten

pinch of salt

25 g/1 oz cocoa powder

125 g/4½ oz self-raising flour

25 g/1 oz dark chocolate, finely chopped

75 g/2¾ oz white chocolate, finely chopped

SAUCE

150 ml/5 fl oz double cream

75 g/2¾ oz soft brown sugar

2 tbsp butter

1 Lightly grease 6 individual 175 ml/6 fl oz pudding basins.

2 In a bowl, cream together the butter and sugar until pale and fluffy. Beat in the eggs a little at a time, beating well after each addition.

3 Sieve the salt, cocoa powder and flour into the creamed mixture and fold through the mixture. Stir in the chopped chocolate until evenly combined.

4 Divide the mixture between the prepared pudding basins. Lightly grease 6 squares of foil and use them to cover the tops of the basins. Press around the edges to seal.

5 Place the basins in a roasting tin and pour in boiling water to come halfway up the sides of the basins.

6 Bake in a preheated oven, 180°/350°F/Gas Mark 4, for 50 minutes, or until a skewer inserted into the centre comes out clean.

7 Remove the basins from the roasting tin and set aside while you prepare the sauce.

8 To make the sauce, put the cream, sugar and butter into a pan and bring to the boil over a gentle heat. Simmer gently until the sugar has dissolved.

9 To serve, run a knife around the edge of each pudding, then turn out on to serving plates. Pour the cream sauce over the top of the puddings and serve immediately.

Chocolate Fruit Dip

These warm, lightly barbecued fruit kebabs are served with a delicious chocolate dipping sauce.

10 mins

5–10 mins

SERVES 4

INGREDIENTS

selection of fruit (choose from oranges, bananas, strawberries, pineapple chunks (fresh or canned), apricots (fresh or canned), dessert apples, pears, kiwi fruit)

1 tbsp lemon juice

CHOCOLATE SAUCE

4 tbsp butter

50 g/1¾ oz dark chocolate, broken into small cubes

½ tbsp cocoa powder

2 tbsp golden syrup

BASTE

4 tbsp clear honey

grated rind and juice of ½ orange

1 To make the chocolate sauce, place the butter, chocolate, cocoa powder and golden syrup in a small pan. Heat gently on a stove or at the side of the barbecue, stirring continuously, until all of the ingredients have melted and are well combined.

2 To prepare the fruit, peel and core if necessary, then cut into large, bite-sized pieces or wedges as appropriate. Dip apples, pears and bananas in lemon juice to prevent discoloration. Thread the pieces of fruit on to skewers.

3 To make the baste, mix together the honey, orange juice and rind, heat gently if required, and brush over the fruit.

4 Barbecue the fruit skewers over warm coals for 5–10 minutes until hot. Serve with the chocolate dipping sauce.

COOK'S TIP

If the coals are too hot raise the rack so that it is about 15 cm/6 inches above the coals or spread out the coals a little to reduce the heat. Do not assemble the fruit skewers more than 1–2 hours before they are required.

Italian Drowned Ice Cream

A classic vanilla ice cream is topped with steaming coffee to make a wonderful instant dessert. Remember to serve in heatproof bowls.

🕐 7½ hrs   ⏱ 10 mins

SERVES 4

I N G R E D I E N T S

about 475 ml/16 fl oz freshly made espresso coffee

chocolate-covered coffee beans, to decorate

V A N I L L A   I C E   C R E A M

1 vanilla pod

6 large egg yolks

150 g/5½ oz caster sugar, or vanilla-flavoured sugar (sugar that has been stored with a vanilla pod)

500 ml/17 fl oz milk

250 ml/8 fl oz plus 2 tbsp double cream

1 To make the ice cream, slit the vanilla pod lengthways and scrape out the tiny brown seeds. Set aside.

2 Put the yolks and sugar in a heatproof bowl that will sit over a saucepan with plenty of room underneath it. Beat the eggs and sugar together until thick and creamy.

3 Put the milk, cream and vanilla seeds in the pan over a low heat and bring to a simmer. Pour the milk over the egg mixture, whisking. Pour 2.5 cm/1 inch of water in the bottom of a pan. Place the bowl on top, ensuring the base does not touch the water. Turn the heat to medium–high.

4 Cook the mixture, stirring constantly, until it is thick enough to coat the back of the spoon. Remove from the heat, transfer to a bowl and leave to cool.

5 Churn the mixture in an ice-cream maker, following the manufacturer's instructions. Alternatively, place it in a freezerproof container and freeze for 1 hour, turn out into a bowl and whisk to break up the ice crystals, then return to the freezer, repeating the process 4 times at 30-minute intervals.

6 Transfer the ice cream to a freezerproof bowl, smooth the top and cover with clingfilm or foil. Freeze for up to 3 months.

7 Soften in the refrigerator for 20 minutes before serving. Place scoops of ice cream in each bowl. Pour over the coffee and sprinkle with coffee beans.

Banana Empanadas

Using filo pastry makes these empanadas light and crisp on the outside, while the filling melts into a scrumptious hot banana-chocolate goo.

10 mins   15 mins

SERVES 4

INGREDIENTS

about 8 sheets of filo pastry, cut into half lengthways

melted butter or vegetable oil, for brushing

2 ripe sweet bananas

1–2 tsp sugar

juice of ½ lemon

175–200 g/6–7 oz dark chocolate, broken into small pieces

icing sugar, for dusting

ground cinnamon, for dusting

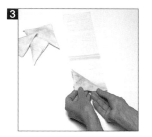

COOK'S TIP

You could use ready-made puff pastry instead of filo for a more puffed-up effect.

1 Working one at a time, lay a long rectangular sheet of filo out in front of you and brush it with butter or oil.

2 Peel and dice and bananas and place in a bowl. Add the sugar and lemon juice and stir well to combine. Stir in the chocolate.

3 Place a couple of teaspoons of the banana and chocolate mixture in one corner of the pastry, then fold over into a triangle shape to enclose the filling. Continue to fold in a triangular shape,

until the filo is completely wrapped around the filling.

4 Dust the parcels with icing sugar and cinnamon. Place on a baking sheet and continue the process with the remaining filo and filling.

5 Bake in a preheated oven, 190°C/375°F/Gas Mark 5, for about 15 minutes or until the little pastries are golden. Remove from the oven and serve hot – warn people that the filling is very hot.

Chocolate Fudge Pears

Melt-in-the-mouth, spicy poached pears are enveloped in a wonderfully self-indulgent chocolate fudge sauce.

🍽 10 mins   ⏱ 30–35 mins

SERVES 4

INGREDIENTS

4 eating pears

1–2 tbsp lemon juice

300 ml/10 fl oz water

5 tbsp caster sugar

5 cm/2 inch piece of cinnamon stick

2 cloves

200 ml/7 fl oz double cream

125 ml/4 fl oz milk

140 g/5 oz light brown sugar

2 tbsp unsalted butter, diced

2 tbsp maple syrup

200 g/7 oz dark chocolate, broken into pieces

1 Peel the pears using a swivel vegetable peeler. Carefully cut out the cores from the base, but leave the stalks intact because they look more attractive. Brush the pears with the lemon juice to prevent discoloration.

2 Pour the water into a large, heavy-based saucepan and add the caster sugar. Stir over a low heat until the sugar has dissolved. Add the pears, cinnamon and cloves and bring to the boil. (Add a little more water if the pears are not almost covered.) Lower the heat and simmer for 20 minutes.

3 Meanwhile, pour the cream and milk into another heavy-based saucepan and add the brown sugar, butter and maple syrup. Stir over a low heat until the sugar has dissolved and the butter has melted. Still stirring, bring to the boil and continue to boil, stirring constantly, for 5 minutes, until thick and smooth. Remove the pan from the heat and stir in the chocolate, a little at a time, waiting until each batch has melted before adding the next. Set aside.

4 Transfer the pears to individual serving plates using a draining spoon and keep warm. Bring the poaching syrup back to the boil and cook until reduced. Remove and discard the cinnamon and cloves, then fold the syrup into the chocolate sauce. Pour the sauce over the pears and serve immediately.

Individual Soufflés

Light-as-air, these delicious little soufflés are the perfect choice for a dinner party dessert.

15 mins   20 mins

SERVES 6

INGREDIENTS

140 g/5 oz unsalted butter, plus 1 tbsp extra for greasing

3 tbsp caster sugar, plus 1 tbsp extra for sprinkling

175 g/6 oz dark chocolate, broken into small pieces

4 large eggs, separated

2 tbsp orange liqueur

¼ tsp cream of tartar

1 tbsp icing sugar, for dusting

300 ml/10 fl oz French Chocolate Sauce (see page 102), to serve

1 Butter 6 ramekins and sprinkle with caster sugar to coat the bases and sides. Tip out any excess. Stand the ramekins on a baking tray.

2 Chop the butter and place it in a heavy-based saucepan with the chocolate. Stir over a very low heat until melted and smooth. Remove the pan from the heat and cool slightly. Beat in the egg yolks, one at a time, and stir in the orange liqueur. Set aside, stirring occasionally.

3 Gently whisk the egg whites until they are frothy, then sprinkle in the cream of tartar and whisk again rapidly until the froth forms soft peaks. Add 1 tablespoon of caster sugar and whisk rapidly again. Add the remaining caster sugar, 1 tablespoon at a time, continuing to whisk until the whites form stiff, glossy peaks. Gently stir about one-quarter of the whisked egg whites into the cooled chocolate mixture, then fold the chocolate mixture into the remaining whites using a metal spoon.

4 Divide the mixture among the ramekins and bake in a preheated oven, 220°C/425°F/Gas Mark 7, for about 10 minutes, until risen and just set. Dust with icing sugar and serve immediately, handing the sauce separately.

Chocolate Crêpes

Serve these sweet, soufflé-filled, golden chocolate crêpes with flambéed summer berries for a superb contrast.

40 mins, plus 30 mins cooling

1 hr

SERVES 6

INGREDIENTS

85 g/3 oz plain flour

1 tbsp cocoa powder

1 tsp caster sugar

2 eggs, lightly beaten

175 ml/6 fl oz milk

2 tsp dark rum

6 tbsp unsalted butter

icing sugar, to dust

FILLING

5 tbsp double cream

225 g/8 oz dark chocolate

3 eggs, separated

2 tbsp caster sugar

BERRY SAUCE

2 tbsp butter

4 tbsp caster sugar

150 ml/5 fl oz orange juice

225 g/8 oz berries, such as raspberries, blackberries and strawberries

3 tbsp white rum

1 To make the crêpes, sieve the flour, cocoa and caster sugar into a bowl. Make a well in the centre and add the eggs, beating them in a little at a time. Add the milk and beat until smooth. Stir in the rum.

2 Melt all the butter and stir 2 tablespoonfuls into the batter. Cover with clingfilm and set aside for 30 minutes.

3 To cook the crêpes, brush the base of an 18 cm/7 inch crêpe pan or non-stick frying pan with melted butter and set over a medium heat. Stir the batter and pour 3 tablespoonfuls into the pan, swirling it to cover the base. Cook for 2 minutes or until the underside is golden, flip over, cook for 30 seconds, then slide on to a plate. Cook another 11 crêpes in the same way. Stack the crêpes interleaved with baking paper.

4 For the filling, pour the cream into a heavy-based pan, add the chocolate and melt over a low heat, stirring. Remove from the heat. In a heatproof bowl, beat the egg yolks with half the sugar until creamy, beat in the chocolate cream and leave to cool.

5 In a separate bowl, whisk the egg whites into soft peaks, add the rest of the sugar, and beat into stiff peaks. Stir a spoonful of the whites into the chocolate mixture, then fold the mixture into the remaining egg whites with a metal spoon.

6 Preheat the oven to 200°C/400°F/Gas Mark 6. Brush a baking tray with melted butter. Spread 1 crêpe with 1 tablespoon of the filling, then fold it in half and in half again to make a triangle. Repeat with the remaining crêpes. Brush the tops with the remaining melted butter, place on the baking tray and bake for 20 minutes.

7 For the berry sauce, melt the butter in a heavy-based frying pan over a low heat, stir in the sugar and cook until golden. Stir in the orange juice and cook until syrupy. Add the berries and warm through, stirring gently. Add the rum, heat gently for 1 minute, then ignite with a long match. Shake the pan until the flames have died down. Transfer the crêpes to serving plates with the sauce and serve immediately.

Chocolate Ravioli

Tempting squares of home-made chocolate pasta are filled with a mouthwatering mixture of mascarpone cheese and white chocolate.

25 mins, plus 1 hr chilling/resting

10 mins

SERVES 4

INGREDIENTS

175 g/6 oz plain flour, plus 2 tbsp extra for dusting

4 tbsp cocoa powder

2 tbsp icing sugar

2 eggs, lightly beaten, plus extra for brushing

1 tbsp vegetable oil

FILLING

175 g/6 oz white chocolate, broken into pieces

225g/8 oz mascarpone cheese

1 egg

1 tbsp finely chopped stem ginger

fresh mint sprigs, to decorate

double cream, to serve

1 Sieve together the flour, cocoa and sugar on to a clean work surface. Make a well in the centre and pour the 2 beaten eggs and the oil into it. Gradually draw in the flour with your fingertips until it is fully incorporated. Alternatively, sieve the flour, cocoa and sugar into a food processor, add the eggs and oil and process until mixed. Knead the dough until it is smooth and elastic, then cover with clingfilm and place in the refrigerator for 30 minutes to chill.

2 Meanwhile, to make the filling, put the white chocolate in the top of a double boiler or in a heatproof bowl set over a pan of barely simmering water. When the chocolate has melted, remove it from the heat and cool slightly, then beat in the mascarpone and the egg. Stir in the chopped ginger.

3 Remove the pasta dough from the refrigerator, cut it in half and keep one half tightly wrapped in clingfilm. Roll out the first half of the dough into a rectangle on a lightly floured surface, then cover with a clean, damp tea towel. Roll out the other half into a rectangle. Spoon the chocolate and ginger filling into a piping bag and pipe small mounds in even rows at intervals of about 4 cm/1½ inches over 1 dough rectangle. Brush the spaces between the mounds with beaten egg, then, using a rolling pin to lift it, position the second dough rectangle on top of the first. Press firmly between the mounds with your finger to seal and push out any pockets of air. Cut the dough into squares around the mounds using a serrated ravioli or pastry cutter or a sharp knife. Transfer the ravioli to a lightly floured tea towel and leave to rest for 30 minutes.

4 Bring a large pan of water to the boil, then lower the heat to medium and cook the ravioli, in batches, stirring to prevent them from sticking together, for 4–5 minutes, until tender but still firm to the bite. Remove with a slotted spoon. Serve immediately on individual plates, garnished with mint sprigs and handing the cream separately.

Chocolate Pudding with Rum

A warming way to end supper on a wintry evening, this steamed pudding is very easy to make.

15 mins   65–70 mins

SERVES 4

INGREDIENTS

4 tbsp unsalted butter, plus 1 tsp extra for greasing

175 g/6 oz self-raising flour, plus 2 tsp extra for dusting

55 g/2 oz dark chocolate

¼ tsp vanilla essence

115 g/4 oz caster sugar

2 eggs, lightly beaten

5 tbsp milk

SAUCE

300 ml/10 fl oz milk

2 tbsp cornflour

2 tbsp caster sugar

2 tbsp dark rum

1 Grease and flour a 1.25 litre/2 pint pudding basin. Put the butter, chocolate and vanilla in the top of a double boiler or in a heatproof bowl set over a pan of barely simmering water. Heat gently until the butter and sugar have melted, then remove from the heat and cool slightly. Stir the sugar into the chocolate mixture, then beat in the eggs. Sieve in the flour, stir in the milk, and mix well. Pour the mixture into the prepared pudding basin, cover the top with foil and tie with string. Steam the pudding for 1 hour, topping up with boiling water if necessary.

2 To make the sauce, pour the milk into a small pan set over a medium heat. Stir in the cornflour, then stir in the sugar until dissolved. Bring to the boil, stirring constantly, then lower the heat and simmer until thickened and smooth. Remove from the heat and stir in the rum.

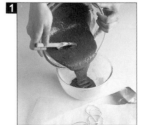

3 To serve, remove the pudding from the heat and discard the foil. Run a round-bladed knife around the side of the basin, place a serving plate on top of the pudding and, holding them together, invert. Serve immediately, handing the sauce separately.

Chocolate Cranberry Sponge

The sharpness of the fruit contrasts deliciously with the sweetness of the chocolate in this wonderful, fluffy sponge pudding.

20 mins   1 hr

SERVES 4

INGREDIENTS

4 tbsp unsalted butter, plus 1 tsp extra for greasing

4 tbsp dark brown sugar, plus 2 tsp extra for sprinkling

85 g/3 oz cranberries, thawed if frozen

1 large cooking apple

2 eggs, lightly beaten

85 g/3 oz self-raising flour

3 tbsp cocoa powder

SAUCE

175 g/6 oz dark chocolate, broken into pieces

400 ml/14 fl oz evaporated milk

1 tsp vanilla essence

½ tsp almond essence

1 Grease a 1.25 litre/2 pint pudding basin, sprinkle with brown sugar to coat the sides and tip out any excess. Put the cranberries in a bowl. Peel, core and dice the apple and mix with the cranberries. Put the fruit in the prepared pudding basin.

2 Place the butter, brown sugar and eggs in a large bowl. Sieve in the flour and cocoa and beat well until thoroughly mixed. Pour the mixture into the basin on top of the fruit, cover the top with foil and tie with string. Steam for about 1 hour, until risen, topping up with boiling water if necessary.

3 Meanwhile, to make the sauce, put the dark chocolate and milk in the top of a double boiler or a heatproof bowl set over a pan of barely simmering water. Stir until the chocolate has melted, then remove from the heat. Whisk in the vanilla and almond essences and continue to beat until the sauce is thick and smooth.

4 To serve, remove the pudding from the heat and discard the foil. Run a round-bladed knife around the side of the basin, place a serving plate on top of the pudding and, holding them together, invert. Serve immediately, handing the sauce separately.

Stuffed Nectarines

This delectable combination of juicy fruit, crunchy amaretti biscuits and continental chocolate is an irresistible summer treat.

15 mins   40–45 mins

SERVES 6

INGREDIENTS

85 g/3 oz dark continental chocolate, finely chopped

55 g/2 oz amaretti biscuit crumbs

1 tsp finely grated lemon rind

1 large egg, separated

6 tbsp amaretto liqueur

6 nectarines, halved and stoned

300 ml/10 fl oz white wine

55 g/2 oz milk chocolate, grated

whipped cream or ice cream, to serve

1 In a large bowl, mix together the chocolate, amaretti crumbs and lemon rind. Lightly beat the egg white and add it to the mixture with half the amaretto liqueur. (Use the yolk in another recipe.) Using a small sharp knife, slightly enlarge the cavities in the nectarines. Add the removed nectarine flesh to the chocolate and crumb mixture and mix well.

2 Preheat the oven to 190°C/375°F/Gas Mark 5. Place the nectarines, cut side up, in an ovenproof dish just large enough to hold them in a single layer. Pile the chocolate and crumb mixture into the cavities, dividing it equally among them. Mix the wine and remaining amaretto and pour it into the dish around the nectarines. Bake in the preheated oven for 40–45 minutes, until the nectarines are tender. Transfer 2 nectarine halves to each individual serving plate and spoon over a little of the cooking juices. Sprinkle over the grated milk chocolate and serve immediately with whipped cream or ice cream.

Chocolate Castle Puddings

Covered in a rich chocolate sauce, these light-as-air individual puddings are a delicious treat on a cold day.

🗊 25 mins   🕐 40 mins

SERVES 4

INGREDIENTS

3 tbsp butter, plus 2 tsp extra for greasing

3 tbsp caster sugar

1 large egg, lightly beaten

85 g/3 oz self-raising flour

55 g/2 oz dark chocolate, melted

SAUCE

2 tbsp cocoa powder

2 tbsp cornflour

150 ml/5 fl oz single cream

300 ml/10 fl oz milk

1–2 tbsp dark brown sugar

1 Grease 4 dariole moulds or small heatproof bowls with butter. In a mixing bowl, cream together the butter and sugar until pale and fluffy. Gradually add the egg, beating well after each addition.

2 In a separate bowl, sift the flour, fold it into the butter mixture with a metal spoon, then stir in the melted chocolate. Divide the mixture among the moulds, filling them to about two-thirds full to allow for expansion during cooking. Cover each mould with a circle of foil, and tie in place with string.

3 Bring a large pan of water to the boil and set a steamer over it. Place the moulds in the steamer and cook for 40 minutes. Check the water level from time to time and top up with boiling water when necessary.

4 To make the sauce, put the cocoa, cornflour, cream and milk in a heavy-based pan. Bring to the boil, then reduce the heat and simmer over a low heat, whisking constantly, until thick and smooth. Cook for a further 2–3 minutes, then stir in brown sugar to taste. Pour the sauce into a jug.

5 Lift the moulds out of the steamer and remove the foil circles from them. Run a knife blade around the sides of the moulds and turn out the puddings onto warmed, individual plates. Serve immediately, handing the sauce separately.

Chocolate Fudge Sauce

This creamy white chocolate sauce adds a touch of luxury and sophistication to the dinner table.

  5 mins, plus 15–20 mins cooling   10–15 mins

MAKES 225 ML/8 FL OZ

INGREDIENTS

150 ml/5 fl oz double cream

4 tbsp unsalted butter, diced

3 tbsp caster sugar

175 g/6 oz white chocolate, broken into pieces

2 tbsp brandy

1 Pour the cream into the top of a double boiler or a heatproof bowl set over a pan of barely simmering water. Add the butter and sugar and stir until the mixture is smooth. Remove from the heat.

2 Stir in the chocolate, a few pieces at a time, waiting until each batch has melted before adding the next. Add the brandy and stir the sauce until smooth. Cool to room temperature before serving.

French Chocolate Sauce

This rich, warm – and alcoholic – sauce is superb with both hot and cold desserts and positively magical with ice cream.

🍐 5 mins   🕐 10–15 mins

MAKES 150 ML/5 FL OZ

INGREDIENTS

6 tbsp double cream

85 g/3 oz dark chocolate, broken into small pieces

2 tbsp orange liqueur

1 Bring the cream gently to the boil in a small, heavy-based saucepan over a low heat. Remove the pan from the heat, add the chocolate and stir until smooth.

2 Stir in the liqueur and serve immediately or keep the sauce warm until required.

Glossy Chocolate Sauce

This simple sauce is a deliciously rich accompaniment to hot and cold desserts and is suitable for all the family.

 5 mins   10–15 mins

MAKES 150 ML/5 FL OZ

INGREDIENTS

100 g/3½ oz caster sugar

4 tbsp water

175 g/6 oz dark chocolate, broken into pieces

2 tbsp unsalted butter, diced

2 tbsp orange juice

1 Put the sugar and water into a small, heavy-based pan set over a low heat and stir until the sugar has dissolved. Stir in the chocolate, a few pieces at a time, waiting until each batch has melted before adding the next. Stir in the butter, a few pieces at a time, waiting until each batch has been incorporated before adding the next. Do not allow the sauce to boil.

2 Stir in the orange juice and remove the pan from the heat. Serve immediately or keep warm until required. Alternatively, leave to cool, transfer to a freezer-proof container and freeze for up to three months. Defrost at room temperature before re-heating to serve.

Savouries

Chocolate may seem an unusual ingredient to use in savoury dishes, but Mexican cooks have long known about its wonderful affinity with chillies and red peppers. It can be used to add a wonderful new flavour to dishes that you may have normally cooked in a more traditional way. Chillies, red peppers and chocolate feature in two of the

recipes in this section, Mole Poblano and Mexican Beef Stew. For a lighter dish that is also suitable for vegetarians, try the Nut and Chocolate Pasta. Finally, the Veal in Chocolate Sauce is perfect for a dinner party, where the chocolate will add an interesting flavour to this meat stew to surprise and satisfy you and your guests.

Mole Poblano

This great Mexican celebration dish, ladled out at fiestas, baptisms and weddings, is known for its combination of chillies and chocolate.

20 mins, plus 1–8 hrs soaking

15 mins

SERVES 4

INGREDIENTS

3 mulato chillies

3 mild ancho chillies

5–6 New Mexico or California chillies

1 onion, chopped

5 garlic cloves, chopped

450 g/1 lb ripe tomatoes

2 tortillas, preferably stale, cut into small pieces

pinch of cloves

pinch of fennel seeds

⅛ tsp each ground cinnamon, coriander and cumin

3 tbsp lightly toasted sesame seeds or tahini

3 tbsp flaked or coarsely ground blanched almonds

2 tbsp raisins

1 tbsp peanut butter, optional

475 ml/16 fl oz chicken stock

3–4 tbsp grated dark chocolate, plus extra for garnishing

2 tbsp mild chilli powder

3 tbsp vegetable oil

about 1 tbsp lime juice

salt and pepper

1 Using metal tongs, toast each chilli over an open flame for a few seconds until the colour darkens. Alternatively, roast in an ungreased frying pan over a medium heat, turning constantly, for about 30 seconds.

2 Place the toasted chillies in a bowl or a pan and pour boiling water over to cover. Cover with a lid and leave to soften for at least 1 hour or overnight. Once or twice lift the lid and rearrange the chillies so that they soak evenly.

3 Remove the softened chillies with a slotted spoon. Discard the stems and seeds and cut the flesh into pieces. Place in a blender.

4 Add the onion, garlic, tomatoes, tortillas, cloves, fennel seeds, cinnamon, coriander, cumin, sesame seeds, almonds, raisins and peanut butter if using, then process to combine. With the motor running, add enough stock through the feed tube to make a smooth paste. Stir in the remaining stock, chocolate and chilli powder.

5 Heat the oil in a heavy-based pan until it is smoking, then pour in the mole mixture. It will splatter and pop as it hits the hot oil. Cook for about 10 minutes, stirring occasionally to prevent it from burning.

6 Season with salt, pepper and lime juice, garnish with grated chocolate and serve.

Mexican Beef Stew

Colourful and richly-flavoured, this stew is somewhat time-consuming, but well worth the effort.

15 mins   2–2¼ hrs

SERVES 4

INGREDIENTS

2 red peppers

1 beef tomato

1 onion, cut into quarters

55 g/2 oz dark chocolate, broken into pieces

2 garlic cloves, roughly chopped

3 tbsp red wine vinegar

3 tbsp vegetable oil

800 g/1 lb 12 oz lean braising steak, diced

375 ml/13 fl oz beef stock

2 cloves

2.5 cm/1 inch piece of cinnamon stick

2 large carrots, peeled and finely chopped

1 large potato, peeled and diced

salt and pepper

1 tbsp chopped fresh coriander, to garnish

2 Meanwhile, cut a cross in the skin on the base of the tomato. Put it in a bowl, cover with boiling water and let it stand for 1 minute. Remove the tomato from the water, then peel and seed it. Dice the tomato flesh, and put it into a food processor. When the peppers are cool enough to handle, peel and seed them, then chop the flesh. Add the peppers to the food processor, together with the onion, chocolate, garlic and vinegar. Process the ingredients to a purée.

3 Heat the oil in a flameproof casserole or large pan. Add the steak, in batches if necessary, and fry over a medium heat, stirring frequently, until browned all over. Season to taste with salt and pepper. Add the chocolate purée and beef stock. Tie the cloves and cinnamon in a small piece of muslin and add to the pan. Bring to the boil, then lower the heat, cover and simmer for 1–1¼ hours.

4 Add the carrots and potato to the pan, stir well and simmer for a further 30 minutes. Remove and discard the cloves and cinnamon. Taste the stew and adjust the seasoning if necessary. Garnish with the fresh coriander and serve immediately with cooked green vegetables such as green beans.

1 Preheat the oven to 240°C/475°F/Gas Mark 9. Arrange the red peppers on a baking tray and cook in the preheated oven for about 20 minutes, until the skins have blackened and are beginning to blister. Using tongs, transfer them to a plastic bag. Tie the top and set aside.

Nut and Chocolate Pasta

This is a popular, main course dish in northern Europe, and makes a satisfying vegetarian supper.

20 mins   35–40 mins

SERVES 4

INGREDIENTS

salt

350 g/12 oz dried ribbon pasta, such as tagliatelle or fettucine

1 tsp butter, for greasing

2–3 tbsp fresh white breadcrumbs

SAUCE

6 tbsp butter

85 g/3 oz icing sugar

4 eggs, separated

85 g/3 oz ground, roasted hazelnuts

85 g/3 oz dark chocolate, grated

4 tbsp fresh white breadcrumbs

½ tsp ground cinnamon

finely grated rind of ½ lemon

1 Bring a large pan of lightly salted water to the boil. Add the pasta and cook for 8–10 minutes or according to the instructions on the packet, until tender, but still firm to the bite. Drain, rinse under cold running water and set aside.

2 To make the sauce, beat together the butter, half the sugar and the egg yolks until frothy.

3 In a separate bowl, whisk the egg whites with the remaining sugar until stiff, then fold them into the butter mixture.

4 In another bowl, mix the hazelnuts, grated chocolate, breadcrumbs, cinnamon and lemon rind, then stir into the egg mixture. Add the pasta and stir gently to mix.

5 Preheat the oven to 200°C/400°F/Gas Mark 6. Grease an ovenproof dish with butter. Sprinkle with breadcrumbs, tapping lightly to coat the base and sides, then tip out any excess. Spoon the pasta mixture into the dish and bake in the preheated oven for 25–30 minutes. Serve immediately, with roasted vine tomatoes (see Cook's Tip), if desired.

COOK'S TIP

To roast vine tomatoes, put 12 small tomatoes in an ovenproof dish, sprinkle with 2 tablespoons of olive oil, and season with salt and pepper to taste. Roast in an oven preheated to 200°C/400°F/Gas Mark 6 for 15–20 minutes, then serve.

Veal in Chocolate Sauce

Chocolate can enrich stews based on a broad range of meats, including game, but it is important to be light-handed or it can become cloying.

🥘 20 mins   🕐 1¾ hrs

SERVES 4

INGREDIENTS

5 tbsp vegetable oil

675 g/1½ lb boneless veal (or pork if veal is unavailable), cut into 2.5 cm/1 inch cubes

1 onion, chopped

2 garlic cloves, chopped

2 carrots, chopped

2 celery sticks, chopped

2 fresh red chillies, seeded and chopped

300–425 ml/10–15 fl oz red wine

125 ml/4 fl oz beef stock

2 tsp chopped fresh thyme

1 bay leaf

4 juniper berries, lightly crushed

2 cloves

2.5 cm/1 inch piece of cinnamon stick

225 g/8 oz chestnuts

8 shallots, quartered

55 g/2 oz dark chocolate, grated

salt and pepper

GARNISH

2 tbsp chopped fresh parsley

2 fresh bay leaves, optional

1 Heat 3 tablespoons of the oil in a large, flameproof casserole. Add the veal and cook over a medium heat, stirring, until lightly browned. Remove from the casserole with and set aside. Add the onion, garlic, carrots, celery and chillies to the casserole and fry, stirring, for 5 minutes, until the onion is softened.

2 Preheat the oven to 200°C/400°F/Gas Mark 6. Stir in 300 ml/10 fl oz of the wine and all of the stock, and return the meat to the casserole. Add the thyme, bay leaf, juniper berries, cloves and cinnamon, and season with salt and pepper. Bring to the boil, stirring, then cook in the oven for 1 hour. Top up the casserole with more wine from time to time, if necessary.

3 Meanwhile, make a cross in the base of the chestnuts, put them on a baking tray, bake at 200°C/400°F/Gas Mark 6 for 20 minutes, then shell them.

4 While the chestnuts are cooking, place the shallots in a small roasting tin and coat them with the remaining oil. Roast at the same oven temperature for 15–20 minutes, until golden and tender.

5 Remove the casserole from the oven and lift out the meat with a draining spoon. Place it in a serving dish, add the chestnuts and shallots and keep warm. Strain the cooking juices into a clean pan. Discard the contents of the strainer. Set the pan over a medium heat, bring to the boil and cook until slightly reduced. Stir in the chocolate until melted and adjust the seasoning, if necessary. Pour the sauce over the meat, sprinkle with the parsley, and bay leaves if using, and serve.

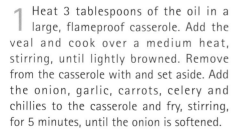

Cold Desserts

Cool, creamy, sumptuous, indulgent are just a few of the words that spring to mind when you think of cold chocolate desserts. The desserts contained in this chapter are a combination of all of these.

Some of the desserts are surprisingly quick and simple to make, while others are more elaborate. One of the best things about these desserts is they can all be made in advance, sometimes days in advance, making them perfect for entertaining. A quick decoration when necessary is all that is needed on the day. Even the Baked Chocolate Alaska can be assembled in advance and popped into the oven just before serving.

Chocolate Mint Swirl

The classic combination of chocolate and mint flavours makes an attractive dessert for special occasions.

45 mins 5 mins

SERVES 6

I N G R E D I E N T S

300 ml/10 fl oz double cream

150 ml/5 fl oz creamy fromage frais

2 tbsp icing sugar

1 tbsp crème de menthe

175 g/6 oz dark chocolate

chocolate, to decorate

1 Place the cream in a large mixing bowl and whisk until standing in soft peaks.

2 Fold in the fromage frais and icing sugar, then place about one-third of the mixture in a smaller bowl. Stir the crème de menthe into the smaller bowl. Melt the dark chocolate and stir it into the remaining mixture.

3 Place alternate spoonfuls of the 2 mixtures into serving glasses, then swirl the mixture together to give a decorative effect. Leave to cool and chill until required.

4 To make the piped chocolate decorations, melt a small amount of chocolate and place in a paper piping bag.

5 Place a sheet of baking paper on a board and pipe squiggles, stars or flower shapes with the melted chocolate. Alternatively, to make curved decorations, pipe decorations on to a long strip of baking paper, then carefully place the strip over a rolling pin, securing with sticky tape. Leave the chocolate to set, then carefully remove from the baking parchment.

6 Decorate each dessert with piped chocolate decorations and serve. The desserts can be decorated and then chilled, if preferred.

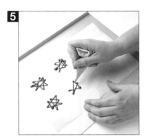

COOK'S TIP
Pipe the patterns freehand or draw patterns on to baking paper first, turn the parchment over and then pipe the chocolate, following the drawn outline.

Chocolate Rum Pots

Wickedly rich little pots, flavoured with a hint of dark rum, are pure indulgence on any occasion!

2 hrs 20 mins ⏱ 5 mins

SERVES 6

INGREDIENTS

225 g/8 oz dark chocolate

4 eggs, separated

6 tbsp caster sugar

4 tbsp dark rum

4 tbsp double cream

TO DECORATE

a little whipped cream

marbled chocolate shapes (see page 114)

1 Melt the chocolate and leave to cool slightly.

2 Whisk the egg yolks with the caster sugar in a bowl until pale and fluffy, using an electric whisk or balloon whisk.

3 Drizzle the chocolate into the mixture and fold in together with the rum and the double cream.

4 Whisk the egg whites in a separate bowl until standing in soft peaks. Fold the egg whites into the chocolate mixture in 2 batches. Divide the mixture between 6 ramekins, or other individual dishes, and leave to chill for at least 2 hours.

5 To serve, decorate with a little whipped cream and small chocolate shapes.

COOK'S TIP

Make sure you use a perfectly clean and grease-free bowl for whisking the egg whites. They will not aerate if any grease is present as the smallest amount breaks down the bubbles in the whites, preventing them from trapping and holding air.

Chocolate & Vanilla Creams

These rich, creamy desserts are completely irresistible. Serve them with crisp dessert biscuits.

40 mins   5–10 mins

SERVES 4

I N G R E D I E N T S

475 ml/16 fl oz double cream

6 tbsp caster sugar

1 vanilla pod

200 ml/7 fl oz crème fraîche

2 tsp gelatine

3 tbsp water

50 g/1¾ oz dark chocolate

MARBLED CHOCOLATE SHAPES

a little melted white chocolate

a little melted dark chocolate

1 Place the cream and sugar in a saucepan. Cut the vanilla pod into 2 pieces and add to the cream. Heat gently, stirring until the sugar has dissolved, then bring to the boil. Reduce the heat and leave to simmer for 2–3 minutes.

2 Remove the pan from the heat and take out the vanilla pod. Stir in the crème fraîche.

3 Sprinkle the gelatine over the water in a small heatproof bowl and leave to go spongy, then place over a pan of hot water and stir until dissolved. Stir into the cream mixture. Pour half of this mixture into another mixing bowl.

4 Melt the dark chocolate and stir it into one half of the cream mixture. Pour the chocolate mixture into 4 individual glass serving dishes and chill for 15–20 minutes until just set. While it is chilling, keep the vanilla mixture at room temperature.

5 Spoon the vanilla mixture on top of the chocolate mixture and chill until the vanilla is set.

6 Meanwhile, make the shapes for the decoration. Spoon the melted white chocolate into a paper piping bag and snip off the tip. Spread some melted dark chocolate on a piece of baking paper. Whilst still wet, pipe a fine line of white chocolate in a scribble over the top. Use the tip of a cocktail stick to marble the white chocolate into the dark. When firm but not too hard, cut into shapes with a small shaped cutter or a sharp knife. Chill the shapes until firm, then use to decorate the desserts.

Chocolate Hazelnut Pots

Chocoholics will adore these creamy desserts consisting of a rich baked chocolate custard with the delicious flavour of hazelnuts.

🥧 15 mins   🕐 35–40 mins

SERVES 6

I N G R E D I E N T S

2 eggs

2 egg yolks

1 tbsp caster sugar

1 tsp cornflour

600 ml/1 pint milk

75 g/3 oz dark chocolate

4 tbsp chocolate and hazelnut spread

T O   D E C O R A T E

grated chocolate or quick chocolate curls
(see page 15)

1 Beat together the eggs, egg yolks, caster sugar and cornflour until well combined. Heat the milk until almost boiling.

2 Gradually pour the milk on to the eggs, whisking as you do so. Melt the chocolate and hazelnut spread in a bowl set over a pan of gently simmering water, then whisk the melted chocolate mixture into the eggs.

3 Pour into 6 small ovenproof dishes and cover the dishes with foil. Place them in a roasting tin. Fill the tin with boiling water to come halfway up the sides of the dishes.

4 Bake in a preheated oven, 170°C/ 325°F/Gas Mark 3, for 35–40 minutes until the custard is just set. Remove from the tin and cool, then chill until required. Serve decorated with grated chocolate or chocolate curls.

COOK'S TIP

This dish is traditionally made in little pots called pots de crème, which are individual ovenproof dishes with a lid. Ramekins are fine. The dessert can also be made in one large dish; cook for about 1 hour or until set.

Mocha Creams

These creamy chocolate and coffee-flavoured desserts make a perfect end to a fine meal.

30 mins   5 mins

SERVES 4

I N G R E D I E N T S

225 g/8 oz dark chocolate

1 tbsp instant coffee

300 ml/10 fl oz boiling water

1 sachet gelatine

3 tbsp cold water

1 tsp vanilla essence

1 tbsp coffee-flavoured liqueur, optional

300 ml/10 fl oz double cream

4 chocolate coffee beans

8 amaretti biscuits

1 Break the chocolate into small pieces and place in a saucepan with the coffee. Stir in the boiling water and heat gently, stirring until the chocolate melts.

2 Sprinkle the gelatine over the cold water and leave to go spongy, then whisk it into the hot chocolate mixture to dissolve it.

3 Stir in the vanilla essence and coffee-flavoured liqueur, if using. Leave to stand in a cool place until just beginning to thicken; whisk from time to time.

4 Whisk the cream until it is standing in soft peaks, then reserve a little for decorating the desserts and fold the remainder into the chocolate mixture. Spoon into serving dishes and leave to set.

5 Decorate with the reserved cream and coffee beans and serve with the amaretti biscuits.

VARIATION

To add a delicious almond flavour to the dessert, replace the coffee-flavoured liqueur with almond-flavoured (amaretto) liqueur.

Layered Chocolate Mousse

Three layers of fabulous rich mousse give this elegant dessert extra appeal. It is a little fiddly to prepare, but well worth the extra effort.

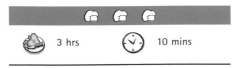

3 hrs   10 mins

SERVES 4

INGREDIENTS

3 eggs

1 tsp cornflour

4 tbsp caster sugar

300 ml/10 fl oz milk

1 sachet gelatine

3 tbsp water

300 ml/10 fl oz double cream

75 g/2¾ oz dark chocolate

75 g/2¾ oz white chocolate

75 g/2¾ oz milk chocolate

chocolate caraque, to decorate
  (see page 15)

1 Line a 450 g/1 lb loaf tin with baking paper. Separate the eggs, putting each egg white in a separate bowl. Place the egg yolks and sugar in a large mixing bowl and whisk until well combined. Place the milk in a pan and heat gently, stirring until almost boiling. Pour the milk on to the egg yolks, whisking.

2 Set the bowl over a pan of gently simmering water and cook, stirring until the mixture thickens enough to thinly coat the back of a wooden spoon.

3 Sprinkle the gelatine over the water in a small heatproof bowl and leave to go spongy. Place over a pan of hot water and stir until dissolved. Stir into the hot mixture. Leave to cool.

4 Whip the cream until just holding its shape. Fold into the egg custard, then divide the mixture into 3. Melt the 3 types of chocolate separately. Fold the dark chocolate into one egg custard portion. Whisk one egg white until standing in soft peaks and fold into the dark chocolate custard until combined. Pour into the

prepared tin and level the top. Chill in the coldest part of the refrigerator until just set. Leave the remaining mixtures at room temperature.

5 Fold the white chocolate into another portion of the egg custard. Whisk another egg white and fold in. Pour on top of the dark chocolate layer and chill quickly. Repeat with the remaining milk chocolate and egg white. Chill for at least 2 hours until set. To serve, carefully turn out on to a serving dish and decorate with chocolate caraque.

Chocolate Marquise

This classic French dish is part way between a mousse and parfait. It is usually chilled in a large mould, but here it is made in individual moulds.

2½ hrs   5 mins

SERVES 6

INGREDIENTS

200 g/7 oz dark chocolate

100 g/3½ oz butter

3 egg yolks

75 g/2¾ oz caster sugar

1 tsp chocolate essence or 1 tbsp chocolate-flavoured liqueur

300 ml/10 fl oz double cream

TO SERVE

crème fraîche

chocolate-dipped fruits

cocoa powder, to dust

1 Break the chocolate into pieces. Place the chocolate and butter in a bowl over a pan of gently simmering water and stir until melted and well combined. Remove from the heat and leave to cool.

2 Place the egg yolks in a mixing bowl with the sugar and whisk until pale and fluffy. Using an electric whisk running on low speed, slowly whisk in the cool chocolate mixture. Stir in the chocolate essence or chocolate-flavoured liqueur.

3 Whip the cream until just holding its shape. Fold into the chocolate mixture. Spoon into 6 small ramekins, or individual metal moulds. Leave to chill for at least 2 hours.

4 To serve, turn out the desserts on to individual serving dishes. If you have difficulty turning them out, dip the moulds into a bowl of warm water for a few seconds to help the marquise to slip out. Serve with chocolate-dipped fruit and crème fraîche and dust with cocoa powder.

COOK'S TIP
The slight tartness of the crème fraîche contrasts well with this very rich dessert. Dip the fruit in white chocolate to give a good colour contrast.

Iced White Chocolate Terrine

This iced dessert is somewhere between a chocolate mousse and an ice cream. Serve it with a chocolate sauce or a fruit coulis and fresh fruit.

12 hrs 50 mins   5 mins

SERVES 8

INGREDIENTS

2 tbsp granulated sugar

5 tbsp water

300 g/10½ oz white chocolate

3 eggs, separated

300 ml/10 fl oz double cream

1 Line a 450 g/1 lb loaf tin with foil or clingfilm, pressing out as many creases as you can.

2 Place the granulated sugar and water in a heavy-based pan and heat gently, stirring until the sugar has dissolved. Bring to the boil and boil for 1–2 minutes until syrupy, then remove the pan from the heat.

3 Break the white chocolate into small pieces and stir it into the syrup, continuing to stir until the chocolate has melted and combined with the syrup. Leave to cool slightly.

4 Beat the egg yolks into the chocolate mixture. Leave to cool completely.

5 Lightly whip the cream until just holding its shape and fold it into the chocolate mixture.

6 Whisk the egg whites in a separate bowl until they are standing in soft peaks. Fold into the chocolate mixture.

Pour into the prepared loaf tin and freeze overnight.

7 To serve, remove from the freezer about 10–15 minutes before serving. Turn out of the tin and cut into slices before serving.

COOK'S TIP

To make a coulis, place 225 g/ 8 oz soft fruit of your choice – strawberries, mangoes or raspberries are ideal – in a food processor or blender. Add 1–2 tablespoons of icing sugar and blend to a purée. If the fruit contains seeds, push the purée through a sieve to remove them. Cool and chill.

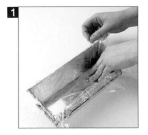

Chocolate Banana Sundae

A banana split in a glass! Choose the best vanilla ice cream you can find, or better still, make your own.

15 mins 5 mins

SERVES 4

INGREDIENTS

GLOSSY CHOCOLATE SAUCE

60 g/2 oz dark chocolate

4 tbsp golden syrup

1 tbsp butter

1 tbsp brandy or rum, optional

SUNDAE

4 bananas

150 ml/5 fl oz double cream

8–12 scoops of good quality vanilla ice cream

75 g/2¾ oz flaked or chopped almonds, toasted

grated or flaked chocolate, for sprinkling

4 fan wafer biscuits

1 To make the chocolate sauce, break the chocolate into small pieces and place in a heatproof bowl with the syrup and butter. Heat over a pan of hot water until melted, stirring until well combined. Remove the bowl from the heat and stir in the brandy or rum, if using.

2 Slice the bananas and whip the cream until just holding its shape. Place a scoop of ice cream in the bottom of 4 tall sundae dishes. Top with slices of banana, some chocolate sauce, a spoonful of cream and a good sprinkling of nuts.

3 Repeat the layers, finishing with a good dollop of cream, sprinkled with nuts and a little grated or flaked chocolate. Serve with fan wafer biscuits.

VARIATION

For a traditional banana split, halve the bananas lengthways and place on a plate with two scoops of ice cream between. Top with cream and sprinkle with nuts. Serve with the glossy chocolate sauce poured over the top.

Rich Chocolate Ice Cream

A rich chocolate ice cream, delicious on its own or served with chocolate sauce. For a special dessert, serve it in these attractive trellis cups.

4–5 hrs   12 mins

SERVES 6

INGREDIENTS

ICE CREAM

1 egg

3 egg yolks

90 g/3 oz caster sugar

300 ml/10 fl oz full cream milk

250 g/9 oz dark chocolate

300 ml/10 fl oz double cream

TRELLIS CUPS

100 g/3½ oz dark chocolate

1 Beat together the egg, egg yolks and caster sugar in a mixing bowl until well combined. Heat the milk until it is almost boiling.

2 Gradually pour the hot milk on to the eggs, whisking as you do so. Place the bowl over a pan of gently simmering water and cook, stirring until the mixture thickens sufficiently to thinly coat the back of a wooden spoon.

3 Break the dark chocolate into small pieces and add to the hot custard. Stir until the chocolate has melted. Cover with a sheet of dampened baking paper and leave to cool.

4 Whip the cream until just holding its shape, then fold into the cooled chocolate custard. Transfer to a freezer container and freeze for 1–2 hours until the mixture is frozen 2.5 cm/1 inch from the sides.

5 Scrape the ice cream into a chilled bowl and beat again until smooth. Re-freeze until firm.

6 Meanwhile, make the trellis cups. Invert a muffin tray and cover 6 alternate mounds with clingfilm. Melt the chocolate, place it in a paper piping bag and snip off the end.

7 Pipe a circle around the base of the mound, then pipe chocolate back and forth over it to form a trellis; carefully pipe a double thickness. Pipe around the base again. Chill until set, then lift from the tray and remove the clingfilm. Serve the ice cream in the trellis cups.

Baked Chocolate Alaska

A cool dessert that leaves the cook completely unflustered – assemble it in advance and freeze until required.

50 mins   12 mins

SERVES 4

INGREDIENTS

2 eggs

4 tbsp caster sugar

5 tbsp plain flour

2 tbsp cocoa powder

3 egg whites

150 g/5½ oz caster sugar

1 litre/1¾ pints good quality chocolate ice cream

1 Grease an 18 cm/7 inch round cake tin and then line the base with baking paper.

2 Whisk the egg and the 4 tablespoons of sugar in a mixing bowl until very thick and pale. Sieve the flour and cocoa powder together and carefully fold in.

3 Pour into the prepared tin and bake in a preheated oven, 220°C/425°F/Gas Mark 7, for 7 minutes or until springy to the touch. Transfer to a wire rack to cool completely.

4 Whisk the egg whites in a clean bowl until they are standing in soft peaks. Gradually add the sugar, whisking until you have a thick, glossy meringue.

5 Place the sponge on a baking tray and pile the ice cream on to the centre in a heaped dome.

6 Pipe or spread the meringue over the ice cream, making sure the ice cream

is completely enclosed. (At this point the dessert can be frozen, if wished.)

7 Return it to the oven for 5 minutes, until the meringue is just golden. Serve immediately.

COOK'S TIP

This dessert is delicious served with a blackcurrant coulis. Cook a few blackcurrants in a little orange juice until soft, purée and push through a sieve, then sweeten to taste with a little icing sugar.

White Chocolate Ice Cream

This white chocolate ice cream is served in a biscuit cup. If desired, top with a chocolate sauce for a true chocolate addict's treat.

🍮 4–5 hrs   🕐 15 mins

SERVES 6

INGREDIENTS

ICE CREAM

1 egg

1 egg yolk

3 tbsp caster sugar

150 g/5½ oz white chocolate

300 ml/10 fl oz milk

150 ml/5 fl oz double cream

BISCUIT CUPS

1 egg white

4 tbsp caster sugar

2 tbsp plain flour, sifted

2 tbsp cocoa powder, sifted

2 tbsp butter, melted

1 Place baking paper on 2 baking trays. To make the ice cream, beat the egg, egg yolks and sugar. Break the chocolate into pieces, place in a bowl with 3 tablespoons of milk and melt over a pan of hot water. Heat the milk until almost boiling and pour on to the eggs, whisking. Place over a pan of simmering water and cook, stirring until the mixture thickens enough to coat the back of a wooden spoon. Whisk in the chocolate. Cover with dampened baking paper and let cool.

2 Whip the cream until just holding its shape and fold into the custard. Transfer to a freezer container and freeze the mixture for 1–2 hours until frozen 2.5 cm/1 inch from the sides. Scrape into a bowl and beat again until smooth. Re-freeze until firm.

3 To make the cups, beat the egg white and sugar together. Beat in the flour and cocoa, then the butter. Place 1 tablespoon of mixture on one tray; spread out to a 12.5 cm/5 inch circle. Bake in a preheated oven, 200°C/400°F/Gas Mark 6, for 4–5 minutes. Remove and mould over an upturned cup. Leave to set, then cool on a wire rack. Repeat to make 6 cups. Serve the ice cream in the cups.

Cardamom Cream Horns

A crisp chocolate biscuit cone encloses a fabulous cardamom-flavoured cream, making this an unusual dessert.

30 mins   4–5 mins

SERVES 6

INGREDIENTS

1 egg white

4 tbsp caster sugar

2 tbsp plain flour

2 tbsp cocoa powder

2 tbsp butter, melted

50 g/1¾ oz dark chocolate

CARDAMOM CREAM

150 ml/5 fl oz double cream

1 tbsp icing sugar

¼ tsp ground cardamom

pinch of ground ginger

25 g/1 oz stem ginger, finely chopped

1 Place a sheet of baking paper on 2 baking trays. Lightly grease 6 cream horn moulds. To make the horns, beat the egg white and sugar in a mixing bowl until well combined. Sieve the flour and cocoa powder together, then beat into the egg followed by the melted butter.

2 Place 1 tablespoon of the mixture on to 1 baking tray and spread out to form a 12.5 cm/5 inch circle. Bake in a preheated oven, 200°C/400°F/Gas Mark 6, for 4–5 minutes.

3 Working quickly, remove the biscuit with a spatula and wrap around the cream horn mould to form a cone. Leave to set, then remove from the mould. Repeat with the remaining mixture to make 6 cones.

4 Melt the chocolate and dip the open edges of the horn in the chocolate.

Place the horn on a piece of baking paper and leave to set.

5 To make the cardamom cream, place the cream in a bowl and sieve the icing sugar and ground spices over the surface. Whisk the cream until standing in soft peaks. Fold in the chopped ginger and use to fill the chocolate cones.

Chocolate Charlotte

This chocolate dessert, consisting of a rich chocolate mousse-like filling enclosed in boudoir biscuits, is a variation of a popular classic.

  5 hrs 40 mins 5 mins

SERVES 8

INGREDIENTS

about 22 boudoir biscuits

4 tbsp orange-flavoured liqueur

250 g/9 oz dark chocolate

150 ml/5 fl oz double cream

4 eggs

150 g/5½ oz caster sugar

TO DECORATE

150 ml/5 fl oz whipping cream

2 tbsp caster sugar

½ tsp vanilla essence

quick dark chocolate curls (see page 15)

chocolate decorations (see page 112), optional

1 Line the base of a Charlotte mould or a deep 18 cm/7 inch round cake tin with a piece of baking paper.

2 Place the boudoir biscuits on a tray and sprinkle with half of the orange-flavoured liqueur. Use to line the sides of the mould or tin, trimming if necessary to make a tight fit.

3 Break the chocolate into small pieces, place in a bowl and melt over a pan of hot water. Remove from the heat and stir in the double cream.

4 Separate the eggs and place the whites in a large grease-free bowl. Beat the egg yolks into the chocolate mixture.

5 Whisk the egg whites until standing in stiff peaks, then gradually add the caster sugar, whisking until stiff and glossy. Carefully fold the egg whites into the chocolate mixture in 2 batches, taking care not to knock out all of the air. Pour into the centre of the mould. Trim the biscuits so that they are level with the chocolate mixture. Leave to chill for at least 5 hours.

6 To decorate, whisk the cream, sugar and vanilla essence until standing in soft peaks. Turn out the Charlotte on to a serving dish. Pipe cream rosettes around the base and decorate with quick chocolate curls and other decorations of your choice.

Marble Cheesecake

A dark and white chocolate cheesecake filling is marbled together to give an attractive finish to this rich and decadent dessert.

🍥 🍥

🍚 2 hrs 30 mins ⏲ 5 mins

SERVES 10

INGREDIENTS

BASE

225 g/8 oz toasted oat cereal

50 g/1¾ oz toasted hazelnuts, chopped

4 tbsp butter

25 g/1 oz dark chocolate

FILLING

350 g/12 oz full fat soft cheese

100 g/3½ oz caster sugar

200 ml/7 fl oz thick yogurt

300 ml/10 fl oz double cream

1 sachet gelatine

3 tbsp water

175 g/6 oz dark chocolate, melted

175 g/6 oz white chocolate, melted

1 Place the toasted oat cereal in a plastic bag and crush with a rolling pin. Pour the crushed cereal into a mixing bowl and stir in the hazelnuts.

2 Melt the butter and chocolate together over a low heat and add to the cereal mixture, stirring until well coated.

3 Using the bottom of a glass, press the mixture into the base and up the sides of a 20 cm/8 inch springform tin.

4 Beat together the cheese and sugar with a wooden spoon until smooth. Beat in the yogurt. Whip the cream until just holding its shape and fold into the mixture. Sprinkle the gelatine over the water in a heatproof bowl and leave to go spongy. Place over a pan of hot water and stir until dissolved. Stir into the mixture.

5 Divide the mixture in half and beat the dark chocolate into one half and the white chocolate into the other half.

6 Place alternate spoonfuls of mixture on top of the cereal base. Swirl the filling together with the tip of a knife to give a marbled effect. Level the top with a scraper or a spatula. Chill for at least 2 hours to set before serving.

Banana Coconut Cheesecake

The exotic combination of banana and coconut goes well with chocolate. Fresh coconut gives a better flavour than dessicated coconut.

2½ hrs   5 mins

SERVES 10

INGREDIENTS

225 g/8 oz chocolate chip cookies

4 tbsp butter

350 g/12 oz medium-fat soft cheese

75 g/2¾ oz caster sugar

50 g/1¾ oz fresh coconut, grated

2 tbsp coconut-flavoured liqueur

2 ripe bananas

125 g/4½ oz dark chocolate

1 sachet gelatine

3 tbsp water

150 ml/5 fl oz double cream

TO DECORATE

1 banana

lemon juice

a little melted chocolate

1 Place the biscuits in a plastic bag and crush with a rolling pin. Pour into a mixing bowl. Melt the butter and stir into the biscuit crumbs until well coated. Firmly press the biscuit mixture into the base and up the sides of a 20 cm/8 inch springform tin.

2 Beat together the soft cheese and caster sugar until well combined, then beat in the grated coconut and coconut-flavoured liqueur. Mash the 2 bananas and beat them in. Melt the dark chocolate and beat in until well combined.

3 Sprinkle the gelatine over the water in a heatproof bowl and leave to go spongy. Place over a pan of hot water and

stir until dissolved. Stir into the chocolate mixture. Whisk the cream until just holding its shape and stir into the chocolate mixture. Spoon over the biscuit base and chill for 2 hours, until set.

4 To serve, carefully transfer to a serving plate. Slice the banana, toss in the lemon juice and arrange around the edge of the cheesecake. Drizzle with melted chocolate and leave to set.

COOK'S TIP

To crack the coconut, pierce 2 of the "eyes" and drain off the liquid. Tap hard around the centre with a hammer until it cracks; lever apart.

Chocolate Brandy Torte

A crumbly ginger chocolate base topped with velvety smooth chocolate brandy cream makes this a blissful cake.

2 hrs 40 mins   5 mins

SERVES 12

INGREDIENTS

BASE

250 g/9 oz gingernut biscuits

75 g/2¾ oz dark chocolate

100 g/3½ oz butter

FILLING

225 g/8 oz dark chocolate

250 g/9 oz mascarpone cheese

2 eggs, separated

3 tbsp brandy

300 ml/10 fl oz double cream

4 tbsp caster sugar

TO DECORATE

100 ml/3½ fl oz double cream

chocolate coffee beans

1 Crush the biscuits in a bag with a rolling pin or in a food processor. Melt the chocolate and butter together and pour over the biscuits. Mix well, then use to line the base and sides of a 23 cm/ 9 inch loose-bottomed fluted flan tin or springform tin. Leave to chill whilst preparing the filling.

2 To make the filling, melt the dark chocolate in a pan, remove from the heat and beat in the mascarpone cheese, egg yolks and brandy.

3 Lightly whip the cream until just holding its shape and fold in the chocolate mixture.

4 Whisk the egg whites in a grease-free bowl until standing in soft peaks. Add the caster sugar a little at a time and whisk until thick and glossy. Fold into the chocolate mixture, in two batches, until just mixed.

5 Spoon the mixture into the prepared base and chill for at least 2 hours. Carefully transfer to a serving plate. To decorate, whip the cream and pipe on to the cheesecake and add the chocolate coffee beans.

VARIATION

If chocolate coffee beans are unavailable, use chocolate-coated raisins to decorate.

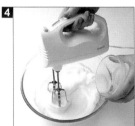

Chocolate Shortcake Towers

Stacks of crisp shortcake are sandwiched with chocolate-flavoured cream and fresh raspberries, and served with a fresh raspberry coulis.

30 mins   10 mins

SERVES 6

INGREDIENTS

SHORTCAKE

225 g/8 oz butter

75 g/2¾ oz light muscovado sugar

50 g/1¾ oz dark chocolate, grated

275 g/9½ oz plain flour

TO FINISH

350 g/12 oz fresh raspberries

2 tbsp icing sugar

3 tbsp milk

300 ml/10 fl oz double cream

100 g/3 oz white chocolate, melted

icing sugar, to dust

1 Lightly grease a baking tray. To make the shortcake, beat together the butter and sugar until light and fluffy. Beat in the dark chocolate. Mix in the flour to form a stiff dough.

2 Roll out the dough on a lightly floured surface and stamp out 18 rounds, 7.5 cm/3 inches across, with a fluted biscuit cutter. Place the rounds on the baking tray and bake in a preheated oven, 200°C/400°F/Gas Mark 6, for 10 minutes until crisp and golden. Leave to cool on the tray.

3 To make the coulis, set aside about 100 g/3½ oz of the raspberries. Purée the remainder in a food processor with the icing sugar, then push through a sieve to remove the seeds. Chill. Set aside 2 teaspoons of the cream. Whip the remainder until just holding its shape. Fold in the milk and the melted chocolate.

4 For each tower, spoon a little coulis on to a serving plate. Drop small dots of the reserved cream into the coulis around the edge of the plate and use a skewer to drag through the cream to make an attractive pattern.

5 Place a shortcake circle on the plate and spoon on a little of the chocolate cream. Top with 2 or 3 raspberries, top with another shortcake and repeat. Place a third biscuit on top. Dust with sugar.

Black Forest Trifle

Try all the delightful flavours of a Black Forest Gateau in this new guise – the results are stunning.

1½ hrs   10 mins

SERVES 6

INGREDIENTS

6 thin slices chocolate butter cream Swiss roll

800 g/1 lb 12 oz canned black cherries

2 tbsp kirsch

1 tbsp cornflour

2 tbsp caster sugar

425 ml/15 fl oz milk

3 egg yolks

1 egg

75 g/2¾ oz dark chocolate

300 ml/10 fl oz double cream, lightly whipped

TO DECORATE

dark chocolate caraque (see page 15)

maraschino cherries, optional

1 Place the slices of chocolate Swiss roll in the bottom of a glass serving bowl.

2 Drain the black cherries, reserving 6 tablespoons of the juice. Place the cherries and the reserved juice on top of the cake. Sprinkle with the kirsch.

3 In a bowl, mix the cornflour and caster sugar. Stir in enough of the milk to mix to a smooth paste. Beat in the egg yolks and the whole egg.

4 Heat the remaining milk in a small saucepan until almost boiling, then gradually pour it on to the egg mixture, whisking well until it is combined.

5 Place the bowl over a pan of hot water and cook over a low heat until the custard thickens, stirring. Add the chocolate and stir until melted.

6 Pour the chocolate custard over the cherries and cool. When cold, spread the cream over the custard, swirling with the back of a spoon. Chill before decorating.

7 Decorate with chocolate caraque and whole maraschino cherries, if using, before serving.

Champagne Mousse

Any dry sparkling wine made by the traditional method used for champagne can be used for this elegant dessert.

🍧 3¼ hrs   ⏱ 8 mins

SERVES 4

I N G R E D I E N T S

S P O N G E

4 eggs

100 g/3½ oz caster sugar

75 g/2¾ oz self-raising flour

2 tbsp cocoa powder

2 tbsp butter, melted

M O U S S E

1 sachet gelatine

3 tbsp water

300 ml/10 fl oz champagne

300 ml/10 fl oz double cream

2 egg whites

6 tbsp caster sugar

TO DECORATE

50 g/2 oz dark chocolate-flavoured cake covering, melted

1 Line a 37.5 x 25 cm/15 x 10 inch Swiss roll tin with greased baking paper. Place the eggs and sugar in a bowl and beat with an electric whisk until the mixture is very thick and the whisk leaves a trail when lifted. If using a balloon whisk, stand the bowl over a pan of hot water whilst whisking. Sieve the flour and cocoa together and fold into the egg mixture. Fold in the butter. Pour into the tin and bake in a preheated oven, 200°C/400°F/Gas Mark 6, for 8 minutes or until springy to the touch. Cool for 5 minutes, then turn out on to a wire rack until cold. Meanwhile, line four 10 cm/ 4 inch baking rings with baking paper. Line the sides with 2.5 cm/1 inch strips of cake and the base with circles.

2 To make the mousse, sprinkle the gelatine over the water and leave to go spongy. Place the bowl over a pan of hot water; stir until dissolved. Stir in the champagne.

3 Whip the cream until just holding its shape. Fold in the champagne mixture. Leave in a cool place until on the point of setting, stirring. Whisk the egg whites until standing in soft peaks, add the sugar and whisk until glossy. Fold into the setting mixture. Spoon into the sponge cases, allowing the mixture to go above the sponge. Chill for 2 hours. Pipe the cake covering in squiggles on a piece of parchment, leave them to set, then use them to decorate the mousses.

Chocolate Freezer Cake

Hidden in a ring of chocolate sponge lies the secret of this freezer cake – chocolate mint ice cream. Use orange or coffee ice cream if preferred.

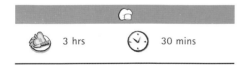

 3 hrs 30 mins

SERVES 8

INGREDIENTS

4 eggs

175 g/6 oz caster sugar

100 g/3½ oz self-raising flour

3 tbsp cocoa powder

500 ml/17 fl oz chocolate and mint ice cream

Glossy Chocolate Sauce (see page 103)

1 Lightly grease a 23 cm/9 inch ring tin. Place the eggs and sugar in a large mixing bowl. If using an electric whisk, whisk the mixture until it is very thick and the whisk leaves a trail. If using a balloon whisk, stand the bowl over a pan of hot water whilst whisking.

2 Sieve the flour and cocoa together and fold into the egg mixture. Pour into the prepared tin and bake in a preheated oven, 180°C/350°F/Gas Mark 4, for 30 minutes or until springy to the touch. Leave to cool in the tin before turning out on to a wire rack to cool completely.

3 Rinse the cake tin and line with a strip of clingfilm, overhanging slightly. Carefully cut off the top 1 cm/½ inch of the cake in one slice, and set aside.

4 Return the cake to the tin. Using a spoon, scoop out the centre of the cake, leaving a shell approximately 1 cm/½ inch thick.

5 Remove the ice cream from the freezer and leave to stand for a few minutes, then beat with a wooden spoon until softened a little. Fill the centre of the cake with the ice cream, levelling the top. Replace the top of the cake.

6 Cover with the overhanging cling film and freeze for at least 2 hours.

7 To serve, turn the cake out on to a serving dish and drizzle over some of the chocolate sauce in an attractive pattern, if you wish. Cut the cake into slices and then serve the remaining sauce separately.

Mississippi Mud Pie

An all-time favourite with chocoholics – the "mud" refers to the gooey, rich chocolate layer of the cake.

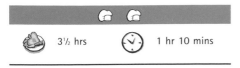

3½ hrs   1 hr 10 mins

SERVES 8

INGREDIENTS

225 g/8 oz plain flour

2 tbsp cocoa powder

150 g/5½ oz butter

2 tbsp caster sugar

about 2 tbsp cold water

FILLING

175 g/6 oz butter

350 g/12 oz dark muscovado sugar

4 eggs, lightly beaten

4 tbsp cocoa powder, sifted

150 g/5½ oz dark chocolate

300ml/10 fl oz single cream

1 tsp chocolate essence

TO DECORATE

425 ml/15 fl oz double cream, whipped

chocolate flakes and quick chocolate curls
   (see page 15)

1 To make the pastry, sieve the flour and cocoa powder into a mixing bowl. Rub in the butter until the mixture resembles fine breadcrumbs. Stir in the sugar and enough cold water to mix to a soft dough. Chill for 15 minutes.

2 Roll out the dough on a lightly floured surface and use to line a deep 23 cm/9 inch loose-bottomed flan tin or ceramic flan dish. Line with foil or baking paper and baking beans. Bake blind in a preheated oven, 190°C/375°F/Gas Mark 5, for 15 minutes. Remove the beans and foil or paper and cook for a further 10 minutes until crisp.

3 Meanwhile, make the filling. Beat the butter and sugar in a bowl and gradually beat in the eggs with the cocoa powder. Melt the chocolate and beat it into the mixture with the single cream and the chocolate essence.

4 Pour the mixture into the cooked pastry case and bake at 170°C/325°F/Gas Mark 3 for 45 minutes or until the filling is set.

5 Leave to cool completely, then transfer the pie to a serving plate, if preferred. Cover with the whipped cream and leave to chill.

6 Decorate the pie with quick chocolate curls and chocolate flakes and then leave it to chill.

Chocolate Fruit Tartlets

Chocolate pastry trimmed with nuts makes a perfect case for fruit in these tasty individual tartlets. You can use fresh or canned fruit.

  1½ hrs 20–25 mins

SERVES 6

INGREDIENTS

250 g/9 oz plain flour

3 tbsp cocoa powder

150 g/5½ oz butter

3 tbsp caster sugar

2–3 tbsp water

50 g/1¾ oz dark chocolate

50 g/1¾ oz chopped mixed nuts, toasted

350 g/12 oz prepared fruit

3 tbsp apricot jam or redcurrant jelly

1 Sieve the flour and cocoa powder into a mixing bowl. Cut the butter into small pieces and rub into the flour with your fingertips until the mixture resembles fine breadcrumbs.

2 Stir in the sugar. Add enough of the water to mix to a soft dough – about 1–2 tablespoons. Cover and chill for 15 minutes.

3 Roll out the pastry on a lightly floured surface and use to line 6 tartlet tins, each 10 cm/4 inches across. Prick the pastry with a fork and line the pastry cases with a little crumpled foil. Bake in a preheated oven, 190°C/375°F/Gas Mark 5, for 10 minutes.

4 Remove the foil and bake for a further 5–10 minutes until the pastry is crisp. Place the tins on a wire rack to cool completely.

5 Melt the chocolate. Spread out the chopped nuts on a plate. Remove the pastry cases from the tartlet tins. Spread melted chocolate on the rims, then dip in the nuts. Leave to set.

6 Arrange the fruit in the tartlet cases. Melt the apricot jam or redcurrant jelly with the remaining 1 tablespoon of water and brush it over the fruit. Chill the tartlets until required.

VARIATION

If liked, you can fill the cases with a little sweetened cream before topping with the fruit. For a chocolate-flavoured filling, blend 225 g/8 oz chocolate hazelnut spread with 5 tablespoons of thick yogurt or whipped cream.

Banana Cream Profiteroles

Chocolate profiteroles are a popular choice. In this recipe they are filled with a delicious banana-flavoured cream – the perfect combination!

45 mins   15–20 mins

SERVES 4

I N G R E D I E N T S

C H O U X   P A S T R Y

150 ml/5 fl oz water

5 tbsp butter

90 g/3 oz strong plain flour, sifted

2 eggs

C H O C O L A T E   S A U C E

100 g/3½ oz dark chocolate, broken into pieces

2 tbsp water

4 tbsp icing sugar

2 tbsp unsalted butter

F I L L I N G

300 ml/10 fl oz double cream

1 banana

2 tbsp icing sugar

2 tbsp banana-flavoured liqueur

1 Lightly grease a baking tray and sprinkle with a little water. To make the pastry, place the water in a pan. Cut the butter into small pieces and add to the pan. Heat gently until the butter melts, then bring to a rolling boil. Remove the pan from the heat and add the flour in one go, beating well until the mixture leaves the sides of the pan and forms a ball. Leave to cool slightly, then gradually beat in the eggs to form a smooth, glossy mixture. Spoon the paste into a large piping bag fitted with a 1 cm/½ inch plain nozzle.

2 Pipe about 18 small balls of the paste on to the baking tray, allowing enough room for them to expand during cooking. Bake in a preheated oven, 220°C/425°F/Gas Mark 7, for 15–20 minutes until crisp and golden. Remove from the oven and make a small slit in each one for steam to escape. Cool on a wire rack.

3 To make the sauce, place all the ingredients in a heatproof bowl, set over a pan of simmering water and heat until combined to make a smooth sauce, stirring constantly.

4 To make the filling, whip the cream until standing in soft peaks. Mash the banana with the sugar and liqueur. Fold into the cream. Place in a piping bag fitted with a 1 cm/½ inch plain nozzle and pipe into the profiteroles. Serve with the sauce poured over.

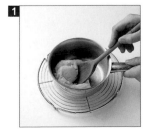

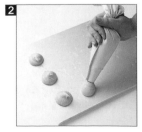

Tiramisu Layers

This is a modern version of the well-known and very traditional chocolate dessert from Italy.

🕑 1 hr 25 mins   🕐 5 mins

SERVES 6

INGREDIENTS

150 ml/5 fl oz double cream

300 g/10½ oz dark chocolate

400 g/14 oz mascarpone cheese

400 ml/14 fl oz black coffee with
   4 tbsp caster sugar, cooled

6 tbsp dark rum or brandy

36 sponge fingers, about 400 g/14 oz

cocoa powder, to dust

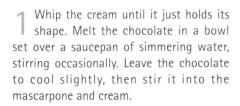

1 Whip the cream until it just holds its shape. Melt the chocolate in a bowl set over a saucepan of simmering water, stirring occasionally. Leave the chocolate to cool slightly, then stir it into the mascarpone and cream.

2 Mix the coffee and rum together in a bowl. Dip the sponge fingers into the mixture briefly so that they absorb the coffee and rum liquid but do not become soggy.

3 Place 3 sponge fingers on 3 serving plates.

4 Spoon a layer of the mascarpone and chocolate mixture over the sponge fingers.

5 Place 3 more sponge fingers on top of the mascarpone layer. Spread another layer of mascarpone and chocolate mixture and place 3 more sponge fingers on top.

6 Leave the tiramisu to chill in the refrigerator for at least 1 hour. Dust all over with a little cocoa powder just before serving.

VARIATION
Try adding 50 g/1¾ oz toasted, chopped hazelnuts to the chocolate cream mixture in step 1, if you prefer.

Rich Chocolate Loaf

Another rich chocolate dessert, this loaf is very simple to make and can be served as a tea-time treat as well.

 1 hr 20 mins 5 mins

MAKES 16 SLICES

INGREDIENTS

150 g/5½ oz dark chocolate

6 tbsp unsalted butter

210 ml/7¼ fl oz condensed milk

2 tsp cinnamon

75 g/2¾ oz almonds

75 g/2¾ oz amaretti biscuits, broken

50 g/1¾ oz dried no-soak apricots, roughly chopped

1 Line a 675 g/1½ lb loaf tin with a sheet of kitchen foil.

2 Using a sharp knife, roughly chop the almonds.

3 Place the chocolate, butter, milk and cinnamon in a heavy-based saucepan.

4 Heat the chocolate mixture over a low heat for 3–4 minutes, stirring with a wooden spoon, or until the chocolate has melted. Beat the mixture well.

COOK'S TIP

To melt chocolate, first break it into manageable pieces. The smaller the pieces, the quicker it will melt.

5 Stir the almonds, biscuits and apricots into the chocolate mixture, stirring with a wooden spoon, until well mixed.

6 Pour the mixture into the prepared tin and leave to chill in the refrigerator for about 1 hour or until set.

7 Cut the rich chocolate loaf into slices to serve.

Chocolate Mousse

This is a light and fluffy mousse with a subtle hint of orange. It is wickedly delicious served with a fresh fruit sauce.

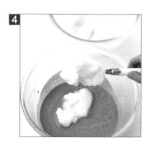

2¼ hours   5 mins

SERVES 8

INGREDIENTS

100 g/3½ oz dark chocolate, melted

300 ml/10 fl oz natural yogurt

150 ml/5 fl oz Quark

4 tbsp caster sugar

1 tbsp orange juice

1 tbsp brandy

1½ tsp gelozone (vegetarian gelatine)

9 tbsp cold water

2 large egg whites

TO DECORATE

roughly grated dark and white chocolate

orange rind

1 Put the melted chocolate, yogurt, Quark, sugar, orange juice and brandy in a food processor or blender and process for 30 seconds. Transfer the mixture to a large bowl.

2 Sprinkle the gelozone over the water and stir until dissolved.

3 In a pan, bring the gelozone and water to the boil for 2 minutes. Cool slightly, then stir into the chocolate.

4 Whisk the egg whites until stiff peaks form and fold into the chocolate mixture using a metal spoon.

5 Line a 500 g/1 lb 2 oz loaf tin with clingfilm. Spoon the mousse into the tin. Chill in the refrigerator for 2 hours, until set. Turn the mousse out on to a serving plate, decorate and serve.

Chocolate Cheesecake

This cheesecake takes a little time to prepare and cook but is well worth the effort. It is quite rich and is good served with a little fresh fruit.

15 mins

1–1¼ hrs

SERVES 12

INGREDIENTS

100 g/3½ oz plain flour

100 g/3½ oz ground almonds

200 g/7 oz raw brown sugar

150 g/5½ oz margarine

675 g/1 lb 8 oz firm tofu

175 ml/6 fl oz vegetable oil

125 ml/4 fl oz orange juice

175 ml/6 fl oz brandy

6 tbsp cocoa powder, plus extra to decorate

2 tsp almond essence

TO DECORATE

icing sugar

Cape gooseberries

1 Put the flour, ground almonds and 1 tablespoon of the sugar in a bowl and mix well. Rub the margarine into the mixture to form a dough.

2 Lightly grease and line the base of a 23 cm/9 inch springform tin. Press the dough into the base of the tin to cover, pushing the dough right up to the edge of the tin.

3 Roughly chop the tofu and put in a food processor with the vegetable oil, orange juice, brandy, cocoa powder almond essence and remaining sugar and process until smooth and creamy. Pour over the base in the tin and cook in a preheated oven, 160°C/325°F/ Gas Mark 3, for 1–1¼ hours, or until set.

4 Leave to cool in the tin for 5 minutes, then remove from the tin and chill in the refrigerator. Dust with icing sugar and cocoa powder. Decorate with Cape gooseberries and serve.

COOK'S TIP

Cape gooseberries make an attractive decoration for many desserts. Peel open the papery husks to expose the bright orange fruits.

Chocolate Cheese Pots

These super-light desserts are just the thing if you have a craving for chocolate. Serve on their own or with a selection of fruits.

40 mins   0 mins

SERVES 4

INGREDIENTS

300 ml/10 fl oz low-fat natural fromage frais

150 ml/5 fl oz low-fat natural yogurt

2 tbsp icing sugar

4 tsp low-fat drinking chocolate powder

4 tsp cocoa powder

1 tsp vanilla essence

2 tbsp dark rum, optional

2 medium egg whites

4 chocolate cake decorations

TO SERVE

pieces of kiwi fruit, orange and banana

strawberries and raspberries

COOK'S TIP

This chocolate mixture would make an excellent filling for a cheesecake. Make the base out of crushed amaretti biscuits and egg white, and set the filling with 2 tablespoons of powdered gelatine dissolved in 2 tablespoons of boiling water.

1 Mix the fromage frais and low-fat yogurt in a bowl. Sift in the sugar, drinking chocolate and cocoa powder and mix well.

2 Add the vanilla essence and rum (if using).

3 In a clean bowl, whisk the egg whites until stiff. Using a metal spoon, fold the egg whites into the chocolate mixture.

4 Spoon the fromage frais and chocolate mixture into 4 small china dessert pots and leave to chill for about 30 minutes.

5 Decorate each chocolate cheese pot with a chocolate cake decoration and serve with an assortment of fresh fruit, such as pieces of kiwi fruit, orange and banana, and a few whole strawberries and raspberries.

Mocha Swirl Mousse

A combination of feather-light yet rich chocolate and coffee mousses, whipped and attractively presented in serving glasses.

🥔 1¼ hours   🕐 0 mins

SERVES 4

INGREDIENTS

1 tbsp coffee and chicory essence

2 tsp cocoa powder, plus extra for dusting

1 tsp low-fat drinking chocolate powder

150 ml/5 fl oz low-fat crème fraîche, plus 4 tsp to serve

2 tsp powdered gelatine

2 tbsp boiling water

2 large egg whites

2 tbsp caster sugar

4 chocolate coffee beans, to serve

1 Place the coffee and chicory essence in one bowl, and 2 teaspoons cocoa powder and the drinking chocolate in another bowl. Divide the crème fraîche between the 2 bowls and mix both well.

2 Dissolve the gelatine in the boiling water and set aside. In a grease-free bowl, whisk the egg whites and sugar until stiff and divide this evenly between the two mixtures.

3 Divide the dissolved gelatine between the 2 mixtures and, using a large metal spoon, gently fold until well mixed.

4 Spoon small amounts of the 2 mousses alternately into 4 serving glasses and swirl together gently. Chill for 1 hour or until set.

5 To serve, top each mousse with a teaspoonful of crème fraîche, a chocolate coffee bean and a light dusting of cocoa powder. Serve immediately.

COOK'S TIP

Vegetarians should not be denied this delicious chocolate dessert. Instead of gelatine use the vegetarian equivalent, gelozone, available from health-food shops. However, be sure to read the instructions on the packet first as it is prepared differently from gelatine.

Panforte di Siena

This famous Tuscan honey and nut cake is a Christmas speciality. In Italy it is sold in pretty boxes, and served in very thin slices.

10 mins   1¼ hours

SERVES 12

INGREDIENTS

125 g/4½ oz split whole almonds

125 g/4½ oz hazelnuts

90 g/3 oz chopped mixed peel

60 g/2 oz no-soak dried apricots

60 g/2 oz glacé or crystallized pineapple

grated rind of 1 large orange

6 tbsp plain flour

2 tbsp cocoa powder

2 tsp ground cinnamon

125 g/4½ oz caster sugar

175 g/6 oz honey

icing sugar, for dredging

1 Toast the almonds under the grill until lightly browned and place in a bowl.

2 Toast the hazelnuts until the skins split. Place on a dry tea towel and rub off the skins. Roughly chop the hazelnuts and add them to the almonds with the mixed peel.

3 Chop the apricots and pineapple fairly finely, add to the nuts with the orange rind and mix well.

4 Sieve the flour with the cocoa and cinnamon, add to the nut mixture, and stir to combine.

5 Line a round 20 cm/8 inch cake tin or deep loose-bottomed flan tin with baking paper.

6 Put the sugar and honey into a saucepan and heat until the sugar dissolves, then boil gently for about 5 minutes or until the mixture thickens and begins to turn a deeper shade of brown. Quickly add it to the nut mixture and mix together evenly. Turn into the prepared tin and level the top using the back of a damp spoon.

7 Cook in a preheated oven, 150°C/300°F/Gas Mark 2, for 1 hour. Remove from the oven and leave in the tin until cold. Take out of the tin and carefully peel off the paper. Before serving, dredge the cake heavily with sifted icing sugar. Serve in very thin slices.

Chocolate & Almond Tart

This is a variation on the classic pecan pie recipe – here, nuts and chocolate are encased in a thick syrup filling.

1½ hrs   1 hr

SERVES 8

INGREDIENTS

PASTRY

150 g/5 oz plain flour

2 tbsp caster sugar

125 g/4½ oz butter, cut into small pieces

1 tbsp water

FILLING

150 g/5½ oz golden syrup

4 tbsp butter

75 g/2¾ oz soft brown sugar

3 eggs, lightly beaten

100 g/3½ oz whole blanched almonds, roughly chopped

100 g/3½ oz white chocolate, roughly chopped

cream, to serve (optional)

VARIATION

You can use a mixture of white and dark chocolate for this tart, if preferred.

1 To make the pastry, place the flour and sugar in a mixing bowl and rub in the butter with your fingers. Add the water and work the mixture together until a soft pastry has formed. Wrap and leave to chill for 30 minutes.

2 On a lightly floured surface, roll out the dough and line a 24 cm/9½ inch loose-bottomed flan tin. Prick the pastry with a fork and leave to chill for 30 minutes. Line the pastry case with foil and baking beans and bake in a preheated oven, 190°C/375°F/Gas Mark 5, for 15 minutes. Remove the foil and baking beans and cook for a further 15 minutes.

3 Meanwhile, make the filling. Gently melt the syrup, butter and sugar together in a saucepan. Remove from the heat and leave to cool slightly. Stir in the beaten eggs, almonds and chocolate.

4 Pour the chocolate and nut filling into the prepared pastry case and cook in the oven for 30–35 minutes or until just set. Leave to cool before removing the tart from the tin. Serve with cream, if wished.

Chocolate & Pear Sponge

What could be better than the lovely combination used in this cake of chocolate and fresh pears in a moist sponge?

1¼ hrs   1 hr

SERVES 6

I N G R E D I E N T S

175 g/6 oz butter, softened

175 g/6 oz soft brown sugar

3 eggs, beaten

150 g/5½ oz self-raising flour

2 tbsp cocoa powder

2 tbsp milk

2 small pears, peeled, cored and sliced

1 Grease a 23 cm/8 inch loose-bottomed cake tin and line the base with baking paper.

2 In a bowl, cream together the butter and soft brown sugar until the mixture is pale and fluffy.

3 Gradually add the beaten eggs to the creamed mixture, beating well after each addition.

4 Sieve the self-raising flour and cocoa powder into the creamed mixture and fold in gently until all of the ingredients are combined.

5 Stir in the milk, then spoon the mixture into the prepared tin. Level the surface with the back of a spoon or a palette knife.

6 Arrange the pear slices on top of the cake mixture, arranging them in a radiating pattern.

7 Bake in a preheated oven, 180°C/350°F/Gas Mark 4, for about 1 hour, until the cake is just firm to the touch.

8 Leave the cake to cool in the tin, then transfer to a wire rack to completely cool before serving.

COOK'S TIP

Serve the cake with melted chocolate drizzled over the top for a delicious dessert.

Mint-chocolate Gelato

Rich, creamy gelati, or ice creams, are one of the great Italian culinary contributions to the world. This version is made with fresh mint.

5–6 hrs   20 mins

SERVES 4

INGREDIENTS

6 large eggs

150 g/5½ oz caster sugar

300 ml/10 fl oz milk

150 ml/5 fl oz double cream

large handful fresh mint leaves, rinsed and dried

2 drops green food colouring, optional

60 g/2 oz dark chocolate, finely chopped

1 Put the eggs and sugar in a heatproof bowl that will sit over a saucepan with plenty of room underneath. Using an electric mixer, beat the eggs and sugar together until thick and creamy.

2 Put the milk and cream in the saucepan and bring to a simmer, where small bubbles appear all around the edge, stirring. Pour on to the eggs, whisking constantly. Rinse the pan and put 2.5 cm/1 inch of water in the bottom. Place the bowl on top, making sure the base does not touch the water. Turn the heat to medium-high.

3 Transfer the mixture to a pan and cook the mixture, stirring constantly, until it is thick enough to coat the back of the spoon and leave a mark when you pull your finger across it.

4 Tear the mint leaves and stir them into the custard. Remove the custard from the heat. Leave to cool, then cover and infuse for at least 2 hours, chilling for the last 30 minutes.

5 Strain the mixture through a small nylon sieve, to remove the pieces of mint. Stir in the food colouring, if using. Transfer to a freezer container and freeze the mixture for 1–2 hours until frozen 2.5 cm/1 inch from the sides.

6 Scrape into a bowl and beat again until smooth. Stir in the chocolate pieces, smooth the top and cover with clingfilm or kitchen foil. Freeze until it is set, for up to 3 months. Soften the ice cream in the refrigerator for 20 minutes before serving.

Chocolate Rice Dessert

What could be more delicious than creamy tender rice cooked in a rich chocolate sauce? This dessert is almost like a dense chocolate mousse.

🍴 2 hrs 5 mins 🕐 1 hr 10 mins

SERVES 8

INGREDIENTS

100 g/3½ oz long-grain white rice

pinch of salt

600 ml/1 pint milk

100 g/3½ oz granulated sugar

200 g/7 oz bitter or dark chocolate, chopped

5 tbsp butter, diced

1 tsp vanilla essence

2 tbsp brandy or Cognac

175 ml/6 fl oz double cream

whipped cream, for piping (optional)

chocolate curls (see page 15), to decorate (optional)

1 Bring a saucepan of water to the boil. Sprinkle in the rice and add the salt; reduce the heat and simmer gently for 15–20 minutes until the rice is just tender. Drain, rinse and drain again.

2 Heat the milk and the sugar in a large heavy-based saucepan over a medium heat until the sugar dissolves, stirring frequently. Add the chocolate and butter and stir until melted and smooth.

3 Stir in the cooked rice and reduce the heat to low. Cover and simmer, stirring occasionally, for 30 minutes until the milk is absorbed and the mixture thickened. Stir in the vanilla extract and brandy. Remove from the heat and allow to cool to room temperature.

4 Using an electric mixer, beat the cream until soft peaks form. Stir one heaped spoonful of the cream into the chocolate rice mixture to lighten it; then fold in the remaining cream.

5 Spoon into glass serving dishes, cover and chill for about 2 hours. If wished, decorate with piped whipped cream and top with chocolate curls. Serve cold.

VARIATION

To mould the chocolate rice, soften 1 sachet of gelatine in about 50 ml/2½ fl oz of cold water and heat gently until dissolved. Stir into the chocolate just before folding in the cream. Pour into a rinsed mould, allow to set, then unmould.

Quick Chocolate Desserts

This rich creamy dessert takes hardly any time to prepare, but you will need to allow time for chilling.

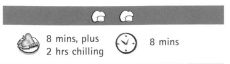

🕐 8 mins, plus 2 hrs chilling   ⏱ 8 mins

SERVES 4

INGREDIENTS

125 ml/4 fl oz water

4 tbsp caster sugar

175 g/6 oz dark chocolate, broken into pieces

3 egg yolks

300 ml/10 fl oz double cream

dessert biscuits, to serve

1 Pour the water into a pan and add the sugar. Stir over a low heat until the sugar has dissolved. Bring to the boil and continue to boil, without stirring, for 3 minutes. Remove the pan from the heat and let it cool slightly.

2 Put the chocolate in a food processor and add the hot syrup. Process until the chocolate has melted, then add the egg yolks and process briefly until smooth. Finally, add the cream and process until fully incorporated.

3 Pour the mixture into 4 glasses or individual bowls, cover with clingfilm and chill in the refrigerator for 2 hours, until set. Serve with dessert biscuits.

Marshmallow Ice Cream

Richly flavoured and with a wonderful texture, this home-made ice cream really couldn't be simpler.

  10 mins, plus 2½ hrs cooling/ freezing

5–10 mins

SERVES 4

INGREDIENTS

85 g/3 oz dark chocolate, broken into pieces

175 g/6 oz white marshmallows

150 ml/5 fl oz milk

300 ml/10 fl oz double cream

1 Put the chocolate and marshmallows in a pan and pour in the milk. Warm over a very low heat until the chocolate and marshmallows have melted. Remove from the heat and leave the mixture to cool completely.

2 Whisk the cream until thick, then fold it into the cold chocolate mixture with a metal spoon. Pour into a 450 g/ 1 lb loaf tin and freeze for at least 2 hours, until firm (it will keep for 1 month in the freezer). Serve with fresh fruit.

Chocolate Sorbet

This is a truly special sorbet and it is worth buying the best possible quality chocolate for it.

10–12 mins, plus 3½ hrs cooling/ freezing

7–10 mins

SERVES 6

I N G R E D I E N T S

140 g/5 oz bitter continental chocolate, roughly chopped

140 g/5 oz dark continental chocolate, roughly chopped

475 ml/16 fl oz water

200 g/7 oz caster sugar

langues de chats biscuits, to serve

1 Put both types of chocolate into a food processor and process briefly until very finely chopped.

2 Pour the water into a heavy-based pan and add the sugar. Stir over a medium heat to dissolve, then bring to the boil. Boil for 2 minutes, without stirring, then remove the pan from the heat.

3 With the motor of the food processor running, pour the hot syrup on to the chocolate. Process for about 2 minutes, until all the chocolate has melted and the mixture is smooth. Scrape down the sides of the food processor, if necessary. Strain the chocolate mixture into a freezerproof container and leave to cool.

4 When the mixture is cool, place it in the freezer for about 1 hour until

slushy, but beginning to become firm around the edges. Tip the mixture into the food processor and process until smooth. Return to the container and freeze for at least 2 hours until firm.

5 Remove the sorbet from the freezer about 10 minutes before serving and let it stand at room temperature to allow it to soften slightly. Serve in scoops with langues de chats biscuits.

Chocolate & Orange Trifle

The slight tartness of satsumas beautifully counterbalances the richness of the trifle, but you could use clementines, if preferred.

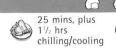

25 mins, plus 1½ hrs chilling/cooling

15–20 mins

SERVES 6

INGREDIENTS

4 trifle sponges

2 large chocolate coconut macaroons, crumbled

4 tbsp sweet sherry

8 satsumas

200 g/7 oz dark chocolate, broken into pieces

2 egg yolks

2 tbsp caster sugar

2 tbsp cornflour

200 ml/7 fl oz milk

250 g/9 oz mascarpone cheese

225 ml/7½ fl oz double cream

TO DECORATE

Marbled Chocolate Shapes (see page 114)

10–12 satsuma segments

2 Put the chocolate in the top of double boiler or a heatproof bowl set over a pan of barely simmering water. Stir over a low heat until melted and smooth. Remove from the heat and let it cool completely.

3 In a separate bowl, mix together the egg yolks, sugar and cornflour to make a smooth paste. Bring the milk to just below boiling point in a small pan. Remove from the heat and pour it into the egg yolk mixture, stirring constantly.

Return the custard to a clean pan and cook over a low heat, stirring constantly, until thickened and smooth. Return to the bowl, then stir in the mascarpone until thoroughly combined. Stir in the cooled chocolate. Spread the chocolate custard evenly over the base of the trifle and chill in the refrigerator for 1 hour until set.

4 Whip the cream until thick, then spread it over the top of the trifle. Decorate with marbled chocolate shapes and satsuma segments.

1 Break up the trifle sponges and place them in a large glass serving dish. Sprinkle the crumbled macaroons on top, then sprinkle with the sherry. Squeeze the juice from two of the satsumas and sprinkle it over the crumbled macaroons. Peel and segment the remaining satsumas and arrange them in the dish.

Strawberry Petits Choux

These little chocolate puffs are filled with a melting mixture of strawberry mousse and fresh fruit.

🥮 35–40 mins, plus 2 hrs chilling/cooling

🕐 40–45 mins

SERVES 6

I N G R E D I E N T S

2 tbsp water

2 tsp gelatine

350 g/12 oz strawberries

225 g/8 oz ricotta cheese

1 tbsp caster sugar

2 tsp crème de fraises de bois or strawberry eau-de-vie

PETITS CHOUX

100 g/3½ oz plain flour

2 tbsp cocoa powder

pinch of salt

6 tbsp unsalted butter

225 ml/8 fl oz water

2 eggs, plus 1 egg white

icing sugar, for dusting

1 Sprinkle the gelatine over the water in a heatproof bowl. Leave to soften for 2–3 minutes. Place the bowl over a pan of barely simmering water and stir until the gelatine dissolves. Remove from the heat.

2 Place 225 g/8 oz of the strawberries in a blender with the ricotta, sugar and liqueur. Process until blended. Add the gelatine and process briefly. Transfer the mousse to a bowl, cover with clingfilm and chill for 1–1½ hours, until set.

3 Meanwhile, to make the petits choux, line a baking tray with baking paper. Sieve the flour, cocoa and salt on to a sheet of greaseproof paper. Put the butter and water into a heavy-based pan and heat gently until the butter has melted.

4 Preheat the oven to 220°C/425°F/Gas Mark 7. Remove the pan from the heat and add the flour mixture all in one go, beating vigorously with a wooden spoon. Return the pan to the heat and beat vigorously until the mixture comes away from the sides of the pan. Remove from the heat and cool slightly.

5 In a separate bowl, beat the eggs with the extra egg white, then gradually add them to the chocolate mixture, beating vigorously until a glossy paste forms. Drop 12 rounded spoonfuls of the mixture onto the prepared baking tray and bake for 20–25 minutes, until puffed up and firm.

6 Remove from the oven and make a slit in the side of each petits choux. Return the petits choux to the oven for 5 minutes to dry out. Transfer to a wire rack to cool.

7 Slice the remaining strawberries. Slice the petits choux in half, removing any uncooked dough from the centres. Divide the set strawberry mousse among the pastries, add a layer of strawberry slices and replace the tops. Dust lightly with icing sugar and place in the refrigerator. Serve within 1½ hours.

Triple Stripe Cream

Layers of chocolate, vanilla and coffee, topped with a swirl of whipped cream, make a simple but elegant dessert.

🧊 15 mins, plus 2 hrs chilling ⏲ 20 mins

SERVES 6

INGREDIENTS

300 g/10½ oz caster sugar

6 tbsp cornflour

900 ml/1½ pints milk

3 egg yolks

6 tbsp unsalted butter, diced

1 heaped tbsp instant coffee granules

2 tsp vanilla essence

2 tbsp cocoa powder

150 ml/5fl oz whipped cream, to decorate

1 Put 100 g/3½ oz of the sugar and 2 tablespoons of the cornflour in a small, heavy-based saucepan. Gradually, whisk in one-third of the milk. Set the pan over a low heat and whisk in one of the egg yolks. Bring to the boil, whisking constantly, and boil for 1 minute. Remove the pan from the heat and stir in 1 tablespoonful of the butter, and all the coffee granules. Set aside to cool slightly, then divide among 6 wine goblets and smooth the surfaces.

2 Place 100 g/3½ oz of the remaining sugar and 2 tablespoons of the remaining cornflour in a small heavy-based saucepan. Gradually, whisk in 300 ml/10 fl oz of the remaining milk. Set the pan over a low heat and whisk in one of the remaining egg yolks. Bring to the boil, whisking constantly, and boil for 1 minute. Remove the pan from the heat and stir in 2 tablespoons of the remaining butter, and all the vanilla. Set aside to cool slightly, then divide among the goblets and smooth the surfaces.

3 Put the remaining sugar and cornflour into a small heavy-based saucepan. Gradually, whisk in the remaining milk. Set the pan over a low heat and whisk in the last egg yolk. Bring to the boil, whisking constantly, and boil for 1 minute. Remove from the heat and stir in the remaining butter, and all the cocoa. Set aside to cool slightly, then divide among the goblets. Cover with clingfilm and chill in the refrigerator for 2 hours, until set.

4 Whip the cream until thick, then pipe a swirl on top of each of the desserts. Serve immediately.

Strawberry Cheesecake

Sweet strawberries are teamed with creamy mascarpone cheese and luxurious white chocolate to make this mouthwatering cheesecake.

  1 hr, plus 2 hrs cooling   1¼ hrs

SERVES 8

INGREDIENTS

BASE

4 tbsp unsalted butter

225 g/8 oz crushed digestive biscuits

55 g/2 oz chopped walnuts

FILLING

450 g/1 lb mascarpone cheese

2 eggs, beaten

3 tbsp caster sugar

250 g/9 oz white chocolate, broken into pieces

225 g/8 oz strawberries, hulled and quartered

TOPPING

175 g/6 oz mascarpone cheese

chocolate caraque (see page 15)

16 whole strawberries

1 To make the base, melt the butter over a low heat and stir in the crushed biscuits and the nuts. Spoon the mixture into a 23 cm/9 inch loose-bottomed cake tin and press evenly over the base with the back of a spoon. Set aside.

2 Preheat the oven to 150°C/300°F/Gas Mark 2. To make the filling, beat the cheese until smooth, then beat in the eggs and sugar. Put the chocolate in the top of a double boiler or in a heatproof bowl set over a pan of barely simmering water. Stir

over a low heat until melted and smooth. Remove from the heat and cool slightly, then stir into the cheese mixture. Finally, stir in the strawberries.

3 Spoon the mixture into the cake tin, spread out evenly and smooth the surface. Bake in the preheated oven for

1 hour, until the filling is just firm. Turn off the oven but leave the cheesecake in it until completely cold.

4 Transfer the cheesecake to a serving plate and spread the mascarpone on top. Decorate with chocolate caraque and whole strawberries.

Chocolate Cloud

This unbelievably easy, but delicious dessert can be made in a matter of a few minutes.

20 mins, plus 1 hr chilling/ cooling		5 mins

SERVES 6

INGREDIENTS

115 g/4 oz dark chocolate, broken into pieces

4 eggs, separated

600 ml/1 pint double cream

toasted slivered almonds, to decorate

1 Put the chocolate in the top of a double boiler or in a heatproof bowl set over a pan of barely simmering water. Stir over a low heat until melted. Remove from the heat and cool slightly, then beat in the egg yolks.

2 In a separate bowl, whisk the egg whites until they are stiff, then fold them into the chocolate mixture. Set aside for 30 minutes until beginning to set.

3 Whip 300 ml/10 fl oz of the double cream until thick, then fold half of the whipped cream into the chocolate mixture. Spoon half the chocolate and cream mixture into 6 sundae glasses. Divide the other half of the whipped cream between the glasses in a layer over the chocolate mixture. Top with the remaining chocolate mixture. Cover with clingfilm and chill in the refrigerator for 30 minutes.

4 Just before serving, whip the remaining cream until it is thick. Pipe a swirl of cream on the top of each dessert and sprinkle with the almonds.

Chocolate Pecan Pie

This classic American dessert is packed with deliciously contrasting flavours and textures and is simply irresistible.

40 mins, plus 2 hrs chilling/cooling

1¼ hrs

MAKES 1 X 25 CM/10 INCH PIE

I N G R E D I E N T S

PASTRY

280 g/10 oz plain flour, plus extra for dusting

6 tbsp cocoa powder

115 g/4 oz icing sugar

pinch of salt

200 g/7 oz unsalted butter, diced

1 egg yolk

FILLING

85 g/3 oz dark chocolate, broken into small pieces

350 g/12 oz shelled pecan nuts

6 tbsp unsalted butter

175 g/6 oz brown sugar

3 eggs

2 tbsp double cream

2 tbsp plain flour

1 tbsp icing sugar, for dusting

1 To make the pastry, sieve the flour, cocoa, sugar and salt into a mixing bowl and make a well in the centre. Put the butter and egg yolk in the well and gradually mix in the dry ingredients. Knead lightly into a ball. Cover with clingfilm and chill in the refrigerator for 1 hour.

2 Unwrap the dough and roll it out on a lightly floured surface. Use it to line a 25 cm/10 inch non-stick springform pie tin and prick the base with a fork. Preheat the oven to 180°C/350°F/Gas Mark 4. Line the pastry case with baking paper and fill with baking beans. Bake in the preheated oven for 15 minutes. Remove from the oven, discard the beans and paper and let it cool.

3 To make the filling, put the chocolate in a heatproof bowl set over a pan of barely simmering water. Stir until melted. Remove from the heat and set aside. Roughly chop 225 g/8 oz of the pecans and set aside. Mix the butter with 55 g/2 oz of the brown sugar. Beat in the eggs, one at a time, then add the remaining brown sugar and mix well. Stir in the cream, flour, melted chocolate and chopped pecans.

4 Spoon the filling into the pastry case and smooth the surface. Cut the remaining pecans in half and arrange in concentric circles over the pie.

5 Bake in the preheated oven at the same temperature for 30 minutes, then remove the pie and cover the top with foil to prevent it from burning. Bake for a further 25 minutes. Remove the pie from the oven and let it cool slightly before removing from the tin and transferring to a wire rack to cool completely. Dust with icing sugar.

Chocolate Ice Cream Roll

This is a family favourite – spiral slices of sponge cake and ice cream never fail to please.

35 mins, plus 35–40 standing time

20–25 mins

SERVES 8

INGREDIENTS

butter, for greasing

115 g/4 oz plain flour, plus extra for dusting

4 eggs

115 g/4 oz caster sugar

3 tbsp cocoa powder

icing sugar, for dusting

600 ml/1 pint chocolate ice cream

chocolate quick curls, to decorate (see page 15)

225 ml/8 fl oz Chocolate Fudge Sauce, to serve (see page 101)

1 Line a 38 x 25 cm/15 x 10 inch Swiss roll tin with greaseproof paper. Grease the base and dust with flour. Put the eggs and caster sugar into the top of a double boiler or in a heatproof bowl set over a pan of barely simmering water. Beat over a low heat for 5–10 minutes until the mixture is pale and fluffy. Remove from the heat and continue beating for 10 minutes until the mixture is cool and the whisk leaves a ribbon trail when lifted. Sieve the flour and cocoa powder over the surface and gently fold it in.

2 Preheat the oven to 190°C/375°F/Gas Mark 5. Pour the mixture into the prepared tin and spread out evenly with a palette knife. Bake in the preheated oven for 15 minutes, until firm to the touch and beginning to shrink from the sides of the tin.

3 Spread out a clean tea towel and cover with a sheet of baking paper. Lightly dust the paper with icing sugar.

Turn out the cake on to the baking paper and carefully peel off the lining paper. Trim off any crusty edges. Starting from a short side, pick up the cake and the baking paper and roll them up together. Wrap the tea towel around the rolled cake and place on a wire rack to cool.

4 Remove the ice cream from the freezer and put it in the refrigerator for 15–20 minutes to soften slightly. Remove the tea towel and unroll the cake.

Spread the ice cream evenly over the cake, then roll it up again without the baking paper. Wrap the cake in foil and place in the freezer.

5 Remove the cake from the freezer about 20 minutes before serving. Unwrap, place on a serving plate and dust with icing sugar. Make the chocolate quick curls and arrange on top. Place in the refrigerator until required. Serve in slices with Chocolate Fudge Sauce.

Blackberry Chocolate Flan

This richly flavoured flan looks superb and tastes wonderful – a perfect choice for a special occasion.

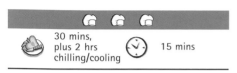

30 mins, plus 2 hrs chilling/cooling

15 mins

SERVES 6

INGREDIENTS

280 g/10 oz plain flour, plus extra for dusting

55 g/2 oz cocoa powder

115 g/4 oz icing sugar

pinch of salt

200 g/7 oz unsalted butter, diced

1 egg yolk

675 g/1 lb 8 oz blackberries

1 tbsp lemon juice

2 tbsp caster sugar

2 tbsp crème de cassis

FILLING

300 ml/10 fl oz double cream

175 g/6 oz blackberry jam

225 g/8 oz dark chocolate, broken into pieces

55 g/2 oz unsalted butter, diced

1 First, make the pastry. Sieve the flour, cocoa, icing sugar and a pinch of salt into a mixing bowl and make a well in the centre. Put the butter and egg yolk in the well and gradually mix in the dry ingredients, using a pastry blender or two forks. Knead lightly and form into a ball. Cover with clingfilm and chill in the refrigerator for 1 hour.

2 When chilled, unwrap the dough. Preheat the oven to 180°C/350°F/Gas Mark 4. Roll the dough out on a lightly floured, non-stick surface and use it to line a 30 x 10 cm/12 x 4 inch rectangular flan tin and prick the base with a fork.

Line the pastry case with baking paper and fill with baking beans. Bake in the preheated oven for 15 minutes. Remove from the oven, remove the beans and paper and set aside to cool.

3 To make the filling, put the cream and jam into a pan and bring to the boil over a low heat. Remove the pan from the heat and stir in the chocolate until melted and smooth. Stir in the butter until melted and smooth. Pour the mixture into the pastry case and set aside to cool.

4 Put 225 g/8 oz of the blackberries, the lemon juice and caster sugar into a food processor and process until smooth. Transfer to a bowl and stir in the crème de cassis. Set aside.

5 Remove the flan from the tin and place on a serving plate. Arrange the remaining blackberries on top and brush with a little of the blackberry and liqueur sauce. Serve the flan and hand the sauce separately.

Zuccotto

This famous Italian ice cream bombe is so named because its shape resembles a pumpkin, or *zucca*.

30 mins, plus 2 hrs chilling | 0 mins

SERVES 8

INGREDIENTS

600 ml/1 pint double cream

2 tbsp icing sugar

55 g/2 oz hazelnuts, toasted

225 g/8 oz cherries, halved and stoned

115 g/4 oz dark chocolate, finely chopped

2 x 20 cm/8 inch round chocolate sponge cakes

4 tbsp brandy

4 tbsp amaretto liqueur

TO DECORATE

2 tbsp icing sugar

2 tbsp cocoa powder

1 In a large bowl, whisk the cream until it is stiff, then fold in the sugar, followed by the hazelnuts, cherries and chocolate. Cover with clingfilm and chill in the refrigerator until required.

2 Meanwhile, cut the cakes in half horizontally and then cut the pieces to fit a 1.25 litre/2 pint pudding basin, so that the base and sides are completely lined. Reserve the remaining sponge cake. Mix together the brandy and amaretto in a small bowl and sprinkle the mixture over the sponge cake lining.

3 Remove the cream filling from the refrigerator and spoon it into the lined basin. Cover the top with the remaining sponge cake, cut to fit. Cover with clingfilm and chill the bombe in the refrigerator for 2 hours, or until ready to serve.

4 For the decoration, sieve the icing sugar into a bowl and the cocoa into another bowl. To serve, remove the bombe from the refrigerator and run a round-bladed knife around the sides to loosen it. Place a serving plate on top of the basin and, holding them firmly together, invert. Dust two opposite quarters of the zuccotto with icing sugar and the other opposite quarters with cocoa to make alternating sections of colour.

Zuccherini

Italians, especially Sicilians and Sardinians, are famous for having a sweet tooth – and for their superb desserts.

30 mins, plus 8½ hrs chilling

10 mins

SERVES 6

INGREDIENTS

175 g/6 oz dark chocolate, broken into pieces

10 amaretti biscuits, crushed

MOUSSE

55 g/2 oz dark chocolate, broken into pieces

1 tbsp cold, strong, black coffee

2 eggs, separated

2 tsp orange-flavoured liqueur

TO DECORATE

150 ml/5 fl oz double cream

2 tbsp cocoa powder

6 chocolate coffee beans

1 To make the chocolate cups, put the 175 g/6 oz dark chocolate in the top of a double boiler or in a heatproof bowl set over a pan of barely simmering water. Stir until melted and smooth, but not too runny, then remove from the heat. Coat the inside of 12 double paper cake cases with chocolate, using a small brush. Stand them on a tray and chill for at least 8 hours or overnight in the refrigerator.

2 To make the mousse, put the chocolate and coffee in the top of a double boiler or in a heatproof bowl set over a pan of barely simmering water. Stir over a low heat until the chocolate has melted and the mixture is smooth, then remove from the heat. Cool slightly, then stir in the egg yolks and liqueur.

3 Whisk the egg whites in a separate bowl until they form stiff peaks. Fold the whites into the chocolate mixture with a metal spoon, then set aside to cool.

4 Remove the chocolate cups from the refrigerator and carefully peel off the paper cases. Divide the crushed amaretti biscuits equally among the chocolate cups and top with the chocolate mousse.

Return to the refrigerator for at least 30 minutes. Just before serving, whip the cream and pipe a star on the top of each chocolate cup. Dust half of the zuccherini with cocoa powder and then decorate the other half with the chocolate-covered coffee beans.

Chocolate & Orange Slices

Contrasting flavours, textures and colours are combined to create this delectable masterpiece.

30–40 mins, plus 3–4 hrs chilling

10 mins

SERVES 8

INGREDIENTS

2 tsp butter, for greasing

450 g/1 lb dark chocolate, broken into pieces

3 small, loose-skinned oranges, such as tangerines, mandarins or satsumas

4 egg yolks

200 ml/7 fl oz crème fraîche

2 tbsp raisins

300 ml/10 fl oz whipped cream, to serve

1 Grease a 450 g/1 lb loaf tin and line it with clingfilm. Put 400 g/14 oz of the chocolate in the top of a double boiler or into a heatproof bowl set over a pan of barely simmering water. Stir over a low heat until melted. Remove from the heat and cool slightly.

2 Meanwhile, peel the oranges, removing all traces of pith. Cut the rind into matchsticks. Beat the egg yolks into the chocolate, one at a time, then add most of the orange rind (reserve the rest for decoration), and all the crème fraîche and raisins and beat until smooth and thoroughly combined. Spoon the mixture into the prepared tin, cover with clingfilm and chill in the refrigerator for 3–4 hours, until set.

3 While the chocolate mixture is chilling, put the remaining chocolate in the top of a double boiler or into a heatproof bowl set over a pan of barely simmering water. Stir over a low heat until melted. Remove the pan from the heat and cool slightly. Meanwhile, segment the oranges. Dip each segment into the melted chocolate and spread out on a sheet of baking paper for about 30 minutes until set.

4 To serve, remove the tin from the refrigerator and turn out the chocolate mould. Remove the clingfilm and cut the mould into slices. Place a slice on each of 8 individual serving plates and decorate with the chocolate-coated orange segments and the remaining orange rind. Serve immediately with whipped cream.

Crispy Chocolate Pie

The whisky-flavoured chocolate filling makes this scrumptious pie very moreish.

25 mins, plus 30 mins cooling

35–40 mins

MAKES 6

INGREDIENTS

2 tsp butter, for greasing

2 egg whites

115 g/4 oz ground almonds

25 g/1 oz ground rice

115 g/4 oz caster sugar

¼ tsp almond essence

225 g/8 oz dark chocolate, broken into small pieces

4 egg yolks

55 g/2 oz icing sugar

4 tbsp whisky

4 tbsp double cream

TO DECORATE

150 ml/5 fl oz whipped cream

55 g/2 oz dark chocolate, grated

1 Preheat the oven to 160°C/325°F/Gas Mark 3. Grease a 20 cm/8 inch flan tin and line the base with baking paper. Whisk the egg whites until they form stiff peaks. Gently fold in the ground almonds, ground rice, caster sugar and almond essence. Spread the mixture over the base and sides of the prepared tin. Bake in the preheated oven for 15 minutes.

2 Meanwhile, put the chocolate in the top of a double boiler or into a heatproof bowl set over a pan of barely simmering water. Stir over a low heat until melted. Remove from the heat and cool slightly, then beat in the egg yolks, icing sugar, whisky and the 4 tablespoons of cream until thoroughly incorporated.

3 Remove the flan tin from the oven and pour in the chocolate mixture. Cover with foil, return to the oven and bake at the same temperature for 20–25 minutes, until set. Remove from the oven and leave to cool completely.

4 Mix together the whipped cream and 25 g/1 oz of the grated chocolate, then spread over the pie. Top with the remaining grated chocolate, and serve immediately.

Chocolate Salami

Don't be alarmed – this Italian dish gets its name from its appearance, not because it contains pork.

25mins,
plus 6–8 hrs
standing/freezing

5–7 mins

SERVES 10

INGREDIENTS

350 g/12 oz dark chocolate, broken into small pieces

4 tbsp amaretto liqueur or brandy

225 g/8 oz unsalted butter, cut into small pieces

24 plain sweet biscuits, such as Petit Beurre, roughly crushed

2 egg yolks

55 g/2 oz toasted flaked almonds, chopped

25 g/1 oz ground almonds

1 tsp vegetable oil or olive oil, for greasing

1 Put the chocolate in the top of a double boiler or in a heatproof bowl set over a pan of barely simmering water. Add the liqueur or brandy and 2 tablespoons of the butter. Stir over a low heat until melted and smooth. Remove from the heat and cool slightly.

2 Stir in the egg yolks, then stir in the remaining butter, a little at a time, making sure each addition is fully incorporated before adding more. Stir in about three-quarters of the crushed biscuits and all the toasted almonds. Cover with clingfilm then set aside for 45–60 minutes, until beginning to set. Meanwhile, put the remaining crushed biscuits into a food processor and process until finely crushed. Transfer them to a bowl and stir in the ground almonds, then set aside.

3 Lightly oil a sheet of baking paper and turn out the chocolate mixture on to

it. Using a palette knife, shape the mixture into a salami about 35 cm/14 inches long. Wrap the salami in the paper and place in the freezer for 4–6 hours, until set.

4 About 1¼ hours before serving, spread out the ground almond mixture on a sheet of baking paper. Remove the salami from the freezer and unwrap. Roll it over the ground almond mixture until thoroughly and evenly coated. Cover with clingfilm then set aside for 1 hour at room temperature. Cut into slices and serve.

Chocolate Loaf

Full of flavour and contrasting textures, this classic Italian dessert is very quick and easy to prepare.

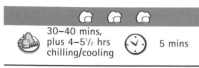

30–40 mins,
plus 4–5½ hrs
chilling/cooling

5 mins

SERVES 8

I N G R E D I E N T S

2 tsp vegetable oil, for brushing

225 g/8 oz dark chocolate, broken into pieces

4 tbsp dark rum

225 g/8 oz unsalted butter

115 g/4 oz caster sugar

2 eggs, separated

175 g/6 oz ground almonds

115 g/4 oz crushed amaretti biscuits or macaroons

2 tbsp icing sugar

pinch of salt

T O   D E C O R A T E

75 g/2¾ oz dark chocolate

8 chocolate-covered cherries

8 chocolate leaves (see page 15)

1 Line a 1 kg/2 lb loaf tin with baking paper, allowing it to overlap the sides. Brush with oil. Put the chocolate in the top of a double boiler or in a heatproof bowl set over a pan of barely simmering water. Stir over a low heat until melted. Remove the pan from the heat, stir in the rum and set aside to cool.

2 Cream together the butter and caster sugar until pale and fluffy, then beat in the egg yolks, one at a time. Add the almonds and beat in the cooled chocolate.

3 Whisk the egg whites with a pinch of salt until they form stiff peaks. Gently fold the whites into the chocolate mixture, then fold in the biscuit crumbs. Spoon the mixture into the prepared tin, spread it out evenly and smooth the top. Cover with clingfilm and chill in the refrigerator for 4–5 hours, until firm.

4 To serve, uncover the tin and run a round-bladed knife around the sides. Dip the base in hot water. Place a serving plate on top of the tin, then, holding them firmly together, invert. Remove the baking paper. Dust with the icing sugar.

5 To decorate, melt the 75 g/2¾ oz dark chocolate as before, and then put spoonfuls along the top of the cake. Top with chocolate-covered cherries and leaves.

Raspberry Chocolate Boxes

Mocha mousse, fresh raspberries and sponge cake all presented in neat little chocolate boxes – almost too good to eat.

50 mins, plus 3 hrs chilling/cooling

45–55 mins

SERVES 12

INGREDIENTS

200g/7 oz dark chocolate, broken into pieces

1½ tsp cold, strong black coffee

1 egg yolk

1½ tsp coffee liqueur

2 egg whites

2 tsp butter, for greasing

200g /7 oz raspberries

SPONGE CAKE

2 tsp butter, for greasing

1 egg, plus 1 egg white

4 tbsp caster sugar

5 tbsp plain flour

1 To make the mocha mousse, melt 55 g /2 oz of the chocolate in a heatproof bowl set over a pan of barely simmering water. Add the coffee and stir over a low heat until smooth, then remove from the heat and cool slightly. Stir in the egg yolk and the coffee liqueur.

2 Whisk the egg whites in a separate bowl into stiff peaks. Fold into the chocolate mixture, cover with clingfilm and chill in for about 2 hours, until set.

3 For the sponge cake, lightly grease a 20 cm/8 inch square cake tin and line the base with baking paper. Put the egg and extra white with the sugar in a heatproof bowl set over a pan of barely simmering water. Whisk over a low heat for 5–10 minutes until pale and thick. Remove from the heat and continue whisking for 10 minutes until cold and the whisk leaves a ribbon trail when lifted.

4 Preheat the oven to 180°C/350°F/Gas Mark 4. Sieve the flour over the egg mixture and gently fold it in. Pour the mixture into the prepared tin and spread evenly. Bake in the preheated oven for 20–25 minutes, until firm to the touch and slightly shrunk from the sides of the tin. Turn out on to a wire rack to cool, then invert the cake, leaving the baking paper in place.

5 To make the chocolate boxes, grease a 30 x 23 cm/12 x 9 inch Swiss roll tin and line with greaseproof paper. Place the remaining chocolate in a heatproof bowl set over a pan of barely simmering water. Stir over a low heat until melted, but not too runny. Pour it into the tin and spread evenly with a palette knife. Set aside in a cool place for about 30 minutes, until set.

6 Turn out the set chocolate onto a clean work surface. Using a ruler and sharp knife, cut it into 36 rectangles, measuring 7.5 x 2.5 cm/3 x 1 inches. Cut 12 of these rectangles in half to make 24 rectangles measuring 3.75 x 2.5 cm/1½ x 1 inches.

7 Trim the crusty edges off the sponge cake, then cut it into 12 slices, measuring 7.5 x 3 cm/3 x 1¼ inches. Spread a little of the set mocha mousse along the sides of each sponge rectangle and gently press 2 long and 2 short chocolate rectangles in place on each side to make boxes. Divide the remaining mousse among the boxes and top with the raspberries. Refrigerate until ready to use.

Filo Nests

Green and black grapes decorate the creamy chocolate filling in these crisp little pastry nests.

25mins, plus 20 mins cooling

15–18 mins

SERVES 4

INGREDIENTS

1 tbsp unsalted butter

6 sheets filo pastry, about 30 x 15 cm/ 12 x 6 inches each

40 g/1½ oz dark chocolate, broken into pieces

115 g/4 oz ricotta cheese

16 seedless green grapes, halved

24 seedless black grapes, halved

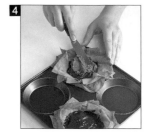

1 Put the butter into a small pan and set over a low heat until melted. Remove from the heat. Preheat the oven to 190°C/375°F/Gas Mark 5. Cut each sheet of pastry into four, to give 24 rectangles, each measuring about 15 x 7.5 cm/ 6 x 3 inches, then stack them all on top of each other. Brush 4 shallow tartlet tins with melted butter. Line 1 tin with a rectangle of pastry, brush with melted butter, and place another rectangle on top at an angle to the first and brush it with melted butter. Continue in this way, lining each tin with 6 rectangles, each brushed with melted butter. Brush the top layers with melted butter.

2 Bake in the preheated oven for 7–8 minutes, until golden and crisp. Remove from the oven and set aside to cool in the tins.

3 Put the chocolate in the top of a double boiler or into a heatproof bowl set over a pan of barely simmering water. Stir over a low heat until melted. Remove from the heat and cool slightly. Brush the insides of the pastry cases with about half the melted chocolate. Beat the ricotta until smooth, then beat in the remaining melted chocolate.

4 Divide the chocolate ricotta among the pastry cases and arrange the grapes alternately around the edges. Carefully lift the pastry cases out of the tins and serve immediately.

Chocolate Pear Tart

The classic partnership of chocolate and pears appears in many forms, both hot and cold. This tart will soon become a family favourite.

25 mins, plus 50–55 mins cooling

30 mins

SERVES 8

INGREDIENTS

PASTRY

115 g/4 oz plain flour, plus 1 tbsp extra for dusting

2 tbsp caster sugar

115 g/4 oz unsalted butter, diced

1 egg yolk

1 tbsp lemon juice

pinch of salt

TOPPING

115 g/4 oz dark chocolate, grated

4 pears

125 ml/4 fl oz single cream

1 egg, plus 1 egg yolk

½ tsp almond essence

3 tbsp caster sugar

1 To make the pastry, sieve the flour and a pinch of salt into a mixing bowl. Add the sugar and butter and mix well with a pastry blender or two forks until thoroughly incorporated. Stir in the egg yolk and the lemon juice to form a dough. Form the dough into a ball, wrap in clingfilm and chill in the refrigerator for 30 minutes.

2 Preheat the oven to 200°C/400°F/Gas mark 6. Roll out the dough on a lightly floured surface and use it to line a 25 cm/10 inch loose-bottomed flan tin. Sprinkle the grated chocolate over the base of the pastry case. Peel the pears, cut them in half lengthways and remove the cores. Thinly slice each pear half crossways and fan the slices out slightly. Using a fish slice

or spatula, scoop up each sliced pear half and arrange in the pastry case.

3 Beat together the cream, egg, extra yolk and almond essence and spoon the mixture over the pears. Sprinkle the sugar over the tart.

4 Bake in the preheated oven for 10 minutes. Lower the temperature to 180°C/350°F/Gas Mark 4 and bake for a further 20 minutes, until the pears are beginning to caramelize and the filling is just set. Remove from the oven and cool to room temperature before serving.

Oeufs à la Neige au Chocolat

In this dessert, poached meringues float on a richly flavoured chocolate custard like little snowballs.

15 mins, plus 2 hrs chilling

15–20 mins

SERVES 6

I N G R E D I E N T S

600 ml/1 pint milk

1 tsp vanilla essence

175 g/6 oz caster sugar

2 egg whites

C U S T A R D

4 tbsp caster sugar

3 tbsp cocoa powder

4 egg yolks

1 Put the milk, vanilla and 5 tablespoons of the sugar into a heavy-based saucepan and stir over a low heat until the sugar has dissolved. Simmer gently.

2 Whisk the egg whites until they form stiff peaks. Whisk in 2 teaspoons of the remaining sugar and continue to whisk until glossy. Gently fold in the rest of the sugar.

3 Drop large spoonfuls of the meringue mixture onto the simmering milk mixture and cook, stirring once, for 4–5 minutes, until the meringues are firm. Remove with a slotted spoon and set aside on kitchen paper to drain. Poach the remaining meringues in the same way, then reserve the milk mixture.

4 To make the custard, mix the sugar, cocoa and egg yolks in the top of a double boiler or in a heatproof bowl. Gradually stir in the reserved milk mixture. Place over barely simmering water and cook for 5–10 minutes, stirring constantly, until thickened. Remove from the heat and cool slightly. Divide the chocolate custard among individual serving glasses and top with the meringues. Cover with clingfilm and chill in the refrigerator for at least 2 hours before serving.

Chocolate & Pernod Creams

This unusual combination of flavours makes a sophisticated and tempting dessert to serve at a dinner party.

10 mins, plus 2 hrs chilling

20 mins

SERVES 4

INGREDIENTS

55 g/2 oz dark chocolate, broken into pieces

250 ml/8 fl oz milk

300 ml/10 fl oz double cream

2 tbsp caster sugar

1 tbsp arrowroot dissolved in 2 tbsp milk

3 tbsp Pernod

langues de chats biscuits, or chocolate-
tipped rolled wafers, to serve

1 Put the chocolate in the top of a double boiler or in a heatproof bowl set over a pan of barely simmering water. Stir over a low heat until melted. Remove the pan from the heat and cool slightly.

2 Pour the milk and cream into a pan over a low heat and bring to just below boiling point, stirring occasionally. Remove the pan from the heat and then set aside.

3 Beat the sugar and the arrowroot mixture into the melted chocolate. Gradually stir in the hot milk and cream mixture, then stir in the Pernod. Return the double boiler to the heat or set the bowl over a pan of barely simmering water and cook, over a low heat, for 10 minutes, stirring constantly, until thick and smooth. Remove from the heat and then set aside to cool.

4 Pour the chocolate and Pernod mixture into 4 individual serving glasses. Cover with clingfilm and chill in the refrigerator for 2 hours before serving with langues de chats biscuits or chocolate-tipped rolled wafers.

White Chocolate Moulds

This pretty, colourful dessert is deliciously refreshing and would make a good finale to an *al fresco* meal.

20 mins, plus 2½ hrs chilling/standing

10–15 mins

SERVES 6

INGREDIENTS

125 g/4½ oz white chocolate, broken into pieces

250 ml/8 fl oz double cream

3 tbsp crème fraîche

2 eggs, separated

3 tbsp water

1½ tsp gelatine

1 tsp oil, for brushing

140 g/5 oz sliced strawberries

140 g/5 oz raspberries

140 g/5 oz blackcurrants

5 tbsp caster sugar

125 ml/4 fl oz crème de framboise

12 blackcurrant leaves, if available

1 Put the chocolate in the top of a double boiler or in a heatproof bowl set over a pan of barely simmering water. Stir over a low heat until melted and smooth. Remove from the heat and set aside.

2 Meanwhile, pour the cream into a pan and bring to just below boiling point over a low heat. Remove from the heat, then stir the cream and crème fraîche into the chocolate and cool slightly. Beat in the egg yolks, one at a time.

3 Pour the water into a small, heatproof bowl and sprinkle the gelatine on the surface. Leave for 2–3 minutes to soften,

then set over a pan of barely simmering water until completely dissolved. Stir the gelatine into the chocolate mixture and then leave until nearly set.

4 Brush the inside of 6 timbales, ramekins, dariole moulds or small cups with oil and line the bases with baking paper. Whisk the egg whites until soft peaks form, then fold them into the chocolate mixture. Divide the mixture evenly among the prepared moulds and smooth the surface. Cover with clingfilm and chill in the refrigerator for 2 hours, until set.

5 Put the strawberries, raspberries and blackcurrants in a bowl and sprinkle with the caster sugar. Pour in the liqueur and stir gently to mix. Cover with clingfilm and then chill in the refrigerator for 2 hours.

6 To serve, run a round-bladed knife around the sides of the moulds and turn out on to individual serving plates. Divide the fruit among the plates and serve immediately, garnished with blackcurrant leaves, if available.

Chocolate Orange Sorbet

Elegant and sophisticated, dark chocolate encloses liqueur-flavoured sorbet to provide this perfect dinner party dessert.

1 hr, plus 12 hours freezing

12–15 mins

SERVES 4

I N G R E D I E N T S

2 tsp vegetable oil, for brushing

225 g/8 oz dark chocolate, broken into small pieces

1 litre/1¾ pints crushed ice

300 ml/10 fl oz freshly squeezed orange juice

150 ml/5 fl oz water

4 tbsp caster sugar

finely grated rind of 1 orange

juice and finely grated rind of 1 lemon

1 tsp gelatine

3 tbsp orange-flavoured liqueur

3 Reserve 3 tablespoons of the orange juice in a small, heatproof bowl. Pour the remainder into a pan and add the water, sugar, orange rind and lemon juice and rind. Stir over a low heat until the sugar has dissolved, then increase the heat and bring the mixture to the boil. Remove the pan from the heat.

4 Meanwhile, sprinkle the gelatine on the surface of the orange juice in the bowl. Set aside for 2 minutes to soften, then set over a pan of barely simmering water until dissolved. Stir the dissolved gelatine and the liqueur into the orange juice mixture. Pour into a freezerproof container and place in the freezer for 30 minutes, until slushy.

5 Remove the sorbet from the freezer, transfer into a bowl and beat thoroughly to break up the ice crystals. Return it to the freezerproof container and put it back in the freezer for 1 hour. Repeat this process 3 more times.

6 Remove the sorbet from the freezer, transfer to a bowl and beat well once more. Remove the mould from the refrigerator and spoon the sorbet into it. Smooth the surface with a palette knife. Place the mould in the freezer and then leave overnight.

7 Remove the mould from the freezer shortly before serving. Place a chilled serving plate on top and, holding them firmly together, invert. Serve immediately.

1 Brush a 900 ml/1½ pint mould with oil, drain well, then chill in the refrigerator. Put the chocolate in the top of a double boiler or into a heatproof bowl set over a pan of barely simmering water. Stir over a low heat until melted, then remove from the heat.

2 Remove the mould from the refrigerator and pour in the melted chocolate. Tip and turn the mould to coat the interior. Place the mould on a bed of crushed ice and continue tipping and turning until the chocolate has set. Return the mould to the refrigerator.

Chocolate & Hazelnut Parfait

Richly flavoured, moulded ice creams make a scrumptious summertime dessert for all the family.

30 mins, plus 8 hrs freezing/standing

10 mins

SERVES 6

I N G R E D I E N T S

175 g/6 oz blanched hazelnuts

175 g/6 oz dark chocolate, broken into small pieces

600 ml/1 pint double cream

3 eggs, separated

250 g/9 oz icing sugar

1 tbsp cocoa powder, for dusting

6 small fresh mint sprigs, to decorate

wafer biscuits, to serve

1 Spread out the hazelnuts on a baking tray and toast under a grill preheated to medium, shaking the tray from time to time for about 5 minutes, until golden all over. Set aside to cool.

2 Put the chocolate in the top of a double boiler or in a heatproof bowl set over a pan of barely simmering water. Stir over a low heat until melted, then remove from the heat and cool. Put the toasted hazelnuts in a food processor and process until finely ground.

3 Whisk the cream until it is stiff, then fold in the ground hazelnuts and set aside. Beat the egg yolks with 3 tablespoons of the sugar for 10 minutes until pale and thick.

4 Whisk the egg whites in a separate bowl until soft peaks form. Whisk in the remaining sugar, a little at a time, until the whites are stiff and glossy. Stir the cooled chocolate into the egg yolk mixture, then fold in the cream and finally, fold in the egg whites. Divide the mixture among six freezerproof timbales or moulds, cover with clingfilm and freeze for at least 8 hours or overnight until firm.

5 Transfer the parfaits to the refrigerator about 10 minutes before serving to soften slightly. Turn out on to individual serving plates, dust the tops lightly with cocoa, decorate with mint sprigs and serve with wafers.

Chocolate Smoothie

Use your favourite fresh fruit in season and dip the pieces in this wonderful malted chocolate mixture.

 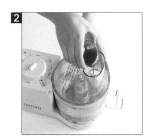 

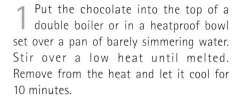 20 mins 5 mins

SERVES 4

INGREDIENTS

55 g/2 oz dark chocolate, broken into pieces

2 large bananas

1 tbsp malt extract

selection of fresh fruit, cut into chunks or slices, as necessary

1 Put the chocolate into the top of a double boiler or in a heatproof bowl set over a pan of barely simmering water. Stir over a low heat until melted. Remove from the heat and let it cool for 10 minutes.

2 Peel and slice the bananas. Place them in a food processor and process until smooth. With the motor still running, pour the malt extract through the feeder tube. Continue to process until fully incorporated, and thick and frothy. With the motor still running, pour the melted chocolate through the feeder tube in a slow, steady stream. Continue to process until thoroughly combined.

3 Scrape the smoothie into a small serving bowl and stand on a large serving plate. Arrange the fruit around the bowl and serve immediately.

Chocolate Chiffon Pie

The nutty crust of this delectable American pie contrasts with the tempting creamy chocolate filling.

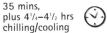

🍐 35 mins, plus 4¼–4½ hrs chilling/cooling ⏲ 12–15 mins

SERVES 8

INGREDIENTS

140 g/5 oz shelled Brazil nuts

2 tbsp granulated sugar

2 tsp melted butter

250 ml/8 fl oz milk

2 tsp gelatine

115 g/4 oz caster sugar

2 eggs, separated

225 g/8 oz dark chocolate, roughly chopped

1 tsp vanilla essence

150 ml/5 fl oz double cream

2 tbsp chopped Brazil nuts

1 Preheat the oven to 200°C/400°F/Gas Mark 6. Put the Brazil nuts into a food processor and process until finely ground. Add the granulated sugar and melted butter and process briefly to combine. Tip the mixture into a 23 cm/9 inch round pie tin or dish and press it on to the base and sides with a spoon or your fingertips. Bake in the preheated oven for 8–10 minutes, until light golden brown. Set aside to cool.

2 Pour the milk into the top of a double boiler or into a heatproof bowl and sprinkle the gelatine over the surface. Allow to soften for 2 minutes, then place over a pan of barely simmering water. Stir in half the caster sugar, both the egg yolks

and all the chocolate. Stir constantly over a low heat for 4–5 minutes, until the gelatine has dissolved and the chocolate has melted. Remove from the heat and beat until the mixture is smooth and thoroughly blended. Stir in the vanilla essence, cover with clingfilm and chill in the refrigerator for 45–60 minutes, until just beginning to set.

3 Whip the cream until it is stiff, then fold all but about 3 tablespoons into

the chocolate mixture. Whisk the egg whites in another bowl until soft peaks form. Add 2 teaspoons of the remaining sugar and whisk until stiff peaks form. Fold in the remaining sugar, then fold the egg whites into the chocolate mixture. Pour the filling into the pie dish and chill in the refrigerator for 3 hours, or until set. Decorate the pie with the remaining whipped cream and the chopped nuts before serving.

Pineapple Chocolate Rings

These pretty fruit desserts make a perfect end to a summertime supper, but can also be served with morning coffee.

25–30 mins, plus 1 hr cooling

30–40 mins

SERVES 10

INGREDIENTS

140 g/5 oz unsalted butter

4 tbsp caster sugar

175 g/6 oz plain flour, plus extra for dusting

3 tbsp ground almonds

½ tsp almond essence

200 g/7 oz dark chocolate, broken into small pieces

10 canned pineapple rings, drained and can juice reserved

10 maraschino cherries

1 tsp cornflour

1 Line a baking tray with baking paper. Cream 115 g/4 oz of the butter with all the sugar until pale and fluffy. Sieve in the flour, add the ground almonds and almond essence and knead the mixture thoroughly until it forms a soft dough.

2 Preheat the oven to 190°C/375°F/Gas Mark 5. Turn out the dough onto a lightly floured board and roll out to about 5 mm/¼ inch thick. Stamp out 20 rounds with a 7.5 cm/3 inch round cutter and place them on the prepared baking tray. Prick the surface of each round with a fork, then bake in the preheated oven for 20 minutes, until lightly browned. Using a spatula, transfer the rounds to a wire rack to cool.

3 Place the remaining butter and the chocolate in the top of a double boiler or in a heatproof bowl set over a pan of barely simmering water. Stir over a low heat until melted and smooth. Remove the pan from the heat. Sandwich the rounds together in pairs, while still moist, with the chocolate mixture spread between them. Place a pineapple ring on top of each pair of rounds before the chocolate sets and place a cherry in the centre of each ring.

4 Put 4 tablespoons of the reserved can juice into a small pan and stir in the cornflour. Bring to the boil over a moderate heat, stirring constantly and cook for 5–7 minutes until thickened. Remove the pan from the heat and let it cool to room temperature. Brush the glaze over the pineapple rings and leave for 10 minutes to set before serving.

Chocolate & Honey Ice Cream

Ice cream is always a popular summer dessert – try this rather different recipe for a change.

30 mins, plus
5 hrs freezing/
cooling

15 mins

SERVES 6

INGREDIENTS

500 ml/18 fl oz milk

200 g/7 oz dark chocolate, broken into pieces

4 eggs, separated

85 g/3 oz caster sugar

2 tbsp clear honey

pinch of salt

12 fresh strawberries, washed and hulled

4 Divide the mixture among 6 individual freezerproof moulds and place in the freezer for at least 4 hours, until frozen. Meanwhile, put the remaining chocolate in the top of a double boiler or in a heatproof bowl set over a pan of barely simmering water. Stir over a low heat until melted and smooth, then dip the strawberries in the melted chocolate so that they are half-coated. Leave to set on a sheet of baking paper. Transfer the ice cream to the refrigerator for 10 minutes before serving. Turn out onto serving plates and decorate with the strawberries.

1 Pour the milk into a pan, add 150 g/5½ oz of the chocolate and stir over a medium heat for 3–5 minutes until melted. Remove the pan from the heat and set aside.

2 In a separate bowl, beat the egg yolks with all but 1 tablespoon of the sugar until pale and thickened. Gradually, beat in the milk mixture, a little at a time. Return the mixture to a clean pan and cook over a low heat, whisking constantly, until smooth and thickened. Remove from the heat and set aside to cool completely. Cover with clingfilm and chill in the refrigerator for 30 minutes.

3 Whisk the egg whites with a pinch of salt until soft peaks form. Gradually whisk in the remaining sugar and continue whisking until stiff and glossy. Remove the chocolate mixture from the refrigerator and stir in the honey, then gently fold in the egg whites.

Small Cakes & Cookies

This chapter contains everyday delights for chocolate fans. You are sure to be tempted by our wonderful array of cookies and small cakes. Make any day special with a home-made chocolate biscuit to be served with coffee, as a snack or to accompany a special dessert. Although some take a little longer to make, most are quick and easy to prepare and

decoration is often simple although you can get carried away if you like!

You'll find recipes for old favourites such as Chocolate Chip Muffins and Chocolate Chip Cookies, Chocolate Butterfly Cakes and Sticky Chocolate Brownies. There are also new biscuits and small cakes, such as Chocolate & Coconut Squares or Malted Chocolate Wedges. Finally, we have given the chocolate treatment to some traditional recipes – try Chocolate Scones or Chocolate Chip Flapjacks.

Chocolate Boxes

Guests will think you have spent hours creating these little boxes, but a few tricks (such as ready-made cake) make them quick to put together.

20 mins   5 mins

SERVES 4

INGREDIENTS

225 g/8 oz dark chocolate

about 225 g/8 oz bought or ready-made plain or chocolate cake

2 tbsp apricot jam

150 ml/5 fl oz double cream

1 tbsp maple syrup

100 g/3½ oz prepared fresh fruit, such as small strawberries, raspberries, kiwi fruit or redcurrants

1 Melt the dark chocolate and spread it evenly over a large sheet of baking paper. Leave to harden in a cool room.

2 When just set, cut the chocolate into 5 cm/2 inch squares and remove from the paper. Make sure that your hands are as cool as possible and handle the chocolate as little as possible.

3 Cut the cake into two 5 cm/2 inch cubes, then cut each cube in half. Warm the apricot jam and brush it over the sides of the cake cubes. Carefully press a chocolate square on to each side of the cake cubes to make 4 chocolate boxes with cake at the bottom. Chill in the refrigerator for 20 minutes.

4 Whip the double cream with the maple syrup until just holding its shape. Spoon or pipe a little of the mixture into each chocolate box.

5 Decorate the top of each box with the prepared fruit. If liked, the fruit can be partially dipped into melted chocolate and allowed to harden before being placed into the boxes.

COOK'S TIP

For the best results, keep the boxes well chilled and fill and decorate them just before you want to serve them.

Chocolate Dairy Wraps

Light chocolate sponge is wrapped around a dairy cream filling. These individual cakes can be served for dessert, if desired.

🍰 40 mins   🕐 6–8 mins

SERVES 6

INGREDIENTS

2 eggs

4 tbsp caster sugar

6 tbsp plain flour

1½ tbsp cocoa powder

4 tbsp apricot jam

150 ml/5 fl oz double cream, whipped

icing sugar, to dust

1 Line 2 baking trays with pieces of baking paper. Whisk the eggs and sugar together until the mixture is very light and fluffy and the whisk leaves a trail when lifted.

2 Sift together the flour and cocoa powder. Using a metal spoon or a spatula, gently fold it into the eggs and sugar in a figure of eight movement.

3 Drop rounded tablespoons of the mixture on to the lined baking trays and spread them into oval shapes. Make sure they are well spaced as they will spread during cooking.

4 Bake in a preheated oven, 220°C/425°F/Gas Mark 7, for about 6–8 minutes or until springy to the touch. Leave to cool on the baking trays.

5 When cold, slide the cakes on to a damp tea towel and allow to stand until cold. Carefully remove them from the dampened paper. Spread the flat side of the cakes with jam, then spoon or pipe the whipped cream down the centre of each one.

6 Fold the cakes in half and place them on a serving plate. Sprinkle them with a little icing sugar and serve.

VARIATION

Fold 4 teaspoons of crème de menthe or 50 g/2 oz melted chocolate into the cream for fabulous alternatives to plain cream.

Chocolate Cup Cakes

A variation on an old favourite, both kids and grown-ups will love these sumptuous little cakes.

1¼ hrs   20 mins

MAKES 18

I N G R E D I E N T S

100 g/3½ oz butter, softened

100 g/3½ oz caster sugar

2 eggs, lightly beaten

50 g/1¾ oz dark chocolate chips

2 tbsp milk

150 g/5½ oz self-raising flour

2 tbsp cocoa powder

WHITE CHOCOLATE ICING

225 g/8 oz white chocolate

150 g/5½ oz low-fat soft cheese

1 Line an 18-hole bun tray with individual paper cup cases.

2 Beat together the butter and sugar until pale and fluffy. Gradually add the eggs, beating well after each addition. Add a little of the flour if the mixture begins to curdle. Add the milk, then fold in the chocolate chips.

3 Sift together the flour and cocoa powder and fold into the mixture with a metal spoon or spatula. Divide the mixture equally between the paper cases and level the tops.

4 Bake in a preheated oven, 180°C/350°F/Gas Mark 4, for 20 minutes, or until well risen and springy to the touch. Leave to cool on a wire rack.

5 To make the white chocolate icing, melt the white chocolate, then leave to cool slightly. Beat the cream cheese until softened slightly, then beat in the melted chocolate. Spread a little of the icing over each cup cake and chill for 1 hour before serving.

VARIATION

Add white chocolate chips or chopped pecan nuts to the mixture instead of the dark chocolate chips, if you prefer. You can also add the finely grated rind of 1 orange for a chocolate and orange flavour.

Chocolate Rum Babas

A little bit fiddly to make but well worth the effort. Indulge in these tasty cakes with coffee, or serve them as a dessert with summer fruits.

3 hrs   15 mins

SERVES 4

INGREDIENTS

100 g/3½ oz strong plain flour

2 tbsp cocoa powder

6 g sachet easy-blend dried yeast

pinch of salt

1 tbsp caster sugar

40 g/1½ oz dark chocolate, grated

2 eggs

3 tbsp tepid milk

4 tbsp butter, melted

SYRUP

4 tbsp clear honey

2 tbsp water

4 tbsp rum

TO SERVE

whipped cream

cocoa powder, to dust

fresh fruit, optional

1 Lightly oil 4 individual ring tins. In a large warmed mixing bowl, sieve the flour and cocoa powder together. Stir in the yeast, salt, sugar and grated chocolate. In a separate bowl, beat the eggs together, add the milk and butter, and beat until mixed.

2 Make a well in the centre of the dry ingredients and pour in the egg mixture, beating to mix to a batter. Beat for 10 minutes, ideally in a electric mixer with a dough hook. Divide the mixture between the tins – it should come halfway up the sides.

3 Place on a baking tray and cover with a damp tea towel. Leave in a warm place until the mixture rises almost to the tops of the tins. Bake in a preheated oven, 200°C/400°F/Gas Mark 6, for 15 minutes.

4 To make the syrup, gently heat all of the ingredients in a small pan. Turn out the babas and place on rack placed above a tray to catch the syrup. Drizzle the syrup over the babas and leave for at least 2 hours for the syrup to soak in. Once or twice, spoon the syrup that has dripped on to the tray over the babas.

5 Fill the centre of the babas with whipped cream and sprinkle a little cocoa powder over the top. Serve the babas with fresh fruit, if desired.

No-bake Chocolate Squares

Children will enjoy making these as an introduction to chocolate cookery, and they keep well in the refrigerator.

    2¼ hrs   5 mins

MAKES 16

INGREDIENTS

275 g/9½ oz dark chocolate

175 g/6 oz butter

4 tbsp golden syrup

2 tbsp dark rum, optional

175 g/6 oz plain biscuits, such as Rich Tea

25 g/1 oz toasted rice cereal

50 g/1¾ oz chopped walnuts or pecan nuts

100 g/3½ oz glacé cherries, roughly chopped

25 g/1 oz white chocolate, to decorate

1 Place the dark chocolate in a large mixing bowl with the butter, syrup and rum, if using, and set over a saucepan of gently simmering water until melted, stirring until blended.

2 Break the biscuits into small pieces and stir into the chocolate mixture along with the rice cereal, nuts and cherries.

VARIATION
Brandy or an orange-flavoured liqueur can be used instead of the rum, if you prefer. Cherry brandy also works well.

3 Line an 18 cm/7 inch square cake tin with baking paper. Pour the mixture into the tin and level the top, pressing down well with the back of a spoon. Chill for 2 hours.

4 To decorate, melt the white chocolate and drizzle it over the top of the cake in a random pattern. Leave to set. To serve, carefully turn out of the tin and remove the baking paper. Cut into 16 squares.

Chocolate Butterfly Cakes

Filled with a tangy lemon cream, these appealing cakes will be a favourite with adults and children alike.

🍰 30 mins   🕐 15 mins

MAKES 12

INGREDIENTS

125 g/4½ oz soft margarine

125 g/4½ oz caster sugar

150 g/5½ oz self-raising flour

2 large eggs

2 tbsp cocoa powder

25 g/1 oz dark chocolate, melted

LEMON BUTTER CREAM

100 g/3½ oz unsalted butter, softened

225 g/8 oz icing sugar, sifted

grated rind of ½ lemon

1 tbsp lemon juice

icing sugar, to dust

1 Place 12 paper cases in a bun tray. Place all of the ingredients for the cakes, except for the melted chocolate, in a large mixing bowl and beat with an electric whisk until the mixture is just smooth. Beat in the chocolate.

2 Spoon equal amounts of the cake mixture into each paper case, filling them three-quarters full. Bake in a preheated oven, 180°C/350°F/Gas Mark 4, for 15 minutes or until springy to the touch. Transfer the cakes to a wire rack and leave to cool.

3 Meanwhile, make the lemon butter cream. Place the butter in a mixing bowl and beat until fluffy, then gradually beat in the icing sugar. Beat in the lemon rind and gradually add the lemon juice, beating well.

4 When cold, cut the top off each cake, using a serrated knife. Cut each cake top in half.

5 Spread or pipe the butter cream icing over the cut surface of each cake and push the 2 cut pieces of cake top into the icing to form wings. Sprinkle the cakes with icing sugar.

VARIATION
For a chocolate butter cream, beat the butter and icing sugar together, then beat in 25 g/1 oz melted dark chocolate.

Sticky Chocolate Brownies

Everyone loves chocolate brownies and these are so gooey and delicious they are impossible to resist!

1 hr 20 mins   25 mins

MAKES 9

INGREDIENTS

100 g/3½ oz unsalted butter

175 g/6 oz caster sugar

75 g/2¾ oz dark muscovado sugar

125 g/4½ oz dark chocolate

1 tbsp golden syrup

2 eggs

1 tsp chocolate or vanilla essence

100 g/3½ oz plain flour

2 tbsp cocoa powder

½ tsp baking powder

1 Lightly grease a 20 cm/8 inch shallow square cake tin and line the base.

2 Place the butter, sugars, dark chocolate and golden syrup in a heavy-based saucepan and heat gently, stirring until the mixture is well blended and smooth. Remove from the heat and leave to cool.

3 Beat together the eggs and chocolate or vanilla essence. Whisk in the cooled chocolate mixture.

4 Sieve together the flour, cocoa powder and baking powder and fold carefully into the egg and chocolate mixture, using a metal spoon or spatula.

5 Spoon the mixture into the prepared tin and bake in a preheated oven, 180°C/350°F/Gas Mark 4, for 25 minutes until the top is crisp and the edge of the cake is beginning to shrink away from the tin. The inside of the cake mixture will still be quite stodgy and soft to the touch.

6 Leave the cake to cool completely in the tin, then cut it into squares to serve.

COOK'S TIP

This cake can be well wrapped and frozen for up to 2 months. Defrost at room temperature for about 2 hours or overnight in the refrigerator.

Chocolate Fudge Brownies

Here, a traditional brownie mixture has a cream cheese ribbon through the centre and is topped with a delicious chocolate fudge icing.

1 hr 20 mins · 40–45 mins

MAKES 16

INGREDIENTS

200 g/7 oz low-fat soft cheese

½ tsp vanilla essence

2 eggs

250 g/9 oz caster sugar

100 g/3½ oz butter

3 tbsp cocoa powder

100 g/3½ oz self-raising flour, sifted

50 g/1¾ oz pecans, chopped

FUDGE ICING

4 tbsp butter

1 tbsp milk

100 g/3½ oz icing sugar

2 tbsp cocoa powder

pecans, to decorate, optional

1 Lightly grease a 20 cm/8 inch square shallow cake tin and line the base.

2 Beat together the cheese, vanilla essence and 25 g/1 oz of the caster sugar until smooth, then set aside.

VARIATION

Omit the cheese layer if preferred. Use walnuts in place of the pecans.

3 Beat the eggs and remaining caster sugar together until light and fluffy. Place the butter and cocoa powder in a small pan and heat gently, stirring until the butter melts and the mixture combines, then stir it into the egg mixture. Fold in the flour and nuts.

4 Pour half of the brownie mixture into the tin and level the top. Carefully spread the soft cheese over it, then cover it with the remaining brownie mixture. Bake in a preheated oven, 180°C/350°F/ Gas Mark 4, for 40–45 minutes. Cool in the tin.

5 To make the icing, melt the butter in the milk. Stir in the icing sugar and cocoa powder. Spread the icing over the brownies and decorate with pecan nuts, if using. Leave the icing to set, then cut into squares to serve.

Chocolate Chip Muffins

Muffins are always popular and are so simple to make. Mini muffins are fabulous bite-sized treats for young children – and perfect for parties.

45 mins   25 mins

MAKES 12

INGREDIENTS

100 g/3½ oz soft margarine

225 g/8 oz caster sugar

2 large eggs

150 ml/5 fl oz whole-milk natural yogurt

5 tbsp milk

275 g/9½ oz plain flour

1 tsp bicarbonate of soda

175 g/6 oz dark chocolate chips

1 Line 12 muffin tins with paper cases.

2 Place the margarine and sugar in a mixing bowl and beat with a wooden spoon until light and fluffy. Beat in the eggs, yogurt and milk until combined.

3 Sieve the flour and bicarbonate of soda together and add to the mixture. Stir until just blended.

4 Stir in the chocolate chips, then spoon the mixture into the paper cases

VARIATION
The mixture can also be used to make 6 large or 24 mini muffins. Bake mini muffins for 10 minutes or until springy to the touch.

and bake in a preheated oven, 190°C/375°F/Gas Mark 5, for 25 minutes or until a fine skewer inserted into the centre comes out clean. Leave to cool in the tin for 5 minutes, then turn out on to a wire rack to cool completely.

Chocolate Scones

A plain scone mixture is transformed into a chocoholics' treat by the simple addition of chocolate chips.

10 mins

10–12 mins

MAKES 4

INGREDIENTS

225 g/8 oz self-raising flour, sifted

5 tbsp butter

1 tbsp caster sugar

50 g/1¾ oz chocolate chips

about 150 ml/5 fl oz milk

1 Lightly grease a baking tray. Place the flour in a mixing bowl. Cut the butter into small pieces and rub it into the flour with your fingertips until the scone mixture resembles fine breadcrumbs.

2 Stir in the caster sugar and chocolate chips.

3 Mix in enough milk to form a soft dough.

4 On a lightly floured surface, roll out the dough to form a rectangle measuring 10 x 15 cm/4 x 6 inches, about 2.5 cm/1 inch thick. Cut into 9 squares.

5 Place the scones spaced well apart on the prepared baking tray.

6 Brush with a little milk and bake in a preheated oven, 220°C/425°F/Gas Mark 7, for 10–12 minutes until the scones are risen and golden.

COOK'S TIP

To be at their best, all scones should be freshly baked and served warm. Split the warm scones and spread them with a little chocolate and hazelnut spread or a good dollop of whipped cream.

Pain au Chocolat

These croissants can be a bit fiddly to make, but the layers of flaky pastry enclosing a fabulous rich chocolate filling are worth the effort.

 3¼ hrs   20–25 mins

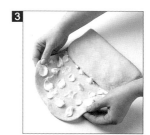

MAKES 12

INGREDIENTS

450 g/1 lb strong plain flour

½ tsp salt

6 g sachet of easy-blend dried yeast

25 g/1 oz white vegetable fat

1 egg, beaten lightly

225 ml/8 fl oz tepid water

175 g/6 oz butter, softened

100 g/3½ oz dark chocolate, broken into 12 squares

beaten egg, to glaze

icing sugar, to dust

1 Lightly grease a baking tray. Sieve the flour and salt into a mixing bowl and stir in the yeast. Rub in the fat with your fingertips. Add the egg and enough of the water to mix into a soft dough. Knead it for about 10 minutes to make a smooth, elastic dough.

2 Roll the dough out to form a rectangle measuring 37.5 x 20 cm/ 15 x 8 inches. Divide the butter into 3 portions and dot one portion over two-thirds of the rectangle, leaving a small border around the edge.

3 Fold the rectangle into 3 by first folding the plain part of the dough over and then the other side. Seal the edges of the dough by pressing with a rolling pin. Give the dough a quarter turn so the sealed edges are at the top and bottom. Re-roll and fold (without adding butter), then wrap the dough and chill for 30 minutes.

4 Repeat steps 2 and 3 until all of the butter has been used, chilling the dough each time. Re-roll and fold twice more without butter. Chill for a final 30 minutes.

5 Roll the dough to a rectangle measuring 45 x 30 cm/18 x 12 inches, trim, and halve lengthways. Cut each half into 6 rectangles and brush with beaten egg. Place a chocolate square at one end of each rectangle and roll up to form a sausage. Press the ends together and place, seamside down, on the baking tray. Cover and leave to rise for 40 minutes in a warm place. Brush with egg and bake in a preheated oven, 220°C/425°F/Gas Mark 7, for 20–25 minutes until golden. Cool on a wire rack. Serve warm or cold.

Chocolate Chip Tartlets

These tasty little tartlets will be a big hit with the kids. Serve as a dessert or as a special teatime treat.

🍐 1 hr   🕐 20 mins

SERVES 6

I N G R E D I E N T S

50 g/1¾ oz toasted hazelnuts

150 g/5½ oz plain flour

1 tbsp icing sugar

6 tbsp soft margarine

FILLING

2 tbsp cornflour

1 tbsp cocoa powder

1 tbsp caster sugar

300 ml/10 fl oz semi-skimmed milk

3 tbsp chocolate and hazelnut spread

2½ tbsp dark chocolate chips

2½ tbsp milk chocolate chips

2½ tbsp white chocolate chips

1 Finely chop the nuts in a food processor. Add the flour, the icing sugar and the margarine. Process for a few seconds until the mixture resembles breadcrumbs. Add 2–3 tablespoons of water and process to form a soft dough. Cover and chill in the freezer for 10 minutes.

2 Roll out the dough and use it to line 6 loose-bottomed 10 cm/4 inch tartlet tins. Prick the bases with a fork and line them with loosely crumpled foil. Bake in a preheated oven, 200°C/400°F/Gas Mark 6, for 15 minutes. Remove the foil and bake for a further 5 minutes until the pastry cases are crisp and golden. Remove from the oven and leave to cool.

3 Meanwhile, mix together the cornflour, cocoa powder and sugar with enough milk to make a smooth paste. Stir in the remaining milk. Pour into a pan and cook gently over a low heat, stirring until thickened. Stir in the hazelnut and chocolate spread.

4 Mix together the chocolate chips and reserve a quarter. Stir half of the remaining chips into the custard. Cover with damp greaseproof paper and leave until almost cold, then stir in the second half of the chocolate chips. Spoon the mixture into the pastry cases and leave to cool. Decorate with the reserved chips, scattering them over the top.

Chocolate Eclairs

Patisserie cream is the traditional filling for éclairs, but if time is short you can fill them with whipped cream.

1 hr   30–35 mins

MAKES 10

INGREDIENTS

CHOUX PASTRY

150 ml/5 fl oz water

5 tbsp butter, cut into small pieces

90 g/3 oz strong plain flour, sifted

2 eggs

PATISSERIE CREAM

2 eggs, lightly beaten

4 tbsp caster sugar

2 tbsp cornflour

300 ml/10 fl oz milk

¼ tsp vanilla essence

ICING

2 tbsp butter

1 tbsp milk

1 tbsp cocoa powder

100 g/3½ oz icing sugar

a little white chocolate, melted

1 Lightly grease a baking tray. Place the water in a saucepan, add the butter and heat gently until the butter melts. Bring to a rolling boil, then remove the pan from the heat and add the flour in one go, beating well until the mixture leaves the sides of the pan and forms a ball. Leave to cool slightly, then gradually beat in the eggs to form a smooth, glossy mixture. Spoon into a large piping bag fitted with a 1 cm/½ inch plain nozzle.

2 Sprinkle the baking tray with a little water. Pipe éclairs 7.5 cm/3 inches long, spaced well apart. Bake in a preheated oven, 200°C/400°F/Gas Mark 6, for 30–35 minutes or until crisp and golden. Make a small slit in each one to let the steam escape. Cool on a wire rack.

3 Meanwhile, make the patisserie cream. Whisk the eggs and sugar until thick and creamy, then fold in the cornflour. Heat the milk until almost boiling and pour on to the eggs, whisking. Transfer to the pan and cook over a low heat, stirring until thick. Remove the pan from the heat and stir in the vanilla essence. Cover with baking paper and cool.

4 To make the icing, melt the butter with the milk in a pan, remove from the heat and stir in the cocoa and sugar. Split the éclairs lengthways and pipe in the patisserie cream. Spread the icing over the top of the éclair. Spoon over the white chocolate, swirl in and leave to set.

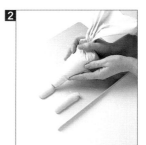

Chocolate Meringues

These melt-in-the-mouth meringues are ideal for a buffet dessert – pile them high in a pyramid for pure, bite-sized magic.

1 hr 25 mins   1 hr

MAKES 8

INGREDIENTS

4 egg whites

225 g/8 oz caster sugar

1 tsp cornflour

40 g/1½ oz dark chocolate, grated

TO COMPLETE

100 g/3½ oz dark chocolate

150 ml/5 fl oz double cream

1 tbsp icing sugar

1 tbsp brandy, optional

1 Line 2 baking trays with baking paper. Whisk the egg whites until standing in soft peaks, then gradually whisk in half of the sugar. Continue whisking until the mixture is very stiff and glossy.

2 Carefully fold in the remaining sugar, cornflour and grated chocolate with a metal spoon or spatula.

3 Spoon the mixture into a piping bag fitted with a large star or plain nozzle. Pipe 16 large rosettes or mounds on the lined baking trays.

4 Bake in a preheated oven, 140°C/275°F/Gas Mark 1, for about 1 hour, changing the position of the baking trays halfway through cooking. Without opening the oven door, turn off the oven and leave the meringues to cool in the oven. Once cold, carefully peel away the baking paper.

5 Melt the dark chocolate and spread it over the base of the meringues. Stand them upside down on a wire rack until the chocolate has set. Whip the cream, icing sugar and brandy (if using), until the cream holds its shape. Spoon into a piping bag and use to sandwich the meringues together in pairs. Serve.

VARIATION

To make mini meringues, use a star shaped nozzle and pipe about 24 small rosettes. Bake for about 40 minutes until crisp.

Mexican Chocolate Meringues

The Mexican name for these delicate meringues is *suspiros*, meaning 'sighs' – supposedly the contented sighs of the nuns who created them.

 1¼ hrs 2 hrs

MAKES 25

I N G R E D I E N T S

4–5 egg whites, at room temperature

a pinch of salt

¼ tsp cream of tartar

¼–½ tsp vanilla essence

175–200 g/6–7 oz caster sugar

⅛–¼ tsp ground cinnamon

115 g/4 oz bitter or dark chocolate, grated

T O   S E R V E

ground cinnamon

115 g/4 oz strawberries

chocolate-flavoured cream (see Cook's Tip)

1 Whisk the egg whites until they are foamy, then add the salt and cream of tartar and beat until very stiff. Whisk in the vanilla, then slowly whisk in the sugar, a small amount at a time, until the meringue is shiny and stiff. This should take about 3 minutes by hand, and less than a minute with an electric whisk.

COOK'S TIP
To make the flavoured cream, simply stir half-melted chocolate pieces into stiffly whipped cream, then chill until solid.

2 Whisk in the cinnamon and grated chocolate. Spoon mounds of about 2 tablespoons on to an ungreased, non-stick baking sheet. Space the mounds well.

3 Place in a preheated oven at 150°C/300°F/Gas Mark 2 and cook for 2 hours until set.

4 Carefully remove from the baking sheet. If the meringues are too moist and soft, return them to the oven to firm up and dry out more. Allow to cool completely.

5 Serve the meringues dusted with cinnamon and accompanied by strawberries and chocolate-flavoured cream.

Rice Pudding Tartlets

These delicious little tartlets have a soft dark chocolate layer covered with creamy rice pudding for a scrumptious special occasion dessert.

30 mins, plus 8 hrs defrosting

50 mins

SERVES 6

INGREDIENTS

1 packet frozen shortcrust pastry

1 litre/1¾ pints milk

pinch of salt

1 vanilla pod, split, seeds removed
   and reserved

100 g/3½ oz arborio or long-grain white rice

1 tbsp cornflour

2 tbsp sugar

cocoa powder, to dust

melted chocolate, to decorate

CHOCOLATE GANACHE

200 ml/7 fl oz double cream

1 tbsp golden syrup

175 g/6 oz bitter or dark chocolate,
   chopped

1 tbsp unsalted butter

1 Defrost the pastry, and then use it to line six 10 cm/4 in tart tins. Fill them with baking beans and bake blind in an oven preheated to 200°C/400°F/Gas Mark 6 for about 20 minutes until the pastry is set and golden at the edges. Transfer to a wire rack to cool.

2 To make the chocolate ganache, bring the double cream and golden syrup to the boil. Remove from the heat and immediately stir in the chopped chocolate; stir until melted and smooth. Beat in the butter. Spoon a 2.5 cm/1 inch thick layer into each tartlet. Set aside.

3 Bring the milk and salt to the boil in a saucepan. Sprinkle in the rice and return to the boil. Add the vanilla seeds and pod. Reduce the heat and simmer until the rice is tender and the milk creamy.

4 Blend the cornflour and sugar in a small bowl and add about 2 tablespoons of water to make a paste. Stir in a few spoonfuls of the rice mixture, then stir the cornflour mixture into the rice. Bring to the boil and cook for about 1 minute until thickened. Cool the pan in iced water, stirring until thick.

5 Spoon into the tartlets, filling each to the brim. Leave to set at room temperature. To serve, dust with cocoa powder and pipe or drizzle with melted chocolate.

Chocolate Hazelnut Palmiers

These delicious chocolate and hazelnut biscuits are very simple to make, yet so effective. For very young children, leave out the chopped nuts.

5 mins   10–15 mins

MAKES 26

INGREDIENTS

TOPPING

375 g/13 oz ready-made puff pastry

8 tbsp chocolate hazelnut spread

50 g/1¾ oz chopped toasted hazelnuts

2 tbsp caster sugar

1 Lightly grease a baking tray. On a lightly floured surface, roll out the puff pastry to a rectangle measuring about 37.5 x 23 cm/15 x 9 inches.

2 Spread the chocolate hazelnut spread over the pastry using a palette knife, then scatter the chopped hazelnuts over the top.

3 Roll up one long side of the pastry to the centre, then roll up the other side so that they meet in the centre. Where the pieces meet, dampen the edges with a little water to join them. Using a sharp

VARIATION

For an extra chocolate flavour, dip the palmiers in melted dark chocolate to half-cover each biscuit.

knife, cut into thin slices. Place each slice on to the prepared baking tray and flatten slightly with a palette knife. Sprinkle the slices with the caster sugar.

4 Bake in a preheated oven, 220°C/425°F/Gas Mark 7, for about 10–15 minutes, until golden. Transfer to a wire rack to cool.

Chocolate Coconut Squares

These biscuits consist of a chewy coconut layer resting on a crisp chocolate biscuit base, cut into squares to serve.

1¼ hrs   30 mins

MAKES 9

INGREDIENTS

225 g/8 oz dark chocolate digestive biscuits

6 tbsp butter or margarine

170 g/6 oz canned evaporated milk

1 egg, beaten

1 tsp vanilla essence

2 tbsp caster sugar

6 tbsp self-raising flour, sifted

125 g/4½ oz desiccated coconut

50 g/1¾ oz dark chocolate, optional

1 Grease a shallow 20 cm/8 inch square cake tin and line the base.

2 Crush the biscuits in a polythene bag with a rolling pin or process them in a food processor.

3 Melt the butter or margarine in a saucepan and stir in the crushed biscuits until well combined.

4 Press the mixture into the base of the cake tin.

5 Beat together the evaporated milk, egg, vanilla and sugar until smooth. Stir in the flour and desiccated coconut. Pour the mixture over the biscuit base and level the top.

6 Bake in a preheated oven, 190°C/375°F/Gas Mark 5, for 30 minutes or until the coconut topping is firm and just golden.

7 Leave to cool in the cake tin for about 5 minutes, then cut into squares. Leave to cool completely in the tin.

8 Carefully remove the squares from the tin and place them on a board. Melt the dark chocolate (if using) and drizzle it over the squares to decorate them. Leave the chocolate to set before serving.

VARIATION

Store the squares in an airtight tin for up to 4 days. They can be frozen, undecorated, for up to 2 months. Defrost at room temperature.

Chocolate & Coconut Cookies

These delicious, melt-in-the-mouth biscuits are finished off with a simple gooey icing and a generous sprinkling of coconut.

 40 mins   12–15 mins

MAKES 24

INGREDIENTS

125 g/4½ oz soft margarine

1 tsp vanilla essence

90 g/3 oz icing sugar, sifted

125 g/4½ oz plain flour

2 tbsp cocoa powder

50 g/1¾ oz desiccated coconut

2 tbsp butter

100 g/3½ oz white marshmallows

25 g/1 oz desiccated coconut

a little white chocolate, grated

1 Lightly grease a baking tray. Beat together the margarine, vanilla and icing sugar in a mixing bowl until fluffy. Sift together the flour and cocoa powder and beat it into the mixture with the coconut.

2 Roll teaspoons of the mixture into balls and place on the baking tray. Allow room for them to spread during cooking.

3 Flatten the rounds slightly and bake in a preheated oven, 180°C/350°F/Gas Mark 4, for 12–15 minutes until just firm.

4 Leave to cool on the baking tray for a few minutes before transferring to a wire rack to cool completely.

5 Place the butter and marshmallows in a small saucepan and heat gently, stirring until melted. Spread a little of the icing mixture over each biscuit and dip in the dessicated coconut. Leave to set. Decorate the biscuits with a little grated white chocolate before serving.

Chocolate Crispy Bites

A favourite with children, this version of crispy bites has been given a new twist which is sure to be popular.

45 mins

5–10 mins

MAKES 16

I N G R E D I E N T S

WHITE LAYER

4 tbsp butter

1 tbsp golden syrup

150 g/5½ oz white chocolate

50 g/1¾ oz toasted rice cereal

DARK LAYER

4 tbsp butter

2 tbsp golden syrup

125 g/dark chocolate, broken into small pieces

75 g/2¾ oz toasted rice cereal

1 Grease a 20 cm/8 inch square cake tin and line with baking paper.

2 To make the white chocolate layer, melt the butter, golden syrup and chocolate in a bowl set over a saucepan of gently simmering water.

3 Remove from the heat and stir in the rice cereal until it is well combined.

COOK'S TIP

These bites can be made up to 4 days ahead. Keep them covered in the refrigerator until ready to use.

4 Press into the prepared tin and level the surface.

5 To make the dark chocolate layer, melt the butter, golden syrup and dark chocolate in a bowl set over a pan of gently simmering water.

6 Remove from the heat and stir in the rice cereal. Pour the dark chocolate layer over the hardened white chocolate layer, and chill until hardened.

7 Turn out of the cake tin and cut into small squares, using a sharp knife.

Dutch Macaroons

These unusual biscuit treats are delicious served with coffee. They also make an ideal dessert biscuit to serve with ice cream.

40 mins   15–20 mins

MAKES 20

INGREDIENTS

rice paper
2 egg whites
225 g/8 oz caster sugar
175 g/6 oz ground almonds
225 g/8 oz dark chocolate

1 Cover 2 baking trays with rice paper. Whisk the egg whites in a large mixing bowl until stiff, then fold in the sugar and ground almonds.

2 Place the mixture in a large piping bag fitted with a 1 cm/½ inch plain nozzle and pipe fingers, about 7.5 cm/ 3 inches long, allowing space for the mixture to spread during cooking.

3 Bake in a preheated oven, 180°C/ 350°F/Gas Mark 4, for 15–20 minutes, until golden. Transfer to a wire rack and leave to cool. Remove the excess rice paper from around the edges.

COOK'S TIP

Rice paper is edible so you can just break off the excess from around the edge of the biscuits. Remove it completely before dipping in the chocolate, if you prefer.

4 Melt the chocolate and dip the base of each biscuit into the chocolate. Place the macaroons on a sheet of baking paper and leave to set.

5 Drizzle any remaining chocolate over the top of the biscuits (you may have to reheat the chocolate in order to do this). Leave to set before serving.

Chocolate Orange Biscuits

These delicious chocolate biscuits have a tangy orange icing. Children love them, especially if different shaped cutters are used.

55 mins   10–12 mins

MAKES 30

INGREDIENTS

6 tbsp butter, softened

6 tbsp caster sugar

1 egg

1 tbsp milk

225 g/8 oz plain flour

2 tbsp cocoa powder

ICING

175 g/6 oz icing sugar, sifted

3 tbsp orange juice

a little dark chocolate, melted

1 Line 2 baking trays with sheets of baking paper.

2 Beat together the butter and sugar until light and fluffy. Beat in the egg and milk until well combined. Sift together the flour and cocoa powder and gradually mix together to form a soft dough. Use your fingers to incorporate the last of the flour and bring the dough together.

3 Roll out the dough on to a lightly floured surface until 6 mm/¼ inch thick. Using a 5 cm/2 inch fluted round cutter, cut out as many cookies as you can. Re-roll the dough trimmings and cut out more cookies.

4 Place the cookies on the prepared baking tray and bake in a preheated oven, 180°C/350°F/Gas Mark 4, for 10–12 minutes or until golden.

5 Leave the cookies to cool on the baking tray for a few minutes, then transfer to a wire rack to cool completely.

6 To make the icing, place the icing sugar in a bowl and stir in enough orange juice to form a thin icing that will coat the back of a spoon. Spread the icing over the cookies and leave to set. Drizzle with melted chocolate. Leave the chocolate to set before serving.

Chocolate Caramel Squares

Wonderfully rich, it is difficult to say "No" to these biscuits, which consist of a crunchy base, a creamy caramel filling and a chocolate top.

40 mins  25 mins

MAKES 16

INGREDIENTS

100 g/3½ oz soft margarine

4 tbsp light muscovado sugar

125 g/4½ oz plain flour

40 g/1½ oz rolled oats

CARAMEL FILLING

2 tbsp butter

2 tbsp light muscovado sugar

200 g/7 oz canned condensed milk

TOPPING

100 g/3½ oz dark chocolate

25 g/1 oz white chocolate, optional

1 Beat together the margarine and muscovado sugar in a bowl until light and fluffy. Beat in the flour and the rolled oats. Use your fingertips to bring the mixture together, if necessary.

2 Press the mixture into the base of a shallow 20 cm/8 inch square cake tin.

3 Bake in a preheated oven, 180°C/350°F/Gas Mark 4, for 25 minutes or until just golden and firm. Cool in the tin.

COOK'S TIP

If liked, you can line the tin with baking paper so that the biscuit can be lifted out before cutting into pieces.

4 Place the ingredients for the caramel filling in a pan and heat gently, stirring until the sugar has dissolved and the ingredients combine. Bring slowly to the boil over a very low heat, then boil very gently for 3–4 minutes, stirring constantly until thickened.

5 Pour the caramel filling over the biscuit base in the tin and leave to set.

6 Melt the dark chocolate and spread it over the caramel. If using the white chocolate, melt it and pipe lines of white chocolate over the dark chocolate. Using a cocktail stick or a skewer, feather the white chocolate into the dark chocolate. Leave to set. Cut into squares to serve.

Chocolate Chip Flapjacks

Turn ordinary flapjacks into something special with the addition of chocolate chips. Use white rather than dark chocolate chips, if preferred.

40 mins   30 mins

MAKES 12

I N G R E D I E N T S

125 g/4½ oz butter

75 g/2¾ oz caster sugar

1 tbsp golden syrup

350 g/12 oz rolled oats

75 g/2¾ oz dark chocolate chips

50 g/1¾ oz sultanas

1 Lightly grease a shallow 20 cm/8 inch square cake tin.

2 Place the butter, caster sugar and golden syrup in a saucepan and cook over a low heat, stirring until the butter and sugar melt and the mixture is thoroughly combined.

3 Remove the pan from the heat and stir in the rolled oats until they are well coated. Add the chocolate chips and the sultanas and mix well to combine everything.

COOK'S TIP
The flapjacks will keep in an airtight container for up to 1 week, but they are so delicious they are unlikely to last that long!

4 Turn into the prepared tin and press down well.

5 Bake in a preheated oven, 180°C/ 350°F/Gas Mark 4, for 30 minutes.

Cool slightly, then mark into fingers. When almost cold, cut into bars or squares and transfer to a wire rack until cold.

Chocolate Chip Cookies

No chocolate cook's repertoire would be complete without a chocolate chip cookie recipe. This recipe can be used to make several variations.

35 mins

10–12 mins

MAKES 18

INGREDIENTS

175 g/6 oz plain flour

1 tsp baking powder

125 g/4½ oz soft margarine

90 g/3 oz light muscovado sugar

5 tbsp caster sugar

½ tsp vanilla essence

1 egg

125 g/4½ oz dark chocolate chips

1 Place all of the ingredients in a large mixing bowl and beat until well combined.

2 Lightly grease 2 baking trays. Place tablespoonfuls of the mixture on to the baking trays, spacing them well apart to allow for spreading during cooking.

3 Bake in a preheated oven, 190°C/375°F/Gas Mark 5, for 10–12 minutes or until the cookies are golden brown.

4 Using a palette knife, transfer the cookies to a wire rack and let them cool completely.

VARIATION

For Choc & Nut Cookies, add 40 g/1½ oz chopped hazelnuts to the basic mixture.

For Double Choc Cookies, beat in 40 g/1½ oz melted dark chocolate.

For White Chocolate Chip Cookies, use white chocolate chips instead of the dark chocolate chips.

Chocolate Shortbread

This buttery chocolate shortbread is the perfect addition to the biscuit tin of any chocoholic.

40 mins   40 mins

MAKES 12

INGREDIENTS

175 g/6 oz plain flour

1 tbsp cocoa powder

4 tbsp caster sugar

150 g/5½oz butter, softened

50 g/1¾ oz dark chocolate, finely chopped

1 Place all of the ingredients in a large mixing bowl and beat together until they form a dough. Knead the dough lightly.

2 Lightly grease a baking tray. Place the dough on the baking tray and roll or press out to form a 20 cm/8 inch circle.

3 Pinch the edges of the dough with your fingertips to form a decorative edge. Prick the dough all over with a fork and then mark it into 12 wedges, using a sharp knife.

4 Bake in a preheated oven, 160°C/ 325°F/Gas Mark 3, for 40 minutes, until firm and golden. Leave to cool slightly before cutting into wedges. Transfer to a wire rack to cool completely.

VARIATION

For round shortbread cookies, roll out the dough on a lightly floured surface to 8 mm/⅜ inch thick. Cut out 7.5 cm/3 inch rounds with a biscuit cutter. Transfer to a greased baking tray and bake as above. If liked, coat half the biscuit in melted chocolate.

Malted Chocolate Wedges

These are perfect with a bedtime drink, although you can enjoy these tasty biscuit wedges at any time of the day.

 45 mins 5 mins

MAKES 16

INGREDIENTS

100 g/3½ oz butter

2 tbsp golden syrup

2 tbsp malted chocolate drink

225 g/8 oz malted milk biscuits

75 g/2¾ oz milk or dark chocolate, broken into pieces

2 tbsp icing sugar

2 tbsp milk

1 Grease a shallow 18 cm/7 inch round cake tin or flan tin and line the base.

2 Place the butter, golden syrup and malted chocolate drink in a small pan and heat gently, stirring all the time until the butter has melted and the mixture is well combined.

3 Crush the biscuits in a plastic bag with a rolling pin, or process them in a food processor until they form crumbs. Stir the crumbs into the chocolate mixture and mix well.

VARIATION

Add chopped pecan nuts to the biscuit crumb mixture in Step 3, if liked.

4 Press the mixture into the prepared tin and then chill in the refrigerator until firm.

5 Place the chocolate pieces in a small heatproof bowl with the icing sugar and the milk. Place the bowl over a pan of gently simmering water and stir until the chocolate melts and the mixture is thoroughly combined.

6 Spread the chocolate icing over the biscuit base and leave to set in the tin. Using a sharp knife, cut into wedges to serve.

Chequerboard Cookies

Children will love these two-tone chocolate biscuits. If you do not mind a little mess, let them help to form the biscuits.

🕐 1 hr 20 mins ⏱ 10 mins

MAKES 18

INGREDIENTS

175 g/6 oz butter, softened

6 tbsp icing sugar

1 teaspoon vanilla essence or
   grated rind of ½ orange

250 g/9 oz plain flour

25 g/1 oz dark chocolate, melted

a little beaten egg white

1 Lightly grease a baking tray. Beat the butter and icing sugar in a mixing bowl until light and fluffy. Beat in the vanilla essence or the grated orange rind.

2 Gradually beat in the flour to form a soft dough. Use your fingers to incorporate the last of the flour and bring the dough together.

3 Divide the dough in half and beat the melted chocolate into one half. Keep each half of the dough separate, cover and leave to chill for about 30 minutes.

4 Roll out each piece of dough to a rectangle 7.5 x 20 cm/3 x 8 inches long and 3 cm/1½ inches thick. Brush one piece of dough with a little egg white and place the other on top.

5 Cut the block of dough in half lengthways and turn over one half. Brush the side of one strip with egg white and butt the other up to it, so that it resembles a chequer-board.

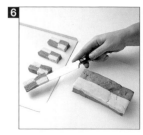

6 Cut the block into thin slices and place each slice flat on the baking tray, allowing enough room for them to spread a little during cooking.

7 Bake in a preheated oven, 180°C/ 350°F/Gas Mark 4, for about 10 minutes, until just firm. Leave to cool on the baking trays for a few minutes, before carefully transferring to a wire rack with a spatula. Leave to cool completely.

Viennese Chocolate Fingers

These biscuits have a fabulously light, melting texture. You can leave them plain, but for real indulgence, dip them in chocolate to decorate.

 1 hr

 12–15 mins

MAKES 18

INGREDIENTS

125 g/4½ oz unsalted butter

6 tbsp icing sugar

175 g/6 oz self-raising flour, sifted

3 tbsp cornflour

200 g/7 oz dark chocolate

1 Lightly grease 2 baking trays. Beat the butter and sugar in a mixing bowl until light and fluffy. Gradually beat in the flour and cornflour.

2 Melt 75 g/2¾ oz of the dark chocolate and beat into the biscuit dough.

3 Place the mixture in a piping bag fitted with a large star nozzle and pipe fingers about 5 cm/2 inches long on the baking trays, slightly spaced apart to allow for spreading.

4 Bake in a preheated oven, 190°C/ 375°F/Gas Mark 5, for 12–15 minutes.

COOK'S TIP

If the biscuit dough is too thick to pipe, beat in a little milk to thin it out a little.

5 Leave to cool slightly on the baking trays, then transfer with a spatula to a wire rack and leave to cool completely.

6 Melt the remaining chocolate and dip one end of each biscuit in the chocolate, allowing the excess to drip back into the bowl.

7 Place the biscuits on a sheet of baking paper and leave to set before serving.

Chocolate Pretzels

If you thought of pretzels as savouries, then think again. These are fun to make and prove that pretzels come in a sweet variety, too.

🍰 1½ hrs   🕐 8–12 hrs

MAKES 30

INGREDIENTS

100 g/3½ oz unsalted butter

100 g/3½ oz caster sugar

1 egg

225 g/8 oz plain flour

2 tbsp cocoa powder

TO FINISH

1 tbsp butter

100 g/3½ oz dark chocolate

icing sugar, to dust

1 Lightly grease a baking tray. Beat together the butter and sugar in a mixing bowl until light and fluffy. Beat in the egg.

2 Sift together the flour and cocoa powder and gradually beat in to form a soft dough. Use your fingers to incorporate the last of the flour and bring the dough together. Chill for 15 minutes.

3 Break pieces from the dough and roll into thin sausage shapes about 10 cm/4 inches long and 6 mm/¼ inch thick. Twist into pretzel shapes by making a circle, then twist the ends through each other to form a letter "B".

4 Place on the prepared baking tray, slightly spaced apart to allow for spreading during cooking.

5 Bake in a preheated oven, 190°C/ 375°F/Gas Mark 5, for 8–12 minutes. Leave the pretzels to cool slightly on the baking tray, then transfer to a wire rack to cool completely.

6 Melt the butter and chocolate in a bowl set over a pan of gently simmering water, stirring to combine.

7 Dip half of each pretzel into the chocolate and allow the excess chocolate to drip back into the bowl. Place the pretzels on a sheet of baking paper and leave to set.

8 When set, dust the non-chocolate coated side of each pretzel with icing sugar before serving.

Chocolate Wheatmeals

A good everyday biscuit, these wheatmeals will keep well in an airtight container for at least 1 week. Dip in white, milk or dark chocolate.

 1 hr 15–20 mins

MAKES 20

INGREDIENTS

6 tbsp butter

100 g/3½ oz demerara sugar

1 egg

25 g/1 oz wheatgerm

125 g/4½ oz wholemeal self-raising flour

6 tbsp self raising flour, sifted

125 g/4½ oz chocolate

1 Lightly grease a baking tray. Beat the butter and sugar until fluffy. Add the egg and beat well. Stir in the wheatgerm and flours. Bring the mixture together with your hands.

2 Roll rounded teaspoons of the mixture into balls and place on the prepared baking tray, allowing room for the biscuits to spread during cooking.

3 Flatten the biscuits slightly with the prongs of a fork. Bake in a preheated oven, 180°C/350°F/Gas Mark 4, for 15–20

COOK'S TIP

These biscuits can be frozen very successfully. Freeze them at the end of Step 3 for up to 3 months. Defrost and then dip them in melted chocolate.

minutes until golden. Leave to cool on the baking tray for a few minutes before transferring to a wire rack to cool completely.

4 Melt the chocolate, then dip each biscuit in the chocolate to cover the bases and come a little way up the sides. Leave the excess chocolate to drip back into the bowl.

5 Place the biscuits on a sheet of baking paper and leave to set in a cool place before serving.

Chocolate Brownies

You really can have a low-fat chocolate treat. These moist bars contain a dried fruit purée, which enables you to bake without adding any fat.

1¼ hrs   35–40 mins

MAKES 12

I N G R E D I E N T S

60 g/2 oz unsweetened pitted dates, chopped

60 g/2 oz no-soak dried prunes, chopped

6 tbsp unsweetened apple juice

4 medium eggs, beaten

300 g/10½ oz dark muscovado sugar

1 tsp vanilla essence

4 tbsp low-fat drinking chocolate powder, plus extra for dusting

2 tbsp cocoa powder

175 g/6 oz plain flour

60 g/2 oz dark chocolate chips

I C I N G

125 g/4½ oz icing sugar

1–2 tsp water

1 tsp vanilla essence

1 Preheat the oven to 180°C/350°F/Gas Mark 4. Grease and line a 18 x 28 cm/7 x 11 inch cake tin with baking paper. Place the dates and prunes in a small saucepan and add the apple juice. Bring to the boil, cover and simmer for 10 minutes until soft. Beat to form a smooth paste, then set aside to cool.

2 Place the cooled fruit in a mixing bowl and stir in the eggs, sugar and vanilla essence. Sift in 4 tablespoons of drinking chocolate, the cocoa and the flour, and fold in along with the chocolate chips until well incorporated.

3 Spoon the mixture into the prepared tin and smooth over the top. Bake for 25–30 minutes until firm to the touch or until a skewer inserted into the centre comes out clean. Cut into 12 bars and leave to cool in the tin for 10 minutes. Transfer to a wire rack to cool completely.

4 To make the icing, sift the sugar into a bowl and mix with sufficient water and the vanilla essence to form a soft, but not too runny, icing.

5 Drizzle the icing over the chocolate brownies and allow to set. Dust with the extra chocolate powder before serving.

COOK'S TIP

Make double the amount, cut one of the cakes into bars and open freeze, then store in plastic bags. Take out pieces of cake as and when you need them – they'll take no time at all to defrost.

Cannoli

No Sicilian celebration is complete without cannoli. If you can't find the moulds, use large dried pasta tubes, covered with foil, shiny side out.

1¾ hrs   15–20 mins

MAKES 20

I N G R E D I E N T S

3 tbsp lemon juice

3 tbsp water

1 large egg

250 g/9 oz plain flour

1 tbsp caster sugar

1 tsp ground mixed spice

pinch of salt

2 tbsp butter, softened

sunflower oil, for deep-frying

1 small egg white, lightly beaten

icing sugar

FILLING

750 g/1 lb 10 oz ricotta cheese, drained

4 tbsp icing sugar

1 tsp vanilla essence

finely grated rind of 1 large orange

4 tbsp very finely chopped glacé fruit

50 g/1¾ oz dark chocolate, grated

pinch of ground cinnamon

2 tbsp marsala or orange juice

1 Combine the lemon juice, water and egg. Put the flour, sugar, spice and salt in a food processor and quickly process. Add the butter, then, with the motor running, pour the egg mixture through the feed tube. Process until the mixture just forms a dough.

2 Turn the dough out on to a lightly floured surface and knead lightly. Wrap and chill for at least 1 hour.

3 Meanwhile, make the filling. Beat the ricotta cheese until smooth. Sift in the icing sugar, then beat in the remaining ingredients. Cover and chill until required.

4 Roll out the dough on a floured surface until 1.5 mm/¹⁄₁₆ inch thick. Using a ruler, cut out 8.5 x 7.5 cm/3 ½ x 3 inch pieces, re-rolling and cutting the trimmings, making about 20 pieces in all.

5 Heat 5 cm/2 inches of oil in a pan to 190°C/375°F. Roll a piece of pastry around a greased cannoli mould, to just overlap the edge. Seal with egg white,

pressing firmly. Repeat with all the moulds you have. Fry 2 or 3 moulds until the cannoli are golden, crisp and bubbly.

6 Remove with a slotted spoon and drain on paper towels. Leave until cool, then carefully slide off the moulds. Repeat with the remaining cannoli.

7 Store unfilled in an airtight container for up to 2 days. Pipe in the filling no more than 30 minutes before serving to prevent the pastry becoming soggy. Sift icing sugar over and serve.

Chocolate Peanut Cookies

These delicious cookies contain two popular ingredients, peanuts and chocolate; the rice flour gives them an original twist.

🍰 1 hr 5 mins   🕐 20 mins

MAKES 50

INGREDIENTS

175 g/6 oz plain flour

250 g/9 oz rice flour

2 tbsp cocoa powder

1 tsp baking powder

pinch of salt

130 g/4¾ oz white vegetable fat

200 g/7 oz caster sugar

1 tsp vanilla essence

140 g/5 oz raisins, chopped

115 g/4 oz unsalted peanuts,
   finely chopped

175 g/6 oz bitter or dark chocolate, melted

1 Sift the flours, cocoa, baking powder and salt into a bowl, then stir well to combine.

2 Using an electric whisk, beat the fat and sugar in a large bowl for about 2 minutes until very light and creamy. Beat in the vanilla. Gradually blend in the flour mixture to form a soft dough. Stir in the raisins.

3 Put the chopped peanuts in a small bowl. Pinch off walnut-sized pieces of the dough and roll into balls. Drop into the peanuts and roll to coat, pressing them lightly to stick. Place the balls about 7.5 cm/3 inches apart on 2 large, greased, non-stick baking sheets.

4 Using the flat bottom of a drinking glass dipped in flour, gently flatten each ball to a round about 5 mm/ ¼ inch thick.

5 Bake in a preheated oven, 180°C/350°F/Gas Mark 4, for about 10 minutes, until golden and lightly set; do not over bake. Cool on the sheets for about 1 minute, then, using a palette knife, transfer to a wire rack to cool. Continue with the remaining dough and peanuts.

6 Arrange the cooled cookies close together on the wire rack and drizzle the tops with the melted chocolate. Allow to set before transferring to an airtight container with greaseproof paper between the layers.

Pine Kernel Tartlets

Pine kernels and orange rind are popular ingredients in Mediterranean dishes – here they add a twist of flavour to luscious chocolate tartlets.

1 hr 40 mins   45 mins

SERVES 8

I N G R E D I E N T S

60 g/2 oz dark chocolate with at least 70% cocoa solids

5 tbsp unsalted butter

175 g/6 oz plus 2 tbsp caster sugar

6 tbsp light brown sugar

6 tbsp milk

3½ tbsp golden syrup

finely grated rind of 2 large oranges and 2 tbsp freshly squeezed juice

1 tsp vanilla essence

3 large eggs, lightly beaten

100 g/3½ oz pine kernels

PASTRY

250 g/9 oz plain flour

pinch of salt

100 g/3½ oz butter

115 g/4 oz icing sugar

1 large egg and 2 large egg yolks

3 Roll the pastry into 8 circles, each 15 cm/6 inch across. Use to line 8 loose-bottomed 10 cm/4 inch tartlet tins. Line each with baking paper to fit and top with baking beans. Chill for 10 minutes.

4 Bake in a preheated oven, 200°C/400°F/Gas Mark 6 for 5 minutes. Remove the paper and beans and bake for a further 8 minutes. Leave to cool on a wire rack. Reduce the oven temperature to 180°C/350°F/Gas Mark 4.

5 Meanwhile, break the chocolate into a saucepan over medium heat. Add the butter and stir until blended.

6 Stir in the remaining ingredients. Spoon the filling into the tartlet cases on a baking tray. Bake for 25–30 minutes, or until the tops puff up and crack and feel set. Cover with baking paper for the final 5 minutes if the pastry is browning too much. Transfer to a wire rack and leave to cool for at least 15 minutes before unmoulding. Serve warm or at room temperature.

1 To make the pastry, sift the flour and a pinch of salt into a bowl. Make a well in the centre and add the butter, icing sugar, whole egg and egg yolks. Using your fingertips, mix the ingredients in the well into a paste.

2 Gradually incorporate the flour to make a soft dough. Quickly and lightly knead the dough. Shape into a ball, wrap in clingfilm and chill for at least 1 hour.

Lemon Chocolate Pinwheels

These stunning biscuits will have your guests guessing as to what the mystery ingredients are that give the pinwheels their exotic flavour!

1¼ hrs ● 10–12 mins

MAKES 40

INGREDIENTS

175 g/6 oz butter, softened

300 g/10½ oz caster sugar

1 egg, beaten

350 g/12 oz plain flour

25 g/1 oz dark chocolate, melted and cooled slightly

grated rind of 1 lemon

1 Grease and flour several baking trays, enough to accommodate 40 biscuits.

2 In a large mixing bowl, cream together the butter and sugar until light and fluffy.

3 Gradually add the beaten egg to the creamed mixture, beating well after each addition.

4 Sieve the flour into the creamed mixture and mix thoroughly until a soft dough forms.

5 Transfer half of the dough to another bowl and then beat in the cooled melted chocolate.

6 Stir the grated lemon rind into the other half of the plain dough.

7 On a lightly floured surface, roll out the 2 pieces of dough to form rectangles of the same size.

8 Lay the lemon dough on top of the chocolate dough. Roll up the dough tightly into a sausage shape, using a sheet of baking paper to guide you. Leave the dough to chill in the refrigerator.

9 Cut the roll into about 40 slices, place them on the baking trays and bake in a preheated oven, 190°C/375°F/Gas Mark 5, for 10–12 minutes or until lightly golden. Transfer the pinwheels to a wire rack and leave to cool completely before serving.

COOK'S TIP

To make rolling out easier, place each piece of dough between 2 sheets of baking paper.

White Chocolate Cookies

These chunky cookies melt in the mouth and the white chocolate gives them a deliciously rich flavour.

40 mins   10–12 mins

MAKES 24

INGREDIENTS

125 g/4½ oz butter, softened

125 g/4½ oz soft brown sugar

1 egg, beaten

200 g/7 oz self-raising flour

pinch of salt

125 g/4½ oz white chocolate, roughly chopped

50 g/1¾ oz brazil nuts, chopped

1 Lightly grease several baking trays, enough to accommodate 24 cookies.

2 In a large mixing bowl, cream together the butter and sugar until light and fluffy.

3 Gradually add the beaten egg to the creamed mixture, beating well after each addition.

4 Sieve the flour and salt into the creamed mixture and blend well.

5 Stir in the white chocolate chunks and the chopped brazil nuts.

6 Place heaped teaspoons of the white chocolate mixture on to the prepared baking trays. Do not put more than 6 teaspoons of the mixture on to each baking tray as the cookies will spread considerably during cooking.

7 Bake in a preheated oven, 190°C/375°F/Gas Mark 5, for 10–12 minutes or until just golden brown.

8 Transfer the cookies to wire racks and leave until completely cold before serving.

VARIATION

Use plain or milk chocolate instead of white chocolate, if you prefer.

Millionaire's Shortbread

These rich squares of shortbread are topped with caramel and finished with chocolate to make a very special treat!

55 mins   30 mins

SERVES 4

INGREDIENTS

175 g/6 oz plain flour

125 g/4½ oz butter, cut into small pieces

4 tbsp soft brown sugar, sifted

TOPPING

4 tbsp butter

4 tbsp soft brown sugar

400 g/14 oz canned condensed milk

150 g/5½ oz milk chocolate

1 Grease a 23 cm/9 inch square cake tin.

2 Sieve the flour into a mixing bowl and rub in the butter with your fingers until the mixture resembles fine breadcrumbs. Add the sugar and mix to form a firm dough.

3 Press the dough into the bottom of the prepared tin and prick with a fork.

4 Bake in a preheated oven, 190°C/375°F/Gas Mark 5, for 20 minutes, until lightly golden. Leave the shortbread to cool in the tin.

COOK'S TIP

Ensure the caramel layer is completely cool and set before coating it with the melted chocolate, otherwise they will mix together.

5 To make the topping, place the butter, sugar and condensed milk in a non-stick saucepan and cook over a gentle heat, stirring constantly, until the mixture comes to the boil.

6 Reduce the heat and cook for 4–5 minutes until the caramel is pale golden and thick and is coming away from the sides of the pan. Pour the topping over the shortbread base and leave to cool.

7 When the caramel topping is firm, melt the milk chocolate in a heatproof bowl set over a saucepan of simmering water. Spread the melted chocolate over the topping, leave to set in a cool place, then cut the shortbread into squares or fingers to serve.

Chocolate Chip Brownies

Choose a good quality chocolate for these chocolate chip brownies to give them a rich flavour that is not too sweet.

45 mins   30–35 mins

MAKES 12

INGREDIENTS

150 g/5½ oz dark chocolate, broken into pieces

225 g/8 oz butter, softened

225 g/8 oz self-raising flour

125 g/4½ oz caster sugar

4 eggs, beaten

75 g/2¾ oz pistachio nuts, chopped

100 g/3½ oz white chocolate, roughly chopped

icing sugar, for dusting

1 Lightly grease a 23 cm/9 inch baking tin and line with greaseproof paper.

2 Melt the dark chocolate and butter in a heatproof bowl set over a saucepan of simmering water. Leave to cool slightly.

3 Sieve the flour into a separate mixing bowl and stir in the caster sugar.

4 Stir the eggs into the melted chocolate mixture, then pour this mixture into the flour and sugar mixture, beating well. Stir in the pistachio nuts and

COOK'S TIP

The brownie won't be completely firm in the middle when it is removed from the oven, but it will set when it has cooled.

white chocolate, then pour the mixture into the tin, using a palette knife to spread it evenly into the corners.

5 Bake in a preheated oven, 180°C/350°/Gas Mark 4, for 30–35 minutes

until firm to the touch. Leave to cool in the tin for 20 minutes, then turn out on to a wire rack.

6 Dust the brownie with icing sugar and cut into 12 pieces when cold.

Chocolate Biscotti

These dry biscuits are delicious served with black coffee after your evening meal.

55 mins   30–40 mins

MAKES 16

INGREDIENTS

1 egg

100 g/3½ oz caster sugar

1 tsp vanilla essence

125 g/4½ oz plain flour

½ tsp baking powder

1 tsp ground cinnamon

50 g/1¾ oz dark chocolate, roughly chopped

50 g/1¾ oz flaked almonds, toasted

50 g/1¾ oz pine kernels

1 Lightly grease a large baking tray.

2 Whisk the egg, sugar and vanilla essence in a mixing bowl with an electric mixer until it is thick and pale – ribbons of mixture should trail from the whisk as you lift it.

3 Sieve the flour, baking powder and cinnamon into a separate bowl, then sieve into the egg mixture and fold in gently. Stir in the chocolate, almonds and pine kernels.

4 Turn on to a lightly floured surface and shape into a flat log, 23 cm/ 9 inches long and 1.5 cm/¾ inch wide. Transfer to the baking tray.

5 Bake in a preheated oven, 180°C/ 350°F/Gas Mark 4, for 20–25 minutes or until golden. Remove from the oven and leave to cool for 5 minutes or until firm.

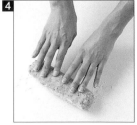

6 Transfer the log to a cutting board. Using a serrated bread knife, cut the log on the diagonal into slices about 1 cm/ ½ inch thick and arrange them on the baking tray. Cook for 10–15 minutes, turning halfway through the cooking time.

7 Leave to cool for about 5 minutes, then transfer to a wire rack to cool completely.

Chocolate Macaroons

Classic gooey macaroons are always a favourite for tea-time: they are made even better by the addition of rich dark chocolate.

🧊 1 hr   🕐 25 mins

MAKES 18

INGREDIENTS

75 g/2¾ oz dark chocolate, broken into pieces

2 egg whites

pinch of salt

200 g/7 oz caster sugar

125 g/4½ oz ground almonds

desiccated coconut, for sprinkling (optional)

1 Grease 2 baking trays and line with baking paper or rice paper.

2 Melt the dark chocolate in a small heatproof bowl set over a saucepan of simmering water. Leave to cool slightly.

3 In a mixing bowl, whisk the egg whites with the salt until they form soft peaks.

4 Gradually whisk the caster sugar into the egg whites, then fold in the almonds and cooled melted chocolate.

5 Place heaped teaspoonfuls of the mixture spaced well apart on the prepared baking trays and spread into circles about 6 cm/2½ inches across. Sprinkle with desiccated coconut, if using.

6 Bake in a preheated oven, 150°C/300°F/Gas Mark 2, for about 25 minutes or until firm.

7 Leave to cool before carefully lifting from the baking trays. Transfer to a wire rack and leave to cool completely before serving.

VARIATION
For a traditional finish, top each macaroon with half a glacé cherry before baking.

Florentines

These luxury biscuits will be popular at any time of the year, but make a particularly wonderful treat at Christmas.

50 mins

10 mins

MAKES 10

INGREDIENTS

4 tbsp butter

4 tbsp caster sugar

3 tbsp plain flour, sifted

50 g/1¾ oz almonds, chopped

50 g/1¾ oz chopped mixed peel

25 g/1 oz raisins, chopped

25 g/1 oz glacé cherries, chopped

finely grated rind of ½ lemon

125 g/4½ oz dark chocolate, melted

1 Line two large baking trays with baking paper.

2 Heat the butter and caster sugar in a small saucepan until the butter has just melted and the sugar dissolved. Remove the pan from the heat.

3 Stir in the flour and mix well. Stir in the chopped almonds, mixed peel, raisins, cherries and lemon rind. Place teaspoonfuls of the mixture well apart on the baking trays.

4 Bake in a preheated oven, 180°C/350°F/Gas Mark 4, for 10 minutes or until lightly golden.

5 As soon as the florentines are removed from the oven, press the edges into neat shapes while still on the baking trays, using a biscuit cutter. Leave to cool on the baking trays until firm, then transfer to a wire rack to cool completely.

6 Spread the melted chocolate over the smooth side of each florentine. As the

chocolate begins to set, mark wavy lines in it with a fork. Leave the florentines until set, chocolate side up.

VARIATION
Replace the dark chocolate with white chocolate or, for a dramatic effect, cover half of the florentines in dark chocolate and half in white.

Fried Chocolate Fingers

Tasty bread fingers flavoured with sherry and coated with chocolate and sugar are surprisingly tasty and very popular.

 15 mins 30 mins

MAKES 24

INGREDIENTS

4 eggs, lightly beaten

600 ml/1 pint milk

5 tbsp sherry

8 x 1 cm/½ inch thick slices of day-old white bread

4 tbsp sunflower oil

115 g/4 oz caster sugar

225 g/8 oz dark chocolate, grated

vanilla ice cream, to serve (optional)

1 Pour the beaten eggs, milk and sherry into a shallow dish and beat lightly to mix. Cut each slice of bread lengthways into three fingers. Soak the bread fingers in the egg mixture until soft, then drain on kitchen paper.

2 Heat the oil in a large, heavy-based frying pan. Carefully add the bread fingers to the pan, in batches, and cook over a medium heat for 12 minutes on each side, until golden. Using tongs, transfer the fingers to kitchen paper to drain.

3 When all the fingers are cooked and thoroughly drained, roll them first in the sugar and then in the grated chocolate. Pile them on a warmed serving plate and serve immediately, with ice cream if desired.

Meringue Fingers

These little tea-time treats can be stored in an airtight container for several days – if they haven't all been eaten!

🕐 15 mins, plus 1 hr setting/cooling

🕐 65–70 mins

MAKES 30

INGREDIENTS

1 egg white

4 tbsp caster sugar

1½ tsp cocoa powder

140 g/5 oz dark chocolate, broken into pieces

1 Line a baking tray with baking paper. Whisk the egg white until it forms soft peaks. Whisk in half the sugar and continue whisking until stiff and glossy. Fold in the remaining sugar and the cocoa.

2 Preheat the oven to 120°C/250°F/Gas Mark ½. Spoon the mixture into a piping bag fitted with a 1 cm/½ inch round nozzle. Pipe fingers about 7.5 cm/3 inches long on the prepared baking tray, spacing them at least 2.5 cm/1 inch apart. Bake in the preheated oven for 1 hour, until completely dry. Remove from the oven and transfer to a wire rack to cool.

3 Put the chocolate in the top of a double boiler or in a heatproof bowl set over a pan of barely simmering water. Heat, stirring constantly, until the chocolate has melted and the mixture is smooth. Remove from the heat. Cool slightly, then dip the meringue fingers into the mixture, one at a time, to half-coat them. You can either coat one end completely, leaving the other plain, or dip the fingers at an angle so half the length is coated. Place the fingers on baking paper to set.

Chestnut Cream Squares

These little cakes look wonderful, and are well worth the preparation time. The magical combination of flavours is out of this world.

45 mins, plus 11–11½ hrs freezing/standing

55–60 mins

MAKES 30

INGREDIENTS

BASE LAYER

85 g/3 oz dark chocolate, broken into pieces

6 tbsp unsalted butter

4 tbsp icing sugar

4 eggs, separated

100 g/3½ oz caster sugar

90 g/3¼ oz plain flour

5 tbsp Morello cherry jam

3 tbsp kirsch

DARK LAYER

100 g/3½ oz dark chocolate

100 ml/3½ fl oz milk

4 tsp caster sugar

¼ tsp vanilla essence

1 egg yolk

1 tbsp cornflour

generous 2 tbsp icing sugar

300 ml/10 fl oz double cream

WHITE LAYER

500 ml/17 fl oz double cream

1 tbsp icing sugar

CHESTNUT LAYER

435 g/15¼ oz chestnut purée

4 tsp dark rum

2 tsp caster sugar

30 cherries, to decorate

1 Line a 30 x 25 x 5 cm/12 x 10 x 2 inch rectangular cake tin with baking paper. To make the base layer, melt the chocolate in a heatproof bowl set over a pan of barely simmering water, then cool slightly. Mix the butter, icing sugar and chocolate together. Beat in the egg yolks, 1 at a time.

2 Preheat the oven to 180°C/350°F/Gas Mark 4. Whisk the egg whites in a separate bowl until soft peaks form, then whisk in the caster sugar until stiff and glossy. Fold into the chocolate mixture. Sieve the flour into a bowl, then fold it into the mixture. Spoon into the tin and smooth the surface. Bake for 30 minutes.

3 Remove the tin from the oven, cool, then cut around the edges with a knife. Invert onto a flat surface. Wash and dry the cake tin and line with baking paper. Return the base layer to the tin. Bring the jam to the boil in a small saucepan, strain and cool. Sprinkle the Kirsch over the base layer, then spread with the jam.

4 Melt the chocolate in a heatproof bowl set over a pan of barely simmering water. Remove from the heat. Put the milk, caster sugar and vanilla into a pan and bring to the boil. Remove from the heat. Mix the egg yolk, cornflour and 2 tablespoons of the hot milk in a bowl, add to the pan of milk and return to a medium heat. Cook, stirring, for 3–5 minutes, until thickened. Stir in the icing sugar and melted chocolate. Remove from the heat. Beat the cream until thick, then stir it into the chocolate mixture. Spread over the layer in the tin, cover and freeze for 1½–2 hours.

5 When the dark layer is half-frozen, make the white layer. Whisk the cream with the sugar until thick, then spread over the dark layer. Cover and freeze for 8 hours.

6 Remove the cake from the tin, with the white layer uppermost. Beat together the chestnut purée, rum and sugar. Press through a garlic press and spread over the white layer. Cut the cake into 30 squares and top each with a cherry. Refrigerate for 30 minutes before serving.

Mocha Rolls

Dark and white chocolate are combined with coffee and Kahlúa liqueur in these attractive sponge-cake rolls.

 35 mins, plus 1½–2¼ hrs chilling/setting

50–55 mins

MAKES 16

INGREDIENTS

150 ml/5 fl oz cold, strong, black coffee

1 tbsp gelatine

1 tsp Kahlúa or other coffee-flavoured liqueur

225 g/8 oz ricotta cheese

280 g/10 oz white chocolate, broken into pieces

25 g/1 oz dark chocolate

SPONGE CAKE

3 eggs, plus 1 egg white

85 g/3 oz caster sugar

115 g/4 oz plain flour

2 tbsp butter, melted

1 For the sponge cake, line the base of a 30 x 20 x 4 cm/12 x 8 x 1½ inch cake tin with baking paper. Put the eggs, egg white and sugar in a heatproof bowl over a pan of barely simmering water. Whisk until pale and thickened.

2 Preheat the oven to 180°C/350°F/Gas Mark 4. Remove the mixture from the heat, then whisk until cool. Sieve the flour over the mixture and fold in. Fold in the melted butter, a little at a time. Pour the mixture into the prepared tin and bake for 25–30 minutes, until the cake is firm to the touch and has shrunk slightly from the sides of the tin. Remove from the oven and transfer to a wire rack, still standing on the baking paper, to cool.

3 Meanwhile, put 2 tablespoons of the coffee into a small heatproof bowl and sprinkle the gelatine on the surface. Leave

to soften for 2 minutes, then set the bowl over a pan of barely simmering water, stir until the gelatine has dissolved, then remove from the heat. Put the remaining coffee, liqueur and ricotta in a food processor or blender and process until smooth. Add the gelatine mixture in a single stream and process briefly. Scrape the mixture into a bowl, cover with clingfilm and refrigerate for 1–1½ hours, until set.

4 Carefully peel the baking paper from the cooled cake. Using a sharp knife, cut horizontally through the cake. Trim off any dried edges. Cut each piece of cake in half lengthways. Place each piece between 2 sheets of baking paper and roll lightly with a rolling pin to make it more flexible.

5 Spread the cut side of each cake piece with an even 5 mm/¼ inch thick layer of the coffee filling, leaving a 5 mm/

¼ inch margin all round. Cut each strip crossways into four, giving a total of 16 pieces. Roll up each piece from the short end, Swiss roll fashion.

6 Put the white chocolate in a heatproof bowl over a pan of barely simmering water. Stir until melted. Remove from the heat. Place 1 roll, seam-side down, on a metal spatula and hold it over the bowl of melted chocolate. Spoon the chocolate over the roll to coat. Transfer the roll to a sheet of baking paper and repeat with the remaining rolls.

7 Put the dark chocolate in a heatproof bowl over a pan of barely simmering water. Stir until melted. Remove from the heat. Spoon it into a greaseproof paper piping bag fitted with a small, plain nozzle and pipe zig-zags along the rolls. Leave to set completely before serving.

Ladies' Kisses

These tiny biscuits sandwiched together with melted chocolate are lovely at tea-time or served as petits fours after dinner.

30 mins, plus 2–2½ hrs chilling/cooling

30–35 mins

MAKES 20

INGREDIENTS

140 g/5 oz unsalted butter

115 g/4 oz caster sugar

1 egg yolk

115 g/4 oz ground almonds

175 g/6 oz plain flour

55 g/2 oz dark chocolate, broken into pieces

2 tbsp icing sugar, to dust

2 tbsp cocoa powder, to dust

1 Line 3 baking trays with baking paper, or use 3 non-stick trays. Cream the butter and sugar together until pale and fluffy. Beat in the egg yolk, then beat in the almonds and flour. Continue beating until thoroughly mixed. Shape the dough into a ball, wrap in clingfilm and chill in the refrigerator for 1½–2 hours.

2 Preheat the oven to 160°C/325°F/Gas Mark 3. Unwrap the dough, break off walnut-sized pieces and roll them into balls between the palms of your hands. Place the dough balls on the prepared baking trays, allowing space for them to spread during cooking. You may need to cook the biscuits in batches. Bake in the preheated oven for 20–25 minutes, until golden. Carefully transfer the biscuits, still on the baking paper if using, to wire racks to cool.

3 Put the chocolate in the top of a double boiler or in a heatproof bowl set over a pan of barely simmering water.

Melt over a low heat, stirring constantly. Remove from the heat. Remove the biscuits from the baking paper, if using. Spread the melted chocolate over the bases, then sandwich them together in pairs. Return to the wire racks to cool. Dust with a mixture of icing sugar and cocoa powder.

Chocolate Pistachio Biscuits

These crisp Italian biscotti are made with polenta – fine cornmeal – as well as flour, to give them an interesting texture.

🍰 25 mins, plus 30 mins cooling   ⏱ 35 mins

MAKES 24

INGREDIENTS

2 tbsp unsalted butter, plus extra for greasing

175 g/6 oz dark chocolate, broken into pieces

300 g/10½ oz self-raising flour, plus extra for dusting

1½ tsp baking powder

85 g/3 oz caster sugar

55 g/2 oz polenta

finely grated rind of 1 lemon

2 tsp amaretto liqueur

1 egg, lightly beaten

85 g/3 oz shelled pistachio nuts, roughly chopped

2 tbsp icing sugar, to dust

1 Lightly grease a baking tray with butter. Put the chocolate and 2 tablespoons of butter in the top of a double boiler or in a heatproof bowl set over a pan of barely simmering water. Stir over a low heat until melted and smooth. Remove from the heat and cool slightly.

2 Sieve the flour and baking powder into a bowl and mix in the caster sugar, polenta, lemon rind, liqueur, egg and pistachios. Stir in the chocolate mixture and mix to a soft dough.

3 Preheat the oven to 160°C/325°F/Gas Mark 3. Lightly dust your hands with flour, divide the dough in half and shape each piece into a 28 cm/11 inch long cylinder. Transfer the dough cylinders to the prepared baking tray and flatten, with the palm of your hand, to about 2 cm/¾ inch thick. Bake in the preheated oven for about 20 minutes, until firm to the touch.

4 Remove the baking tray from the oven and allow the cooked pieces to cool.

When cool, put the cooked pieces onto a cutting board and slice them diagonally into thin biscuits. Return them to the baking tray and bake for a further 10 minutes, until crisp. Remove from the oven, and transfer to a wire rack to cool. Dust lightly with icing sugar.

Sweets & Drinks

There is nothing quite as nice as home-made chocolates and sweets – they leave the average box of chocolates in the shade! You'll find recipes in this chapter to suit everybody's taste. Wonderful, rich, melt-in-the-mouth Italian Chocolate Truffles, Chocolate Marzipans, Nutty

Chocolate Clusters and rich Chocolate Liqueurs – they're all here. There is even some Easy Chocolate Fudge, so there is no need to fiddle about with sugar thermometers.

Looking for something to wash it all down? We have included delightfully cool summer chocolate drinks and for warmth and comfort on winter nights hot drinks that will simply put instant hot chocolate to shame. Enjoy!

Rocky Road Bites

Young children will love these chewy bites. You can vary the ingredients and use different nuts and dried fruit according to taste.

40 mins   5 mins

MAKES 18

INGREDIENTS

FILLING

125 g/4½ oz milk chocolate

50 g/2½ oz mini multi-coloured
   marshmallows

25 g/1 oz chopped walnuts

25 g/1 oz no-soak apricots, chopped

1 Line a baking tray with baking paper and set aside.

2 Break the milk chocolate into small pieces and place in a large mixing bowl. Set the bowl over a pan of simmering water and stir until the chocolate has melted.

3 Stir in the marshmallows, walnuts and apricots and toss in the melted chocolate until well covered.

VARIATION

Light, fluffy marshmallows are available in white or pastel colours. If you cannot find mini marshmallows, use large ones and snip them into smaller pieces with kitchen scissors before mixing them into the melted chocolate in step 3.

4 Place heaped teaspoons of the mixture onto the prepared baking tray.

5 Leave the sweets to chill in the refrigerator until set.

6 Once set, carefully remove the sweets from the baking paper.

7 The chewy bites can be placed in paper sweet cases to serve, if desired.

Easy Chocolate Fudge

This is the easiest fudge to make – for a really rich flavour, use a good dark chocolate with a high cocoa content, ideally at least 70 per cent.

1 hr 10 mins   5 mins

MAKES 25 PIECES

INGREDIENTS

500 g/1 lb 2 oz dark chocolate

75 g/2¾ oz unsalted butter

400 g/14 oz canned condensed milk

½ tsp vanilla essence

1 Lightly grease a 20 cm/8 inch square cake tin.

2 Break the chocolate into pieces and place in a large saucepan with the butter and condensed milk.

3 Heat gently, stirring until the chocolate and butter melts and the mixture is smooth. Do not allow to boil.

4 Remove from the heat. Beat in the vanilla essence, then beat the mixture for a few minutes until thickened. Pour it into the prepared tin and level the top.

5 Chill the mixture in the refrigerator until firm.

6 Tip the fudge out on to a chopping board and cut into squares to serve.

COOK'S TIP
Store the fudge in an airtight container in a cool, dry place for up to 1 month. Do not freeze.

Fruit & Nut Fudge

Chocolate, nuts and dried fruit – the perfect combination – are all found in this simple-to-make fudge.

1 hr 10 mins   5 mins

MAKES 25 PIECES

INGREDIENTS

250 g/9 oz dark chocolate

2 tbsp butter

4 tbsp evaporated milk

450 g/1 lb icing sugar, sifted

50 g/1¾ oz roughly chopped hazelnuts

50 g/1¾ oz sultanas

1 Lightly grease a 20 cm/8 inch square cake tin.

2 Break the chocolate into pieces and place it in a bowl with the butter and evaporated milk. Set the bowl over a pan of gently simmering water and stir until the chocolate and butter have melted and the ingredients are well combined.

3 Remove the bowl from the heat and gradually beat in the icing sugar. Stir the hazelnuts and sultanas into the mixture. Press the fudge into the prepared tin and level the top. Chill until firm.

4 Tip the fudge out on to a chopping board and cut into squares. Place in paper sweet cases. Chill until required.

VARIATION

Vary the nuts used in this recipe; try making the fudge with almonds, brazil nuts, walnuts or pecans.

Nutty Chocolate Clusters

Nuts and crisp biscuits encased in chocolate make these sweets rich, chocolatey and quite irresistible!

1½ hrs   5 mins

MAKES 30

INGREDIENTS

175 g/6 oz white chocolate

100 g/3½ oz digestive biscuits

100 g/3½ oz macadamia nuts or brazil nuts, chopped

25 g/1 oz stem ginger, chopped (optional)

175 g/6 oz dark chocolate

1 Line a baking tray with a sheet of baking paper. Break the white chocolate into small pieces and place in a large mixing bowl set over a pan of gently simmering water; stir until melted.

2 Break the digestive biscuits into small pieces. Stir the biscuits into the melted chocolate with the chopped nuts and stem ginger, if using.

3 Place heaped teaspoons of the mixture on to the prepared baking tray.

4 Chill the mixture until set, then carefully remove from the baking paper.

COOK'S TIP

Macadamia and brazil nuts are both rich and high in fat, which makes them particularly popular for confectionery, but other nuts can be used, if preferred.

5 Melt the dark chocolate and leave it to cool slightly. Dip the clusters into the melted chocolate, allowing the excess to drip back into the bowl. Return the clusters to the baking tray and chill in the refrigerator until set.

Chocolate Cherries

These tasty cherry and marzipan sweets are easy to make. Serve as petits fours at the end of a meal or as an indulgent nibble at any time of day.

🕐 1½ hrs   🕐 5 mins

MAKES 24

INGREDIENTS

12 glacé cherries

2 tbsp rum or brandy

250 g/9 oz marzipan

125 g/5½ oz dark chocolate

extra milk, dark or white chocolate, to decorate (optional)

1 Line a baking tray with a sheet of baking paper.

2 Cut the cherries in half and place in a small bowl. Add the rum or brandy and stir to coat. Leave the cherries to soak for at least 1 hour, stirring occasionally.

3 Divide the marzipan into 24 pieces and roll each piece into a ball. Press half a cherry into the top of each marzipan ball.

4 Break the chocolate into pieces, place in a bowl and set over a pan of hot water. Stir until all the chocolate has melted.

5 Dip each sweet into the melted chocolate using a cocktail stick,

VARIATION

Flatten the marzipan and use it to mould around the cherries to cover them, then dip in the chocolate as above.

allowing the excess to drip back into the bowl. Place the coated cherries on the baking paper and chill until set.

6 If liked, melt a little extra chocolate and drizzle it over the top of the coated cherries. Leave to set.

Chocolate Marzipans

These delightful little morsels make the perfect gift, if you can resist eating them all yourself!

50 mins

5 mins

MAKES 30

INGREDIENTS

450 g/1 lb marzipan

25 g/1 oz glacé cherries, very finely chopped

25 g/1 oz stem ginger, very finely chopped

50 g/1¾ oz no-soak dried apricots, very finely chopped

350 g/12 oz dark chocolate

25 g/1 oz white chocolate

icing sugar, to dust

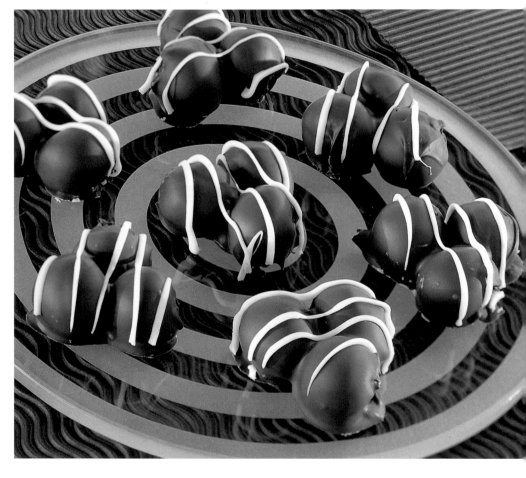

1 Line a baking tray with a sheet of baking paper. Divide the marzipan into 3 balls and knead each ball to soften it.

2 Work the glacé cherries into one portion of the marzipan by kneading on a surface lightly dusted with icing sugar.

3 Do the same with the stem ginger and another portion of marzipan and then the apricots and the third portion of marzipan.

4 Form each flavoured portion of marzipan into small balls, keeping the different flavours separate.

5 Break the dark chocolate into pieces, place in a bowl and set over a pan of hot water. Stir until the chocolate has melted. Dip one of each flavoured ball of marzipan into the melted chocolate by spiking each one with a cocktail stick, allowing the excess chocolate to drip back into the bowl.

6 Place the balls in clusters of the three flavours on the baking tray. Repeat with the remaining balls. Chill until set.

7 Melt the white chocolate and drizzle a little over the tops of each cluster of marzipan balls. Chill until hardened, then remove from the baking paper and dust with sugar to serve.

VARIATION

Coat the marzipan balls in white or milk chocolate and drizzle with dark chocolate, if you prefer.

Chocolate Liqueurs

These tasty chocolate cups are filled with a delicious liqueur-flavoured filling. Use your favourite liqueur to flavour the cream.

1 hr   5 mins

MAKES 40

INGREDIENTS

100 g/3½ oz dark chocolate

about 5 glacé cherries, halved

about 10 hazelnuts or macadamia nuts

150 ml/5 fl oz double cream

2 tbsp icing sugar

4 tbsp liqueur

TO FINISH

50 g/1¾ oz dark chocolate, melted

a little white chocolate, melted or white chocolate quick curls (see page 15) or extra nuts and cherries

1 Line a baking tray with a sheet of baking paper. Break the chocolate into pieces, place in a bowl and set over a pan of hot water. Stir until melted. Spoon into 20 paper sweet cases, spreading up the sides with a small spoon or pastry brush. Place upside down on the prepared baking tray and leave to set.

2 Carefully peel away the paper cases. Place a cherry or nut in the base of each cup.

3 To make the filling, place the double cream in a bowl and sieve the icing sugar on top. Whisk the cream until it is just holding its shape, then whisk in the liqueur.

4 Place the cream in a piping bag fitted with a 1 cm/½ inch plain nozzle and pipe a little into each chocolate case. Leave to chill for 20 minutes.

5 To finish, spoon the melted dark chocolate over the cream to cover it and pipe the melted white chocolate on top, swirling it into the dark chocolate with a cocktail stick. Leave to harden. Alternatively, cover the cream with the melted dark chocolate and decorate with white chocolate curls before setting. Or, place a small piece of nut or cherry on top of the cream and then cover with dark chocolate.

COOK'S TIP

Sweet cases can vary in size. Use the smallest you can find for this recipe.

Chocolate Mascarpone Cups

Mascarpone – the velvety smooth Italian cheese – makes a rich, creamy filling for these tasty chocolates

40 mins   5 mins

MAKES 20

INGREDIENTS

100 g/3½ oz dark chocolate

FILLING

100 g/3½ oz milk or dark chocolate

¼ tsp vanilla essence

200 g/7 oz mascarpone cheese

cocoa powder, to dust

1 Line a baking tray with a sheet of baking paper. Break 100 g/3½ oz dark chocolate into pieces, place in a bowl and set over a pan of hot water. Stir until the chocolate has melted. Spoon the melted chocolate into 20 paper sweet cases, spreading up the sides with a small spoon or pastry brush. Place upside down on the prepared baking tray and leave to set.

2 When set, carefully peel away the paper cases.

3 For the filling, melt the dark or milk chocolate. Place the mascarpone in a bowl and beat in the vanilla essence and melted chocolate until well combined. Leave the mixture to chill, beating occasionally until firm enough to pipe.

4 Place the mascarpone filling in a piping bag fitted with a star nozzle and pipe the mixture into the cups. Decorate with a dusting of cocoa powder.

VARIATION
Mascarpone is a rich Italian soft cheese made from fresh cream, so it has a high fat content. Its delicate flavour blends well with chocolate.

Mini Chocolate Cones

These unusual cone-shaped mint-cream chocolates make a change from the more usual cup shape, and are perfect as an after-dinner chocolate.

40 mins

5 mins

MAKES 10

INGREDIENTS

75 g/2¾ oz dark chocolate

100 ml/3½ fl oz double cream

1 tbsp icing sugar

1 tbsp crème de menthe

chocolate coffee beans, to decorate (optional)

1 Cut ten 7.5 cm/3 inch circles of baking paper. Shape each circle into a cone shape and secure with sticky tape.

2 Break the chocolate into pieces, place in a bowl and set over a pan of hot water. Stir until the chocolate has melted. Using a small pastry brush or clean artists' brush, brush the inside of each cone with the melted chocolate.

3 Brush a second layer of chocolate on the inside of the cones and leave to chill until set. Carefully peel away the paper.

4 Place the double cream, icing sugar and crème de menthe in a mixing bowl and whip until just holding its shape.

COOK'S TIP

The chocolate cones can be made in advance and kept in the refrigerator for up to 1 week. Do not fill them more than 2 hours before you are going to serve them.

Place in a piping bag fitted with a star nozzle and pipe the mixture into the chocolate cones.

5 Decorate the cones with chocolate coffee beans (if using) and chill until required.

Collettes

A creamy, orange-flavoured chocolate filling in white chocolate cups makes a wonderful treat.

🍰 40 mins   🕐 5 mins

MAKES 20

INGREDIENTS

100 g/3½ oz white chocolate

FILLING

150 g/5½ oz orange-flavoured dark chocolate

150 ml/5 fl oz double cream

2 tbsp icing sugar

1 Line a baking tray with a sheet of baking paper. Break the chocolate into pieces, place in a bowl and set over a pan of hot water. Stir until melted, and spoon into 20 paper sweet cases, spreading up the sides with a small pastry brush. Place upside down on the prepared baking tray and leave to set.

2 When set, carefully peel away the paper cases.

3 To make the filling, melt the orange-flavoured chocolate and place in a mixing bowl with the double cream and the icing sugar. Beat until smooth. Chill until the mixture becomes firm enough to pipe, stirring occasionally.

4 Place the filling in a piping bag fitted with a star nozzle and pipe a little into each case. Leave to chill until they are required.

COOK'S TIP

If they do not hold their shape well, use 2 cases to make a double thickness mould. Foil cases are firmer, so use these if you can find them.

Mini Chocolate Tartlets

Small pastry cases are filled with a rich chocolate filling to serve as petits fours. Use small individual tartlet tins to make the pastry cases.

🍰 🍰 🍰

🧈 1½ hrs   🕐 15 mins

MAKES 18

INGREDIENTS

175 g/6 oz plain flour

6 tbsp butter

1 tbsp caster sugar

about 1 tbsp water

FILLING

100 g/3½ oz full-fat soft cheese

2 tbsp caster sugar

1 small egg, lightly beaten

50 g/1¾ oz dark chocolate

TO DECORATE

100 ml/10 fl oz double cream

dark chocolate quick curls (see page 15)

cocoa powder, to dust

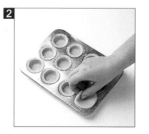

1 Sieve the flour into a mixing bowl. Cut the butter into small pieces and rub in with your fingertips until the mixture resembles fine breadcrumbs. Stir in the sugar. Add enough water to mix to a soft dough, then cover and chill for 15 minutes.

2 Roll out the pastry on a lightly floured surface and use to line 18 mini tartlet tins or mini muffin tins. Prick the bases with a cocktail stick.

3 Beat together the full-fat soft cheese and the sugar. Beat in the egg. Melt the chocolate and beat it into the mixture. Spoon into the pastry cases and bake in a preheated oven, 190°C/375°F/Gas Mark 5, for 15 minutes, until the pastry is crisp and the filling set. Place the tins on a wire rack to cool completely.

4 Chill the tartlets. Whip the cream until it is just holding its shape. Place in a piping bag fitted with a star nozzle. Pipe rosettes of cream on top of the tartlets. Decorate with chocolate curls and dust with cocoa powder.

COOK'S TIP

The tartlets can be made up to 3 days ahead. Decorate on the day of serving, preferably no more than 4 hours in advance.

Mini Florentines

Serve these biscuits at the end of a meal with coffee, or arrange in a shallow presentation box for an attractive gift.

⏱ 30 mins   🕐 10–12 mins

MAKES 40

I N G R E D I E N T S

6 tbsp butter

75 g/2¾ oz caster sugar

2 tbsp sultanas or raisins

2 tbsp glacé cherries, chopped

2 tbsp crystallised ginger, chopped

25 g/1 oz sunflower seeds

100 g/3½ oz flaked almonds

2 tbsp double cream

175 g/6 oz dark or milk chocolate

1 Grease and flour 2 baking trays or line with baking paper.

2 Place the butter in a small pan and heat gently until melted. Add the sugar, stir until dissolved, then bring the mixture to the boil. Remove from the heat and stir in the sultanas or raisins, cherries, ginger, sunflower seeds and almonds. Mix well, then beat in the cream.

3 Place small teaspoons of the fruit and nut mixture on to the prepared baking tray, allowing plenty of space for the mixture to spread. Bake in a preheated oven, at 180°C/350°F/Gas Mark 4, for 10–12 minutes or until they are light golden in colour.

4 Remove from the oven and, while still hot, use a circular biscuit cutter to pull in the edges to form perfect circles. Leave to cool and go crisp before removing from the baking tray.

5 Break the chocolate into pieces, place in a bowl and set over a pan of hot water. Stir until the chocolate has melted. Spread most of the chocolate on to a sheet of baking paper. When the chocolate is on the point of setting, place the biscuits flat-side down on the chocolate and leave to harden completely.

6 Cut around the florentines and remove from the baking paper. Spread a little more melted chocolate on the coated sides and use a fork to mark waves in the chocolate. Leave to set. Arrange the florentines on a plate with alternate sides facing upwards. Keep cool.

Rum Truffles

Truffles are always popular. They make a fabulous gift or, served with coffee, they are a perfect end to a meal.

45 mins   5 mins

MAKES 20

INGREDIENTS

125 g/5½ oz dark chocolate

small knob of butter

2 tbsp rum

50 g/1¾ oz desiccated coconut

100 g/3½ oz cake crumbs

6 tbsp icing sugar

2 tbsp cocoa powder

1 Break the chocolate into pieces and place in a bowl with the butter. Set the bowl over a pan of gently simmering water, stir until melted and combined.

2 Remove from the heat and beat in the rum. Stir in the desiccated coconut, cake crumbs and two-thirds of the icing sugar. Beat until combined. Add a little extra rum if the mixture is stiff.

3 Roll the mixture into small balls and place them on a sheet of baking paper. Leave to chill until firm.

4 Sieve the remaining icing sugar on to a large plate. Sieve the cocoa powder on to another plate. Roll half of the truffles in the icing sugar until coated and roll the remaining truffles in the cocoa powder.

5 Place the truffles in paper sweet cases and leave to chill until required.

VARIATION

Make the truffles with white chocolate and replace the rum with coconut liqueur or milk, if you prefer. Roll them in cocoa powder or dip in melted milk chocolate.

White Chocolate Truffles

These delicious creamy white truffles will testify to the fact that there is nothing quite as nice as home-made chocolates.

🕐 2³/₄ hrs   🕒 5 mins

MAKES 20

I N G R E D I E N T S

2 tbsp unsalted butter

5 tbsp double cream

225 g/8 oz good quality Swiss white chocolate

1 tbsp orange-flavoured liqueur, optional

T O   F I N I S H

100 g/3½ oz white chocolate

1 Line a Swiss roll tin with baking paper.

2 Place the butter and cream in a small saucepan and bring slowly to the boil, stirring constantly. Boil for 1 minute, then remove from the heat.

3 Break the chocolate into pieces and add to the cream. Stir until melted, then beat in the liqueur, if using.

4 Pour into the prepared tin and chill for about 2 hours until firm.

5 Break off pieces of mixture and roll them into balls. Chill for a further 30 minutes before finishing the truffles.

6 To finish, melt the white chocolate. Dip the balls in the chocolate, allowing the excess to drip back into the bowl. Place on non-stick baking paper and swirl the chocolate with the prongs of a fork. Leave to harden.

7 Drizzle a little melted dark chocolate over the truffles if you wish and leave to set. Place the truffles in paper cases to serve.

COOK'S TIP

The truffle mixture needs to be firm but not too hard to roll. If the mixture is too hard, allow it to stand at room temperature for a few minutes to soften slightly. During rolling the mixture will become sticky but will reharden in the refrigerator before coating.

Italian Chocolate Truffles

These tasty morsels are flavoured with almonds and chocolate, and are simplicity itself to make. Serve with coffee for the perfect end to a meal.

50 mins

5 mins

MAKES 24

I N G R E D I E N T S

175 g/6 oz dark chocolate

2 tbsp amaretto liqueur or
orange-flavoured liqueur

3 tbsp unsalted butter

4 tbsp icing sugar

50 g/1¾ oz ground almonds

50 g/1¾ oz grated chocolate

1 Melt the dark chocolate with the liqueur in a bowl set over a saucepan of hot water, stirring until well combined.

2 Add the butter and stir until it has melted. Stir in the icing sugar and the ground almonds.

3 Leave the mixture in a cool place until firm enough to roll into about 24 balls.

4 Place the grated chocolate on a plate and roll the truffles in the chocolate to coat them.

5 Place the truffles in paper sweet cases and chill.

VARIATION
Almond-flavoured liqueur gives these truffles an authentic Italian flavour. The original almond liqueur, Amaretto di Saronno, comes from Saronno in Italy.

Candied Citrus Peel

The Mediterranean sun produces some of the most flavourful citrus fruit in the world, and this is a traditional way to preserve the peel.

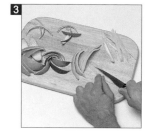

🕑 6½ hrs   🕐 35 mins

MAKES 60

INGREDIENTS

1 large unwaxed, thick-skinned orange

1 large unwaxed, thick-skinned lemon

1 large unwaxed, thick-skinned lime

600 g/1 lb 5 oz caster sugar

300 ml/10 fl oz water

125 g/4½ oz best-quality dark chocolate, chopped (optional)

1 Cut the orange into quarters lengthways and squeeze the juice into a cup to drink, or to use in another recipe. Cut each quarter in half lengthways to make 8 pieces.

2 Cut the fruit and pith away from the rind. If any of the pith remains on the rind, lay the knife almost flat on the white-side of the rind and gently "saw" backwards and forwards to slice it off because it will taste bitter.

3 Repeat with the lemon and lime, only cutting the lime into quarters. Cut each piece into 3 or 4 thin strips to make 60–80 strips in total. Place the strips in a pan of water and boil for 30 seconds. Drain thoroughly.

4 Dissolve the sugar in the water in a pan over a medium heat, stirring. Increase the heat and bring to the boil, without stirring. When the syrup becomes clear, turn the heat to its lowest setting.

5 Add the citrus strips, using a wooden spoon to push them in without stirring. Simmer in the syrup for 30 minutes, without stirring. Turn off the heat and set aside for at least 6 hours until completely cool.

6 Line a baking sheet with kitchen foil. Skim off the thin crust on top of the syrup without stirring. Remove the rind strips, one by one, from the syrup, shaking off any excess. Place the strips on the foil to cool.

7 If you want to dip candied peel in chocolate, melt the chocolate. Working with one piece of candied peel at a time, dip the peel half-way into the chocolate. Return to the foil and leave to dry. Store in an airtight container.

Cocochoc Pyramids

This is a traditional favourite. In this recipe, coconut ice is deliciously dipped in melted chocolate to make a two-tone treat.

35 mins, plus 1½–2½ hrs setting/standing

15–25 mins

MAKES 12

INGREDIENTS

150 ml/5 fl oz water

450 g/1 lb granulated sugar

pinch of cream of tartar

115 g/4 oz desiccated coconut

1 tbsp double cream

few drops of yellow liquid food colouring

85 g/3 oz dark chocolate, broken into pieces

1 Pour the water into a heavy-based pan, add the sugar and stir over a low heat until the sugar has dissolved. Stir in a pinch of cream of tartar and bring to the boil. Boil steadily, without stirring, until the temperature reaches 119°C/238°F on a sugar thermometer. If you do not have a sugar thermometer, test the syrup frequently by dropping a small quantity into a bowl of cold water. If the mixture can then be rolled between your finger and thumb to make a soft ball, it is ready.

2 Remove the pan from the heat and beat in the coconut and cream. Continue to beat for 5–10 minutes until the mixture becomes cloudy. Beat in a few drops of yellow food colouring, then leave to cool. When cool enough to handle, take small pieces of the mixture and form them into pyramids. Place on a sheet of baking paper and leave to harden.

3 Put the chocolate in the top of a double boiler or in a heatproof bowl set over a pan of barely simmering water. Stir over a low heat until melted, then remove from the heat. Dip the bases of the pyramids into the melted chocolate and leave to set.

Dried Fruit Petits Fours

Irresistibly sweet and unbelievably tempting, these fruity little chocolates can be served with coffee at the end of a dinner party.

 20–25 mins, plus 30 mins setting

5 mins

SERVES 30

INGREDIENTS

175 g/6 oz ready-to-eat dried apricots

115 g/4 oz ready-to-eat dried figs

115 g/4 oz ready-to-eat dried dates

85 g/3 oz walnuts, roughly chopped

3 tbsp finely chopped candied orange peel

3 tbsp apricot brandy, plus extra for moistening

icing sugar, to dust

115 g/4 oz milk chocolate, broken into pieces

4 tbsp chopped hazelnuts, toasted

1 Chop the dried fruits by hand or in a food processor. Place the chopped fruit in a bowl and add the walnuts, candied peel and apricot brandy and mix well.

2 Gather the mixture together and turn out on to a surface lightly dusted with icing sugar. Divide the mixture into 3 pieces and form each piece into a roll about 20 cm/8 inches long. Then cut each roll into slices about 2 cm/¾ inch thick. Moisten your hands with a little apricot brandy and roll each slice into a ball between your palms.

3 Place the chocolate in the top of a double boiler or in a heatproof bowl set over a pan of barely simmering water. Stir over a low heat until melted. Remove from the heat and cool slightly. Spear each fruit ball with a fork or skewer and dip it in the melted chocolate to coat it. Place on a sheet of baking paper and sprinkle over the hazelnuts. Leave for 30 minutes, or until set.

Double Chocolate Truffles

Marzipan, honey and dark and light chocolate are combined into little morsels of sheer delight.

 25 mins, plus 1 hr cooling

10 mins

SERVES 60

INGREDIENTS

175 g/6 oz unsalted butter

100 g/3½ oz marzipan, grated

4 tbsp clear honey

½ tsp vanilla essence

200 g/7 oz dark chocolate, broken into pieces

350 g/12 oz milk chocolate, broken into pieces

1 Line 2 baking trays with baking paper. Beat together the butter and marzipan until thoroughly combined and fluffy. Stir in the honey, a little at a time, then stir in the vanilla.

2 Place the dark chocolate and 200 g/7 oz of the milk chocolate in the top of a double boiler or in a heatproof bowl set over a pan of barely simmering water. Stir over a low heat until melted and smooth. Remove from the heat and let it cool slightly.

3 Stir the melted chocolate into the marzipan mixture, then spoon the chocolate/marzipan mixture into a piping bag fitted with a large, round nozzle and pipe small balls on to the prepared baking trays. Leave to cool and set.

4 Put the remaining milk chocolate into the top of a double boiler or into a heatproof bowl set over a pan of barely simmering water. Stir over a low heat until melted, then remove from the heat. Dip the truffles, 1 at a time, in the melted chocolate to coat them, then texture some of them by gently tapping them with a fork. Place on the baking trays and leave to cool and set.

Rum & Chocolate Cups

Use firm foil confectionery cases, rather than paper ones, to make the chocolate cups, because they offer extra support.

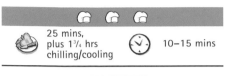

25 mins, plus 1¾ hrs chilling/cooling

10–15 mins

SERVES 12

I N G R E D I E N T S

55 g/2 oz dark chocolate, broken into pieces

12 toasted hazelnuts

F I L L I N G

115 g/4 oz dark chocolate, broken into pieces

1 tbsp dark rum

4 tbsp mascarpone cheese

1 To make the chocolate cups, place the chocolate in the top of a double boiler or in a heatproof bowl set over a pan of barely simmering water. Stir over a low heat until the chocolate is just melted but not too runny, then remove from the heat. Spoon about ½ a teaspoon of melted chocolate into a foil confectionery case and brush it over the base and up the sides. Coat 11 more foil cases in the same way and leave for 30 minutes to set. Chill in the refrigerator for 15 minutes. If necessary, reheat the chocolate in the double boiler or heatproof bowl to melt it again, then coat the foil cases with a second, slightly thinner coating. Chill in the refrigerator for a further 30 minutes.

2 Meanwhile, make the filling. Place the chocolate in the top of a double boiler or in a heatproof bowl set over a pan of barely simmering water. Stir over a low

heat until melted, then remove from the heat. Let it cool slightly, then stir in the rum and beat in the mascarpone until fully incorporated and smooth. Set aside to cool completely, stirring occasionally.

3 Spoon the filling into a piping bag fitted with a 1 cm/½ inch star nozzle. Carefully peel away the confectionery cases from the chocolate cups. Pipe the filling into the cups and top each one with a toasted hazelnut.

Chocolate-dipped Prunes

A much underrated dried fruit, prunes make delicious and very attractive after-dinner treats.

  30 mins, plus 30 mins cooling   55–65 mins

SERVES 24

INGREDIENTS

225 ml/8 fl oz water

125 g/4½ oz granulated sugar

2 cinnamon sticks, each 7.5 cm/3 inches long

1 vanilla pod

450 g/1 lb whole prunes

75 g/2¾ oz leftover sponge cake

85 g/3 oz ground, toasted walnuts

5 tbsp slivovitch or brandy

½ tsp vanilla essence

100 g/3½ oz white chocolate, broken into pieces

1 Pour the water into a pan, add the sugar and stir over a low heat until the sugar has dissolved. Add the cinnamon sticks and vanilla pod, raise the heat and bring to the boil. Then lower the heat and simmer for 5 minutes.

2 Add the prunes, bring back to the boil and simmer for 5 minutes. Lift out 24 large, well-shaped prunes with a slotted spoon and set aside to cool. Simmer the remaining prunes for 30–40 minutes, until very tender. Meanwhile, slit the 24 reserved prunes and remove the stones, leaving a neat cavity for the filling.

3 Drain the soft-cooked prunes and discard the syrup. Remove the stones and place the prunes in a food processor with the sponge cake, ground walnuts, slivovitch (or brandy if using) and vanilla.

Process to a smooth purée. Divide the filling among the reserved prunes, carefully pressing it into the cavities and gently reshaping the prunes around it.

4 Put the chocolate in the top of a double boiler or in a heatproof bowl set over a pan of barely simmering water.

Stir over a low heat until melted, then remove from the heat. Dip the base of each prune into the melted chocolate to half-coat, then spoon the remaining chocolate into a piping bag fitted with a fine nozzle. Pipe thin lines over the tops of the prunes, then place them on a sheet of baking paper until set.

Mexican Chocolate Corn

If you can obtain Mexican chocolate, it is worth doing so, but otherwise use any good-quality, dark chocolate.

5 mins   10–15 mins

SERVES 6

INGREDIENTS

750 ml/1¼ pints water

55 g/2 oz tortilla flour

5 cm/2 inch piece of cinnamon stick

750 ml/1¼ pints milk

85 g/3 oz dark chocolate, grated

sugar, to taste

1 Pour the water into a large pan, stir in the tortilla flour and add the cinnamon. Stir over a low heat for 5–10 minutes until thickened and smooth. Gradually stir in the milk, then beat in the grated chocolate, a little at a time, until melted and fully incorporated. Remove and discard the cinnamon.

2 Remove the pan from the heat and ladle the mixture into heatproof glasses. Sweeten to taste with sugar.

Chocolate Eggnog

The perfect pick-me-up on a cold winter's night, this delicious drink will get the taste buds tingling.

🥚 10 mins   🕐 5 mins

SERVES 4

INGREDIENTS

8 egg yolks

200 g/7 oz sugar

1 litre/1¾ pints milk

225 g/8 oz dark chocolate, grated

150 ml/5 fl oz dark rum

1 Beat the egg yolks with the sugar until thickened.

2 Pour the milk into a large pan, add the grated chocolate and bring to the boil. Remove from the heat and gradually beat in the egg yolk mixture. Stir in the rum and pour into heatproof glasses.

Hot Brandy Chocolate

Brandy and chocolate have a natural affinity, as this richly flavoured drink amply demonstrates.

 10 mins 7–10 mins

SERVES 4

INGREDIENTS

1 litre/1¾ pints milk

115 g/4 oz dark chocolate, broken into pieces

2 tbsp sugar

5 tbsp brandy

TO DECORATE

6 tbsp whipped cream

4 tsp cocoa powder

1 Pour the milk into a pan and bring to the boil, then remove from the heat. Place the chocolate in a small pan and add 2 tablespoons of the hot milk. Stir over a low heat until the chocolate has melted. Stir the chocolate mixture into the remaining milk and add the sugar.

2 Stir in the brandy and pour into 4 heatproof glasses. Top each with a swirl of whipped cream and sprinkle with a little sieved cocoa.

Hot Chocolate Drinks

Rich and soothing, a hot chocolate drink in the evening can be just what you need to help ease away the stresses of the day.

5 mins each　　5 mins each

SERVES 2

INGREDIENTS

SPICY HOT CHOCOLATE

600 ml/1 pint milk

1 tsp ground mixed spice

100 g/3½ oz dark chocolate

4 cinnamon sticks

100 ml/3½ fl oz double cream,
　lightly whipped

HOT CHOCOLATE & ORANGE TODDY

75 g/2½ oz orange-flavoured dark chocolate

600 ml/1 pint milk

3 tbsp rum

2 tbsp double cream

grated nutmeg

1 To make Spicy Hot Chocolate, pour the milk into a small pan. Sprinkle in the mixed spice.

2 Break the dark chocolate into squares and add to the milk. Heat the mixture over a low heat until the milk is just boiling, stirring all the time to prevent the milk burning on the bottom of the pan.

3 Place 2 cinnamon sticks in 2 cups and pour in the spicy hot chocolate. Top with the whipped double cream and serve.

4 To make Hot Chocolate & Orange Toddy, break the orange-flavoured dark chocolate into squares and place in a small saucepan with the milk. Heat the mixture over a low heat until just boiling, stirring constantly.

5 Remove the pan from the heat and stir in the rum. Pour into cups.

6 Pour the cream over the back of a spoon or swirl on to the top so that it sits on top of the hot chocolate. Sprinkle with grated nutmeg and serve at once.

COOK'S TIP

Using a cinnamon stick as a stirrer will give any hot chocolate drink a sweet, pungent flavour of cinnamon without overpowering the flavour of the chocolate.

Cold Chocolate Drinks

These delicious chocolate summer drinks are perfect for making a chocoholic's summer day!

5 mins each   0 mins

SERVES 2

I N G R E D I E N T S

CHOCOLATE MILK SHAKE

450 ml/16 fl oz ice cold milk

3 tbsp drinking chocolate powder

3 scoops chocolate ice cream

cocoa powder, to dust (optional)

CHOCOLATE ICE CREAM SODA

5 tbsp Glossy Chocolate Sauce (see
   page 103)

soda water

2 scoops of chocolate ice cream

double cream, whipped

dark or milk chocolate, grated

1 To make the Chocolate Milk Shake, place half of the ice-cold milk in a blender.

2 Add the drinking chocolate powder to the blender with 1 scoop of the chocolate ice cream. Blend until the mixture is frothy and well mixed. Stir in the remaining milk.

3 Place the remaining 2 scoops of chocolate ice cream in 2 serving glasses and carefully pour the chocolate milk over the ice cream.

4 Sprinkle a little cocoa powder (if using) over the top of each drink and serve at once.

5 To make the Chocolate Ice Cream Soda, divide the Glossy Chocolate Sauce equally between two glasses.

6 Add a little soda water to each glass and stir to combine the sauce and soda water. Place a scoop of ice cream in each glass and then top up with more soda water.

7 Place a dollop of whipped heavy cream on the top, if liked, and sprinkle with a little grated dark or milk chocolate.

COOK'S TIP
Served in a tall glass, a milk shake or an ice cream soda makes a scrumptious snack in a drink. Serve with straws, if wished.

Index